Women and the
New German Cinema

QUESTIONS FOR FEMINISM

Edited by Michèle Barrett, Annette Kuhn, Anne Phillips and Ann Rosalind Jones, this socialist feminist series aims to address, in a lively way and on an international basis, the wide range of political and theoretical questions facing contemporary feminism.

Women and the
New German Cinema

JULIA KNIGHT

VERSO
London · New York

First published by Verso 1992
© Julia Knight 1992
All rights reserved

Verso
UK: 6 Meard Street, London W1V 3HR
USA: 29 West 35th Street, New York, NY 10001-2291

Verso is the imprint of New Left Books

ISBN 0-86091-352-X
ISBN 0-86091-568-9 (pbk)

British Library Cataloguing in Publication Data
A catalogue record for this book is available from the British Library

Library of Congress Cataloging-in-Publication Data
A catalogue record for this book is available from the Library of Congress

Typeset by Leaper & Gard Ltd, Bristol
Printed in Great Britain by Biddles Ltd

For Marjorie Knight and
in loving memory of Peter Knight (1921–90).
Thank you for the support you've always given me.

Contents

Acknowledgements

For their assistance in helping me with my research I would particularly like to thank Birgit Hein, Claudia Schillinger, Monika Treut, Helke Sander, Jutta Brückner, Ulrike Ottinger, Claudia Richarz, Ulrike Zimmermann, Maria Vedder and Annebarbe Kau, as well as Birgit Durbahn and Tanja Schmidt of Bildwechsel, Karin Bruns of Femme Totale, Katja Mildenberger and Dagmar Röper of the Feminale, Christiane Ensslin of the Association of Women Film Workers, Frau Wilhelmina of the DFFB Library, Ruth Becht, Leonore Poth, Margit Weber and Ira Zamjatnins of Trick 17, Dr Torsten Teichert of the Hamburg Film Office, and the staff of both 235 Media and the Neuer Berliner Kunstverein. I am also deeply indebted to The British Academy for their financial assistance in the form of a small research grant, which enabled me to make an invaluable research trip to West Germany. Additional thanks are due to Ken MacKinnon, Richard Collins and Thomas Elsaesser for their support, encouragement and interest. I am also very grateful to Rebecca Coyle, Julian Stringer, Caroline Cooper, Electric Pictures and the London Filmmakers' Coop for their help in supplying information and research material, and to Annette Kuhn, Anne Phillips and Phil Hayward for their advice and very helpful comments on my manuscript.

Finally, additional thanks are due to Phil Hayward for his encouragement, support and help, for which I am extremely grateful; and special thanks go to Val Martin for her understanding and immense patience, which were invaluable and without which this book would never have been finished.

Stills and photographs are reproduced with the kind permission of the following:

Zur Sache Schätzchen: Peter Schamoni-Filmproduktion Munich; *Die allseitig Reduzierte Persönlichkeit – Redupers*: Helke Sander Filmproduktion; *Die Macht der Männer ist die Geduld der Frauen*: Cinema of Women; *Reise nach Lyon*: Cinema of Women; *Bildnis einer Trinkerin – Aller jamais retour*: Ulrike Ottinger Filmproduktion; *Die bleierne Zeit*: Bioskop Film; Ulrike Ottinger: Ulrike Ottinger Filmproduktion; Elfi Mikesch: Elfi Mikesch; *Novembermond*: Cinema of Women; *Mano Destra*: Cleo Übelmann; *Männer*: Olga-Film GmbH; Doris Dörrie: Olga-Film GmbH; Monika Treut: Hyäne I/II Filmproduktion GbR; *Die Jungfrauen Maschine*: Hyäne I/II Filmproduktion GbR; *Die Kali-Filme*: Birgit Hein; *Die Deutschen und ihre Männer*: Helke Sander Filmproduktion.

INTRODUCTION

The Absent Directors

Over the last two decades the New German Cinema has established itself on the international film scene as a body of work marked by its stylistic and thematic diversity. Unlike cinema movements such as Italian Neo-Realism or Latin American Cinema Novo, however, its films have resisted clear generic delineations. Critics have attempted to identify a variety of aspects as common denominators. Eric Rentschler, for example, has argued that the filmmakers' 'quest for alternative images and counter-representations' has been a common factor.[1] Taking another tack, Thomas Elsaesser has suggested that the apparent heterogeneity of style and genre has been determined by funding criteria and opportunities combined with the need to experiment in order to find audiences.[2] Despite such differences, most critics nevertheless agree that the cinema was based on an artisanal mode of production and demonstrates a deep concern with social and political questions.

Although critics may have encountered difficulties in characterizing the essential elements of the New German Cinema, its most successful directors are easier to identify. Prime among those who have risen to prominence through the international film festival and art cinema circuits are Rainer Werner Fassbinder, Werner Herzog, Alexander Kluge, Volker Schlöndorff, Jean-Marie Straub, Hans-Jürgen Syberberg and Wim Wenders. The name of Edgar Reitz can now also be included in this group as a result of the international success of his

1984 film epic *Heimat / Homeland*. These directors can be characterized as a generation, as they were all born around the time of World War Two and grew up in a divided post-war Germany.

Belonging to the same generation, however, is a group of women directors (and of course a number of male directors) whose work – although excluded from many accounts – equally forms part of the New German Cinema. Along with other women directors discussed in later chapters, these women include Claudia von Alemann, Jutta Brückner, Ingemo Engström, Danièle Huillet, Elfi Mikesch, Ulrike Ottinger, Cristina Perincioli, Erika Runge, Helke Sander, Helma Sanders-Brahms, Ula Stöckl and Margarethe von Trotta. Their work, like that of their male colleagues, is also marked by 'alternative images and counter-representations' and reflects an intense concern with socio-political questions. Many of them have also trained, worked and/ or collaborated with their better-known male counterparts. Alemann and Stöckl trained at the Ulm Film Institute where Kluge and Reitz taught; and Stöckl went on to co-direct two films with Reitz.[3] Similarly, Wenders trained with Engström at the Munich film school and acted in her film *Candy Man* (1968). Such partnerships have also been established on a long-term basis; von Trotta has collaborated extensively with her husband Schlöndorff, while Huillet and Straub have shared the writing and directing of most of their films.

However, the work of these women arguably has a significance beyond that of a merely national cinema 'movement'. Although their work contributed to a new German cinema, it also gave rise to a whole feminist film culture and produced a critically acclaimed women's cinema. Furthermore, despite the persistent marginalization of women as directors in international cinema, during the New German Cinema era West Germany came to possess 'proportionally more women film-makers than any other film-producing country'.[4] This is all the more remarkable given that prior to the emergence of the country's 'new cinema' literally only a handful of women had succeeded in making films. As the following brief survey demonstrates, from the early days of silent cinema women in Germany – despite the undoubted ability of many of them – had traditionally managed to make only occasional and usually highly limited contributions as directors.

The honour of being Germany's first woman director probably goes to Olga Wohlbrück who made *Ein Mädchen zu verschenken / A Girl for*

Giving Away in 1913. This appears to be her one and only film, although very little is currently known about women working during this era. Among the small number of women who followed in Wohlbrück's footsteps were Fern Andra, who made her directorial debut two years later. Born in the US, Andra settled in Germany after touring Europe as a tight-rope artist. She started working there as a film actress, setting up her own production company in 1915. During the next four years she directed five of her own films, before deciding to concentrate on acting.

A few years later Marie Luise Droop also moved into directing after working extensively as a scriptwriter during the 1910s. Like Andra, setting up her own production company gave her the opportunity to direct: she made *Das Fest der schwarzen Tulpe/ The Festival of the Black Tulip* and *Die Teufelsanbeter/Devil Worshippers* in 1920. However, the films were not financial successes, and Droop returned to scriptwriting.

Hanna Henning, however, was one of the very few exceptions in the history of women's film production in Germany. She managed to pursue a career as a film director, making over forty films before her death in 1925. She started by directing so-called *Bubi* films, a series of shorts which revolved around a young rascal character's various adventures. After establishing her own production company, Henning moved into feature film production in 1916 and undertook her first major production, *Die Siebzehnjährigen / The Seventeen-Year-Olds*, in 1919.

In the same year, Lotte Reiniger also made her first film, *Das Ornament des verliebten Herzens/ The Ornament of the Loving Heart* (1919). Reiniger's films were short animated silhouette films often based on myths or fairy tales. She created all the figures, objects and background detail in her films using only a pair of scissors. Her skill at cutting paper silhouettes has since become legendary and caused French film-maker Jean Renoir to comment: 'Her fingers clasping her only tool, scissors, make me think of a graceful classical dancer.'[5] Her work also impressed a Berlin banker, Louis Hagen, who asked if she would consider making a feature-length silhouette film. As Reiniger has recalled, however:

> We had to think twice. This was a never heard of thing. Animated films were supposed to make people roar with laughter, and nobody had dared to entertain an audience with them for more than ten minutes.

Everybody to whom we talked in the industry about that proposition was horrified.[6]

Nevertheless, Reiniger and her collaborators rose to the challenge. They combined a number of stories from the Arabian Nights to produce *Die Geschichte des Prinzen Achmed/ The Adventures of Prince Achmed* in 1926, a highly captivating sixty-five minute film full of fantastical creatures brought to life through Reiniger's beautiful and complex silhouettes. Although no German cinema was initially interested in screening the film, it was well received at a privately arranged German premiere and enjoyed a six-month run in Paris. However, as the project took three years to complete, this was Reiniger's only feature-length film and soon after its completion she left Germany.

During the thirties and forties even fewer women managed to direct for the German cinema. Born in Austria, Leontine Sagan trained as a theatre actress and director. She subsequently moved to Germany where she became a popular figure in the Berlin theatre scene. There she made her only film for German cinema, *Mädchen in Uniform/ Maidens in Uniform* (1931). After being withdrawn from distribution, the film enjoyed a revival in the seventies due to its focus on the relationship that develops between two women: Manuela, a new student at a girls' boarding school, and Fräulein von Bernburg, the girl's favourite and most adored teacher. Von Bernburg opposes the authoritarian Prussian codes endorsed by the school and embodied in its totalitarian principal. Manuela falls in love with her teacher, an emotion which is both returned and discouraged by von Bernburg. Manuela, however, publicly declares her passion. For this, she is punished by being confined to the infirmary and denied visitors. After an interview with the principal, von Bernburg tells Manuela that their relationship cannot continue. Distraught, Manuela attempts to commit suicide, but is saved by her schoolfriends and protected from the principal by von Bernburg.

On its release in 1931 *Maidens in Uniform* was discussed as a film which addressed the problems of adolescence and took issue with the Prussian education system.[7] With hindsight, the film's anti-authoritarian stance has also been regarded as prophetically anti-fascist. In the seventies, however, the film was re-evaluated as an early example of radical lesbian cinema. Although the film's iconography and the figure of the principal clearly indicate that real power lies with absent patriarchy, Anglo-American feminist film critics have argued that *Maidens in Uniform* is supportive of women's right to emotional and sexual freedom.[8]

When the Nazi party came to power in 1933, the opportunities for women to pursue any kind of career began rapidly to diminish. Only two women are known to have worked as film directors during the Third Reich: Thea von Harbou and Leni Riefenstahl. Von Harbou is better known for her extensive collaboration with her film-director husband Fritz Lang, and as scriptwriter for films by F.W. Murnau, Carl Theodor Dreyer and Arthur von Gerlach during the silent era. In the early thirties she joined the Nazi party and subsequently had the opportunity of directing two features: *Elisabeth und der Narr/Elisabeth and the Fool* (1933) and *Hanneles Himmelfahrt/Hannele's Journey to Heaven* (1933–4). Like Marie Luise Droop's two films a decade earlier, von Harbou's efforts achieved little success and she returned to script-writing.

Riefenstahl, however, met with far more success in pursuing a directing career and has subsequently become one of Germany's most famous (some would argue, infamous) directors. After a short and successful dance career, Riefenstahl turned film actress and then moved into directing. Her first film was the feature *Das blaue Licht/The Blue Light* in 1932, about a young woman who is persecuted as a witch by the inhabitants of a remote mountain village. However, it was her subsequent documentary epics for the Nazi regime that have secured her notoriety. Although she made four such films, two in particular have repeatedly attracted the attention of critics: her film of the 1934 Nazi party rally at Nuremberg, *Triumph des Willens/Triumph of the Will* (1934–5) and her two-part film of the 1936 Olympic Games, *Olympia* (1936–8).

Critics have been divided in their evaluation of Riefenstahl's work. Some have hailed the films as cinematic masterpieces in formal terms, while others have condemned them for their political content and clear espousal of Nazi ideology. When her work aroused renewed interest in the sixties, Riefenstahl attempted to play down the propagandistic nature of her film work and her involvement with the Nazi party. Although she admitted she was fascinated by Hitler, she denied having been a Nazi herself. In an interview given in 1972 she also claimed to believe in an absolute distinction between art and politics, arguing that 'true art and real artists are unpolitical.'[9] With specific regard to *Triumph of the Will* she asserted:

> I showed what was happening then in front of our eyes, what everyone heard about ... It was, certainly, a film commissioned by Hitler ... But you will notice, if you see the film today, that *it doesn't contain a single reconstructed scene. Everything in it is real ... It is history. A purely historical film.*[10] (my emphasis)

However, Riefenstahl exercised an enormous degree of control over her work. She not only directed, but edited and produced her films as well. As editor of *Triumph of the Will* she was responsible for selecting extracts from Hitler's speech at the rally for inclusion in the final version. According to Peter Nowotny, the extracts she chose demonstrate a 'precise knowledge of the propagandistic intention of the party rally'.[11] Riefenstahl also made several attempts to conceal the extensive support she received from the regime for her film work. She maintained, for instance, that the *Olympia* film was commissioned by the International Olympic Committee. Although the finance was channelled through a private company, it was actually commissioned by Goebbel's Ministry of Propaganda who placed one and a half million reich marks at Reifenstahl's disposal.

In a divided post-war Germany, the opportunities for women to direct in the Federal Republic remained limited. Although several women did work in film during the fifties, none managed to make feature-length films. Instead their films were mostly cultural shorts, documentaries or educational programmes. Like most of their few predecessors moreover, none of them pursued a lengthy filmmaking career, making usually only one or two films at most.

As is evident from the brevity of this history, up to the end of the fifties professional women filmmakers can be characterized by their virtual absence. Indeed, of the aforementioned women, only two are cited by most German film historians: Leontine Sagan and Leni Riefenstahl. Of these two, the former made only one film and the latter is almost universally considered a 'special case'.[12] Lotte Reiniger is in fact also relatively well known, but discussions of her work are usually confined to histories of film animation.

One German distributor even tried to capitalize upon this absence as a marketing strategy for one of their films. After working as assistant director to her filmmaker husband Helmut Käutner, Erica Balqué made her only feature, *Zu jung für die Liebe?/Too Young for Love?* in 1961, an unremarkable film about thwarted young love and teenage pregnancy. As the subject matter was hardly new, the distribution company played up the novelty of a woman director. In the hope of attracting the curious, Balqué's film was promoted as an experiment undertaken by its producer to establish whether women's general absence as film directors resulted from a lack of ability or a lack of opportunity!

During the sixties, however, the situation began to change with the emergence of the critically acclaimed New German Cinema. The conditions that gave rise to and supported this cinema opened up new opportunities for women to direct. Although many women were unable to take advantage of these opportunities until the seventies, Danièle Huillet, May Spils and Ula Stöckl all made their directorial debuts within a few years. The work of each is very different and only the films of Stöckl give any indication of the feminist film culture that was to emerge in the seventies.

French by birth, Huillet moved to Germany in 1959 to join her partner, filmmaker Jean-Marie Straub, and they commenced (and have continued) working as a filmmaking team. Their first collaboration resulted in *Machorka Muff* in 1962. Based on Heinrich Böll's story *Hauptstädtisches Journal/Bonn Diary*, the film focuses on the visit of Colonel Machorka-Muff to the capital and reveals the continuing presence of the old army network in the new, supposedly democratic state. Not only did this make the film highly provocative, but its formally experimental nature led one critic to describe it as 'the worst film since 1895'.[13] Their subsequent work continued to provoke and challenge, but generally met with critical acclaim among New German Cinema supporters.

After doing some theatre work and fashion modelling, May Spils moved to Munich where she worked as a film extra and met filmmakers Peter Schamoni, Klaus Lemke and her future collaborator Werner Enke. In 1965 she visited the Oberhausen Film Festival with Lemke and later recalled: 'I took a look at all the films and said, I can do that too.'[14] The following year she made her first film, *Das Portrait/*

The Portrait (1966), a ten-minute short about a young woman (played by Spils) who wants to become a painter: she tries to produce what she thinks is 'high art', but eventually sticks her own photo on the canvas and signs it. The film won a prize at the 1966 Mannheim Film Festival.

Encouraged by her success, Spils made a second short, *Manöver/ Maneuver* (1966). The film focuses on a young man, played by Werner Enke who, with the help of his girlfriend, played by Spils, tries to prepare for his first proper job by acting out various work situations. With its combination of off-beat humour and slapstick comedy, the film met with a positive response from both critics and audiences. Spils's first feature, *Zur Sache Schätzchen/Go to it, Baby* (1967), elaborated on the comic style and male character developed in *Maneuver*. Produced by Peter Schamoni, *Go to it, Baby* revolves around a day in the life of Martin, a laid-back, anti-establishment young man, played again by Enke. His day basically comprises a number of comic escapades which include outsmarting the police, meeting a young woman at a swimming pool and kidnapping a goat at the zoo. These are interspersed with several chase sequences played for visual comedy and punctuated by Martin's humorous throw-away observations.

A low-budget black-and-white film, *Go to it, Baby* initially had difficulties finding a distributor. But once it got into the cinemas it was a phenomenal success, outstripping all American films at the box office in 1969 and running in one Hamburg cinema for ninety-six consecutive weeks. Critics also responded favourably. It won prizes for its dialogue and male lead, and many found it a refreshing change from the work of Huillet, Straub and other new directors. One critic, for example, reported:

> At the beginning of the glut of young filmmakers May Spils has earned a small note of distinction for herself: she has delivered the first light entertainment film in the midst of a large supply of self-reflexive sorrow and satirical generation mustiness.[15]

Due to this success, Spils was able to continue directing features and several films followed, all of which built on and refined the original Enke character.

In 1963 Ula Stöckl was among the first students to enrol at the Ulm Film Institute, a film school set up with the specific aim of training directors for the New German Cinema. Stöckl made several shorts at the Institute before directing her first feature in 1968, *Neun Leben hat die Katze/ The Cat has Nine Lives*. Based on her own experiences, the film was originally intended to focus on a single protagonist, contrasting her dreams of independence with a reality that offered few opportunities to women. However, Stöckl carried out extensive research for the film in the form of interviews with other women, the results of which led her to introduce four female characters, each of whom offers a different possible role model. Katherina is an ambitious journalist who lives alone and is involved with Stephan, a married man; her friend Ann is recently divorced and unsure of her future, but soon becomes involved in a new relationship; Magdalene is Stephan's deceived wife, who sits at home contemplating suicide; and Gabriele is a popular and glamorous singer who Katherina interviews. Filmed in both black and white and colour, and combining both action and dream sequences to form an episodic narrative, *The Cat has Nine Lives* explores the relationships between the women, the dissatisfaction they experience in their respective lives and their inability to effect real change. Most of Stöckl's subsequent films have similarly focused on the lives of women.

In addition to the Ulm Film Institute, the emergence of the New German Cinema also precipitated the setting up of two further film schools. The German Film and Television Academy in Berlin (DFFB) opened in September 1966 and the College of Television and Film in Munich (HFF) in November 1967.[16] These schools were the first of their kind in the Federal Republic and provided invaluable training opportunities. A number of women who later established themselves as filmmakers were among their first students. Claudia von Alemann, Recha Jungmann and Jeanine Meerapfel trained with Stöckl at Ulm; Helke Sander, Cristina Perincioli, Gisela Tuchtenhagen, Gardi Deppe, Barbara Kasper and Marianne Lüdcke attended the DFFB; while Gloria Behrens, Ingemo Engström, Gabi Kubach and Uschi Reich studied at the Munich school. Furthermore, the schools offered women a rare opportunity to work together with other women rather than in positions of isolation within a male-dominated profession.

Despite this promising start and the additional impulse provided by the women's movement, however, women were in fact acutely under-represented within the New German Cinema until well into the seventies. During the sixties and early seventies most women worked only in those areas highly peripheral to or quite separate from the new cinema. Helma Sanders-Brahms, Erika Runge, Gloria Behrens, Gabi Kubach, Gertrud Pinkus, Edith Schmidt and others worked for television companies making TV documentaries, series, films and news reports. Birgit Hein and Dore O were both highly active contributors to West Germany's avant-garde cinema, *Das andere Kino*, which emerged in the mid to late sixties. Dore O was in fact instrumental in making Hamburg a centre for independent filmmakers. She started making films with her husband Werner Nekes in 1967, subsequently branching out on her own. The same year she and Nekes moved to Hamburg where they met up with other independent filmmakers such as Hellmuth Costard, Helmut Herbst and Klaus Wyborny. Their flat quickly became a centre for the emergent *Das andere Kino*, and Dore O co-founded the Hamburg Filmmakers' Cooperative to distribute its films.

At the beginning of the seventies a number of women also started working with video, often coming to the medium from a background in performance art. In the course of the decade Valie Export, Friederike Pezold, Rebecca Horn and Ulrike Rosenbach established themselves as leading video artists.

Women were also in a distinct minority at the new film schools. In the DFFB's first year of operation, for instance, only two of its thirty students were female; the following year, 1967, no women were accepted; in 1968 five out of seventeen new students were female; and in 1969 only three out of eleven.[17] Of the few women who did get places, some initially found it difficult to acquire any reasonable degree of technical expertise during their training. One female student at Ulm reported that her male colleagues usually ended up operating the cameras. In order to learn camera herself, she eventually bought her own super-8 kit.[18] A similar situation at the Berlin school led female students to organize their own women-only work groups.

Nevertheless, the number of professional women filmmakers clearly increased during the sixties and seventies. By 1975 Claudia von Alemann confidently asserted that, 'Off the cuff, I could mention twenty women in the FRG alone who make films professionally, to say nothing of the women who are still at film school or work as journalists in television.'[19] However, as relatively few had broken into the prestigious area of feature film production, women filmmakers could still be characterized by 'their virtual, if not total, absence'.[20] In direct contrast to Alemann, Helke Sander asserted that women in the film sector were still 'on the other side of the camera: looked at, used, and directed by men'.[21]

Even though Danièle Huillet, May Spils and Ula Stöckl became the Federal Republic's very first professional female directors, their existence was barely noticed. Huillet was overshadowed by her male partner: 'In those days it was not fashionable to mention the women. No one noticed ... that I was always listed in the credits.'[22] Spils became almost as much of a 'special case' as Riefenstahl due to her reputation as a sexploitation film director. The reputation stems from a combination of her predilection for sexually suggestive film titles, the large number of women in her films dressed only in bikinis or underwear, and her own preference for wearing a bikini while working. The actual films in fact 'reveal minimal sexual content'.[23] Stöckl, on the other hand, suffered from trying to explore the concerns of women too soon. With the women's movement barely in its birth throes when she made her directorial debut, a critical audience had not yet emerged capable of appreciating her work.

The decisive breakthrough came in 1977. A number of women succeeded in making their first feature films and participating in the mainstream of New German Cinema activity: Helma Sanders-Brahms made *Heinrich* (1976–77), Helke Sander made *Die allseitig reduzierte Persönlichkeit/ The All-Round Reduced Personality*, Heidi Genée made *Grete Minde*, Margarethe von Trotta made *Das zweite Erwachen der Christa Klages/ The Second Awakening of Christa Klages*, and Ulrike Ottinger made *Madame X – Eine absolute Herrscherin/ Madame X – An Absolute Ruler*. Of these, both Sander's and von Trotta's films garnered considerable critical acclaim; Genée's film won a Silver Film Ribbon in the Federal film awards, and Sanders-Brahms's became the first film by a woman to win the top Federal film prize, the Golden Cup for best feature film, in the history of West German cinema.

It was not altogether surprising that these films should meet with so much success, since their directors had frequently served long 'apprenticeships' before making their first features. By the time she made *Heinrich*, Sanders-Brahms, for example, had already established herself as a highly competent professional filmmaker. She had started her career as a television announcer and moved into filmmaking by training with

Italian directors Sergio Corbucci and Pier Paolo Pasolini. In 1969 she started work on her first film, a documentary which took a critical look at the everyday life of a young working woman. Although a television department expressed initial interest in the project, they eventually decided that Sanders-Brahms's treatment was too 'ordinary' and not exciting enough. She refused, however, to compromise and financed the project herself. Upon completion, Sanders-Brahms sent the finished film, *Angelika Urban, Verkäuferin, verlobt/Angelika Urban, Salesgirl, Engaged to be Married* (1969–70), to a television station, Westdeutscher Rundfunk (WDR), who offered to buy a shortened version of the programme. Again the director refused to compromise and submitted it instead to the 1970 Oberhausen Film Festival where it won two prizes. Subsequently, another television company, Zweites Deutsches Fernsehen (ZDF), bought the film, screened it in its entirety, and commissioned Sanders-Brahms to make another.

A string of films for television followed and by 1976 Sanders-Brahms was a relatively well-known filmmaker in the Federal Republic. Her career had been given a particular boost by her fiction film of 1975, *Shirins Hochzeit/Shirin's Wedding*, which was broadcast in January 1976. Made in black and white, the film focuses on Shirin, a young Turkish woman, who travels to Germany in search of Mahmud, the man she was betrothed to as a child. Mahmud works as a guest worker in Germany and on his last visit home appeared to have forgotten all about Shirin. The film follows her from a relatively promising start in Germany through her gradual 'descent' into prostitution as the only means of survival. Using a combination of low-key realism and conversational voice-over, the film not only offers a moving portrait of its central protagonist but also operates as an observation on the meeting of two alien cultures. Although the film elicited an extremely negative response from the Turkish community (including death threats for the actress who played Shirin), it achieved exceptionally high viewing figures and was selected as 'television film of the month'.

In 1977, the success of Sanders-Brahms and her colleagues clearly demonstrated that women directors had arrived in the national arena and could compete with the best of West Germany's male directors. In the wake of their success even more women who had served filmmaking apprenticeships – either in television like Sanders-Brahms, or at film school, or by making shorts – started to break into feature film directing. Their films continued to win prizes and started to attract considerable media attention. At the same time, women working in virtually all areas of the audio-visual media started to work together to improve their professional opportunities and raise awareness of the feminist consciousness that informed much of their work.

By the early eighties West Germany boasted a highly acclaimed women's cinema and a vibrant feminist film culture as part of its new cinema. A catalogue compiled in 1980 listed no less than fourteen women who were working as film directors within the Federal Republic's new cinema: Claudia von Alemann, Jutta Brückner, Doris Dörrie, Claudia Holldack, Elfi Mikesch, Dorothea Neunkirchen, Ulrike Ottinger, Cristina Perinciola, Helga Reidemeister, Erika Runge, Helke Sander, Helma Sanders-Brahms, Ula Stöckl and Margarethe von Trotta.[24] In a subsequent catalogue a further five women were added to the list: Ingemo Engström, Heidi Genée, Petra Haffter, Recha Jungmann and Jeanine Meerapfel.[25] Women film-makers could no longer be characterized as absent.

Despite the significance of this emergence of women directors as a professional group in West Germany and their substantial contribution to the country's cinema, the work of these new directors has been largely overlooked or marginalized in Britain and the US. The major British and US studies of the New German Cinema have focused almost exclusively on the small number of male directors already mentioned: Fassbinder, Herzog, Kluge, Schlöndorff, Straub, Syberberg and Wenders. Women directors have, on the whole, been accorded serious critical attention only in a small number of specialist academic journals, if at all.

The fact that Helma Sanders-Brahms's film *Heinrich* was the first film by a woman to win the top Federal film award is an event hardly mentioned by Anglo-American observers. In all fairness, there is some justification for this. The film was not well received in Germany, and many critics (and fellow filmmakers) vehemently disagreed with the jury's selection of the film for the best feature prize. Although 'perfectly crafted and elegantly photographed',[26] *Heinrich* was based on the letters, documents and literature of the nineteenth-century writer Heinrich von Kleist. Not only was the film perceived to have very little contemporary relevance, but it was also made at a time when the German cinema was coming under attack for the large number of films based on literary sources. Furthermore, the film's content, together with its director's self-confessed careerist attitudes, place Sanders-Brahms somewhat at odds with the emergent feminist film culture and the women's cinema that followed.

However, such factors obviously cannot account for the *general* critical neglect of Sanders-Brahms and the many other women who subsequently established themselves as filmmakers. With a few rare exceptions, films by female directors have been represented by observers as a homogeneous body of work that exists on the periphery of New German Cinema and is of only marginal interest. John Sandford's book, *The New German Cinema*, is a prime example of this tendency.[27] Published in 1980, the book devotes a chapter each to Fassbinder, Kluge, Herzog, Schlöndorff, Straub, Syberberg and Wenders. Women directors are relegated to a section curiously entitled 'Peculiarities', which also deals with a miscellaneous collection of other filmmakers and areas of interest, such as the so-called Berlin School and the new *Heimat* or homeland film. As Anton Kaes observes 'such accomplished directors as Helke Sander, Helma Sanders-Brahms, or Margartha [sic] von Trotta are not represented as major directors but merely as illustrations of the women's film.'[28]

Published three years later, Timothy Corrigan's *New German Film: The Displaced Image* is even more selective and specific in its focus, offering analyses of just six films by male directors: Wenders's *Kings of the Road* (1976), Fassbinder's *The Bitter Tears of Petra von Kant* (1972), Schlöndorff's *Coup de Grâce* (1976), Kluge's *Strongman Ferdinand* (1975), Herzog's *The Enigma of Kaspar Hauser* (1974) and Syberberg's *Hitler, A Film from Germany* (1977) – while the work of women directors is totally excluded.[29] Although Corrigan clearly states in his introduction that the book is not a comprehensive study of the New German Cinema, the films he includes inevitably come to be considered in some way representative.[30] This further reinforces the marginalization of women's filmmaking.

In *New German Cinema: From Oberhausen to Hamburg*, also published in 1983, James Franklin does at least make some acknowledgement, albeit briefly, of women's contribution to the development of New German Cinema. He lists 'the most prominent women filmmakers presently at work in Germany'[31] and notes their previous work as actresses, scriptwriters, editors and producers for male directors. But the same seven male directors are still the main focus of his book. His main discussion of women filmmakers is confined to two brief pages in his introduction, where he identifies them as a group on the basis of their documentary background and the socially and politically committed nature of their films. Such categorization, however, obscures the diversity of their work – particularly their breakthrough into feature film production – and suggests that their films can be discussed more as a genre.

Neither do two of West Germany's own film historians, Hans Helmut Prinzler and Hans Günther Pflaum, give much coverage to their country's women filmmakers. In their book *Cinema in the Federal Republic of Germany*, translated into English in 1983, the main discussion of women directors is left to three short pages at the very end of their introductory survey of West German cinema.[32] Although they maintain that 'women's films do not constitute a specific category in the New German Cinema',[33] their approach to this particular area of filmmaking tends to suggest that it does. The relegation of the discussion to the end of the survey also implies that it is one of marginal interest.[34]

Special New German Cinema issues of academic journals have also tended to follow this general trend, despite the fact that such journals have been one of the few places where women directors have received at least some serious critical attention. *Literature / Film Quarterly*'s special issue in 1979,[35] for instance, includes an article on *The Lost Honour of Katherina Blum* (1975) which was co-directed by Margarethe von Trotta; but otherwise, it deals only with Fassbinder, Herzog and Wenders. Moreover, the *Katherina Blum* article restricts itself to an analysis of the way in which Heinrich Böll's novel has been adapted to the visual medium, rather than offering any discussion of von Trotta's involvement. Although the writer does acknowledge von Trotta's role as co-director – something the editor does not mention in his preface to the issue – his primary concern is with the filmic product, not its originators. The following year, *Wide Angle*'s New German Cinema issue focused exclusively on the work of male directors.[36]

Quarterly Review of Film Studies[37] and *New German Critique*[38] start to redress the balance in their special issues, but both are limited in their scope. The former includes a single essay on women filmmakers which looks at just four Berlin-based directors: Ulrike Ottinger, Cristina

Perinciola, Helga Reidemeister and Helke Sander. In the latter, only two out of eight articles deal with the work of women directors. One offers an analysis of Helke Sander's first feature, *The All-Round Reduced Personality* (1977); the other is a round-table discussion which addresses reception as well as production and also references the US situation. The remainder focus predictably on Kluge, Fassbinder, Herzog, Wenders and Syberberg. In a similar vein, *Discourse*'s special issue in 1983 includes two articles that examine the work of Helke Sander, but discussions of any other women directors are noticeably absent.[39] The rest of the issue deals with the work of Kluge, Fassbinder and Herbert Achternbusch, together with the collectively-made film *Deutschland im Herbst/Germany in Autumn* (1978).

This is not to suggest that the aforementioned studies are not valuable accounts and analyses of the work of some of West Germany's most prominent male directors. Rather, it is to argue that the work of Fassbinder, Herzog, Kluge, Schlöndorff, Straub, Syberberg and Wenders has largely come to be considered as constituting the New German Cinema. This is particularly apparent in the way that most writers now eschew the use of the New German Cinema label if they are discussing any other director or a wider spectrum of directors. As American academic Marc Silberman has observed, it also means that 'most fans of the new wave German film ... would be hard pressed to name a woman film director – perhaps with the exception of two film-makers who have had some popular success, Margarethe von Trotte [sic] ... and Helma Sanders-Brahms.'[40]

Silberman goes on to ask, 'Why haven't they become better known following the critical acclaim accorded to German cinema for the past several years?'[41] As if in response, several New German Cinema commentators have been quick to point to the fact that many women directors did not make their first feature film until well after their more famous male colleagues. Franklin, for instance, observes that although many women directors 'belong to the same generation as the male directors of the New Cinema, the majority of them did not manage to make their first feature films until the mid and late 1970s ... most women of this generation were able to make only short films or tele-vision films.'[42] This was due to the fact that the extremely restrictive social, economic and institutional conditions that had denied most women access to the means of feature film production throughout the history of German cinema persisted, on the whole, during the early years of the New German Cinema. Consequently, the new women directors lagged substantially behind their male colleagues in establishing themselves as film directors within the new cinema. When the first studies of the New German Cinema began to appear, women's feature film production was still a relatively recent phenomenon.

In the course of the eighties, the critical neglect of West Germany's women directors at least began to be recognized. In his book *West German Film in the Course of Time: Reflections on the Twenty Years since Oberhausen*, published in 1984, Eric Rentschler describes feminist filmmaking in the Federal Republic as 'a subject rarely broached in the scrutiny of New German films'.[43] Although the parameters of his discussion do not permit Rentschler to rectify the situation, he does repeatedly draw attention to the neglect of this 'other history of West German film'.[44]

More constructively, other observers actually began to study the subject itself. In the mid eighties, due largely to the enthusiasm of Marc Silberman, the American film journal *Jump Cut* carried a special section (spread over three issues) on women's cinema and feminist filmmaking in West Germany.[45] Alongside interviews with directors Jutta Brückner, Helga Reidemeister, Cristina Perinciola, Erika Runge, Ula Stöckl, Helke Sander and Ulrike Ottinger, Silberman included articles on various films and translations of extracts from the feminist film journal *Frauen und Film* (*Women and Film*). Klaus Phillips's book *New German Filmmakers*, published in 1984, also included a chapter on Ula Stöckl, together with joint chapters on Volker Schlöndorff and Margarethe von Trotta, Jean-Marie Straub and Danièle Huillet, and May Spils and Werner Enke.[46] Similarly, the winter 1984–85 issue of *Film Criticism* carried a West German Women's film section which looks at the work of von Trotta and two new films by Sander and Ottinger.[47] *Literature/Film Quarterly*'s second special issue on Germany's new cinema also included an article which highlights the work of fifteen women directors[48] and Thomas Elsaesser's recent book, *New German Cinema: A History* devoted more space to a discussion of women's film production than has hitherto been the case in such studies.[49]

Nevertheless, West Germany's new female directors appear to remain – even after nearly fifteen years of a flourishing women's cinema – of marginal interest to most New German Cinema observers in Britain and the US. Although other histories of West Germany's new cinema are beginning to be written, as yet none have focused specifically on the country's feminist film culture. Apart from Elsaesser's book, women's film production still barely figures in studies of West German film. Two other recent books, Eric Rentschler's edited anthology *German Film and Literature: Adaptations and Transformations*, and Anton Kaes's new book *From 'Hitler' to 'Heimat': The Return of History as Film*, both explore their subject through a series of analyses of individual films.[50] The only film by a woman included in each is Helma Sanders-Brahms's *Deutschland, bleiche Mutter/Germany, Pale Mother* (1979–80).[51] An observation made by Rentschler in 1984 still rings true today: 'feminist filmmakers receive, at best, patronizing pats on the back, but little serious discussion.'[52]

Obviously, which films and directors receive the attention of British and US observers is dependent to a large extent on which films get screened at festivals, included in special seasons of films, or taken into distribution in those countries. John Sandford stresses, for instance, that his selection of directors for inclusion in his book 'has been guided more than anything by the international reputation of the directors concerned ... the seven directors to whom the bulk of this book is devoted are internationally the "big names" of the New German Cinema.'[53] But even though a number of women directors have risen to positions of prominence in their homeland, most have been far less successful at achieving international profiles.

Nevertheless, awareness of women filmmakers' work did increase in Britain and the US during the eighties. In Britain, for example, cinema releases were given to films by Margarethe von Trotta, Helma Sanders-Brahms and Doris Dörrie; a number of women's films were broadcast on television; and various programmes of women's films were screened at repertory cinemas and film festivals.[54] Although still less well known than Fassbinder, Wenders and Herzog, women such as von Trotta, Sanders-Brahms and Dörrie have entered the international arena. Indeed, a sneak preview of Monika Treut's *Die Jungfrauen Maschine/ Virgin Machine* (1988) at London's National Film Theatre proved so popular it sold out.

Despite the extenuating circumstances, the fact remains that Anglo-American observers have tended to ignore or marginalize the work of

Germany's new women directors. The marginalization of women's filmmaking is of course not peculiar to West Germany: rather, it is a specific example of a general trend that has prevailed throughout the history of cinema. To reiterate probably the most frequently cited example of this, the contribution of French filmmaker Alice Guy to early cinema has, for instance, effectively been written out of dominant film history. A prolific filmmaker whose career spanned the years 1896 to 1920, Guy was one of the first directors to make narrative-based fiction films and played an extensive role in developing the early French film industry.[55] However, she is not even included in Richard Roud's major historical reference book, *Cinema, A Critical Dictionary: The Major Filmmakers*, aside from a single reference under the entry for Louis Feuillade.[56] Moreover, some of her films have even been attributed to male colleagues and it has largely been the work of feminist film critics that have rescued her, together with many other women film directors, from virtual obscurity. This general trend persists and is not only evident in discussions of the New German Cinema. Jill Forbes has identified the same tendency in the British reception of Agnes Varda's films. Despite being a major French filmmaker, Varda's films are, according to Forbes, 'often simply ignored. Frequently, in fact, Varda is literally invisible, either because her movies do not find a distributor ... or, more subtly, through a damaging critical silence.'[57]

In the case of the New German Cinema, however, the critical neglect of women filmmakers is particularly surprising given that, after a prolonged historical absence, the German cinema suddenly possessed 'proportionally more women filmmakers than any other film-producing country.' The first part of this book, comprising chapters one and two, therefore explores the conditions specific to the New German Cinema that have functioned to marginalize the work of women directors despite their relatively substantial number. The first chapter outlines the development of the new cinema and explores women's experience within it, showing why women were unable to break into feature film production until the late seventies. Chapter two demonstrates how the critical reception of the New German Cinema in Britain and the US has been singularly unconducive to the inclusion of women within its ranks once they started directing features.

The second part of the book constitutes a discussion of certain aspects of the women's cinema and feminist film culture that emerged in West Germany during the seventies and eighties. In view of the prevailing critical neglect of this area, there is now an extensive 'other history' that needs to be documented and explored. Since it is obviously impossible to do this in a single book, chapters three, four, five and six focus only on the main characteristics of and significant trends within women's filmmaking. This approach is not intended to deny the formal and thematic diversity of women's film work, but rather to highlight the shared concerns and experiences that give rise to, shaped and directed West Germany's feminist film culture. I should like to stress that, as with any book of this nature, there are inevitably imbalances and omissions: some directors and films are discussed more fully than others, while some have only been referenced or mentioned briefly. Hopefully, the imbalances and omissions will be corrected in future publications.

Before proceeding, it is necessary to make a few observations. On page 197 there is a list of women film- and videomakers, who have worked in West Germany during the past twenty-five years. It is by no means exhaustive, but is intended to give some background information where available on the women discussed or mentioned in this book. It includes date of birth; place of birth if outside Germany; brief education, training and career details; and a filmography. Original film titles are given in the filmographies, followed by either the UK release title if applicable or a literal translation (this practice has also been adopted throughout the book, although after the first mention of a film in each chapter it is subsequently referred to by its English title or translation). If an English title only is given, it is the original film title. However, in the case of more experimental film- and videomakers, such as Valie Export, Birgit Hein, Rebecca Horn, Dore O, Friederike Pezold, Ulrike Rosenbach and Claudia Schillinger, only original film/video titles have been given (unless an English-language title has entered common usage). This is partly because the films are usually referred to by their original titles in English language sources, but also because many of them are virtually untranslatable.

Also, some of the women directors included in the list and whose work is discussed or mentioned in the book are not in fact West German nationals. Cristina Perincioli, for instance, is Swiss, while Valie Export is Austrian. But these women have either worked and/or lived in the Federal Republic, and their work has consequently had an impact on or become associated with West Germany's feminist film culture. Furthermore, not all women included in the book would necessarily describe themselves or their work as feminist. However, this usually has less to do with the politics or preoccupations of the filmmakers than with a rejection of the practice of labelling. Most would argue that feminism is both an important and an unavoidable context for their work.

Finally, the recent reunification of Germany obviously has implications for film production and culture in both halves of the country. While it is impossible to foresee how reunification will effect women's filmmaking specifically, it is now a highly appropriate moment to carry out this long overdue examination of women's position in and contribution to West German cinema.

PART ONE

New German Cinema

'Why do feminist filmmakers receive, at best,
patronizing pats on the back, but little
serious discussion?'

Eric Rentschler

ONE

A Divided History

Although the work of women directors forms an important part of the New German Cinema, women's filmmaking has developed along a course different from that of their male colleagues, and this has contributed significantly to its marginalization in most studies of the new cinema. In order to demonstrate this divided history it is necessary first to outline the factors that gave rise to the New German Cinema and the institutional structures that supported it. Through the work of film academics and critics such as Jan Dawson, Thomas Elsaesser, Sheila Johnston and Eric Rentschler, a body of work now exists that offers a highly complex and sophisticated analysis of this area; and the first half of this chapter is heavily indebted to this work.

The New German Cinema came into being as a result of a body of criticism that was directed at West German cinema in the late fifties and early sixties. This criticism eventually precipitated the introduction of a complex network of public subsidies which attempted to promote a national cinema that was both culturally motivated and economically viable. The origins of this criticism stemmed largely from the Allies' handling of the film industry after World War Two. Their policies, guided by a combination of ideological and economic considerations, left West German cinema artistically impoverished and economically vulnerable.

At the end of the war it had been deemed necessary to 're-educate' the German people in order both to denazify Germany and to build up the western zones as a capitalist stronghold to counter Soviet influence in eastern Europe. American films were quickly identified as a potential means of 'indoctrinating people into the free way of life and instil[ling] in them a compelling desire for freedom'.[1] Hollywood, however, proved reluctant to send films to West Germany for this purpose until its economic interests had been secured. Only when guarantees were made that American companies would be free to transfer their profits out of Germany did American films start to pour into the western zones. As the German market had been closed to Hollywood during the war, distributors had a whole backlog of films to draw upon. These had already gone into profit in their home and other overseas markets and could therefore be made available at prices which undercut their European competitors. Consequently, American companies rapidly achieved a position of economic dominance in Germany; by 1951, over two hundred American films were being released per annum.

The American Motion Picture Export Association was eager to protect this new market. Measures were therefore taken to prevent the imposition of an import quota on American films, a safeguard which was introduced by other European countries after the war to protect their own film industries. In line with American policy on other German industries, the Allies also insisted on the dismantling of the remnants of the Nazi film industry which had been centralized and state controlled via a giant conglomerate called Universum Film AG (UFA). Decartelization laws were passed; the production, distribution and exhibition branches of the industry were separated; and only small independent production companies were licensed. It was hoped that these measures would promote an industry which would operate on the basis of capitalist free enterprise, but would at the same time prevent the re-emergence of a strong German film industry that could threaten America's monopoly of the German market.

This pursuit of both political aims and economic interests by the Americans had far-reaching effects on the fledgling West German film industry. Forced to remain small in scale, and with production dispersed around the country, the German industry was an unattractive prospect for investment. This was exacerbated as the country's economic recovery got underway, since other industries prospered and offered safer investment prospects than the high-risk area of film production. Unlike in Britain and France, where their profits were frozen, American distributors also had little incentive to invest in West German production as they could transfer any profits back to the US. In an attempt to stimulate production the government introduced a system of guaranteed credits in 1950 to encourage producers to raise finance for film projects. Owing to its administrative unwieldiness, however, the system proved unsuccessful in its aims, and after equally unsuccessful modifications two years later, was ultimately withdrawn in the mid fifties.

In the absence of more decisive government intervention, the German film was unable to compete with the glamour and spectacle of the expensively produced Hollywood product. Consequently, indigenous production quickly became orientated towards the home market. This rendered German films largely unsuitable for export, which meant that producers had to try to break even on national box-office receipts alone. The resulting national cinema was therefore marked by low production values. Films produced during this period included *Heimatfilme* or homeland films which depicted 'the unproblematic activities of simple country folk in settings of natural magnificence and pastoral bliss',[2] adventure films based on the novels of Karl May, so-called *Sissi* films set in imperial Austria (which were basically a variation of the homeland films), together with romantic adventures and comedies set in picturesque locations. This orientation towards 'escapism' moved one contemporary foreign critic to observe that in West German films 'events of the thirties and forties are either ignored or treated as something remote, regrettable, and faintly unmentionable.'[3]

To a certain extent this was hardly surprising. Although UFA was eventually laid to rest, denazification of the film industry workforce apparently proved more difficult to implement since according to one American officer, 'virtually all directors, writers, actors, cameramen and technicians had been more or less active members of the NSDAP.'[4] Although it has been argued that many employees of the Nazi film industry were in fact less than enthusiastic about the party and its nationalistic policies,[5] it remains undeniable that most of these people were re-employed. With the escalation of the cold war the recruitment of ex-Nazis was also considered distinctly preferable to the risk of communist infiltration. By 1960 over 40 per cent of working film directors had been prominent in Nazi cinema, and according to Helmut Herbst the industry became 'a "closed shop", firmly controlled by the old UFA generation. There was never a cultural rebirth of the West German film industry after the war.'[6]

This lack of a 'cultural rebirth' in German cinema was compounded by the introduction of 'quality' ratings. From 1955, these entitled a producer to considerable relief from entertainment tax. Since government representatives sat on the committees which awarded these ratings, the state helped determine what constituted 'quality'. As a result, this supposed financial inducement functioned to inhibit producers addressing 'difficult' subjects, such as the Nazi past, or adopting a critical stance on contemporary issues. According to Elsaesser, 'Instead of quality and experiment, it encouraged mediocrity and conformism, and the official list of "valuable" films for the 1950s reads more like a roll call of the world's worst movies than a guide to a nation's film culture.'[7]

These films, however, proved popular on the home market with the *Heimatfilm* in particular attracting audiences to the cinema in record numbers. Indeed, the industry experienced a brief boom period during the mid fifties: feature film production reached an all-time high in 1955 with 122 productions[8] and cinema attendance peaked the following year with an average of sixteen visits per person.[9]

Yet compared with the output of Hollywood the films looked decidedly provincial – 'drab' and even 'shoddy' are adjectives that have been used by some critics – and did little for the international reputation of West German cinema. There were a handful of notable exceptions to this general trend, for instance, Bernhard Wicki's *Die Brücke/ The Bridge*, made in 1959, became the classic anti-war film of West German cinema. In the same year, Wolfgang Staudte's *Rosen für den Staatsanwalt/ Roses for the Prosecutor* also attracted attention for addressing the fact that former Nazi officers had attained positions of power in the Federal Republic. Exceptions such as these, however, could not halt what became a steady decline in the international standing of West German film.

As the fifties progressed, production figures and box-office receipts also started to decline. By 1963 both had fallen by 50 per cent, and gradually cinemas began to close. Although other factors were involved in this economic decline, the advent of television (as in the rest of

Europe and in the US) played a major role. Whereas in 1956 there had been less than 0.7 million television sets in West Germany, by 1960 this number had risen to 4.6 million, and by 1963 to 9 million.[10]

Even by the mid fifties it had become clear that government intervention would be necessary if the German cinema was to survive. Representatives from the industry established a parliamentary lobby, and by the end of the fifties criticism of West German cinema was rapidly mounting. In 1959, Haro Senft and Ferdinand Khittl formed Doc 59, an organization which stressed both the need to improve the quality of films and to obtain state subsidies for film projects. Two years later film critic Joe Hembus published a pamphlet which sought to pinpoint the causes of the malaise that had struck West German cinema. In particular he condemned the industry's 'factory-like production system where standardized models are turned out on an assembly line'.[11] By 1961 the industry's output was such that the organizers of the Venice Film Festival rejected all entries submitted by the Federal Republic, while at home the Federal Film Prize given annually by the Federal Ministry of the Interior (BMI) went unawarded for best feature film, best director and best screenplay because none were considered to be of sufficient quality.[12]

In February 1962 a group of twenty-six filmmakers, writers and artists, led by Alexander Kluge and including Ferdinand Khittl, Edgar Reitz, Detten Schleiermacher and Haro Senft, drew up and published a manifesto during the eighth Oberhausen Short Film Festival, now known as the Oberhausen Manifesto. They not only added their voices to the mounting condemnation of West German film, but also argued that given the opportunity they could create a new cinema to replace what they dismissively termed *Papas Kino* (papa's cinema):

> The collapse of the conventional German film finally removes the economic justification from a mentality which we reject. The new German film thereby has a chance of coming to life.
>
> In recent years German short films by young authors, directors and producers have received a large number of prizes at international festivals and have won international critical acclaim. These works and their success shows that the future of the German film lies with those who have demonstrated that they speak a new film language.
>
> In Germany, as in other countries, the short film has become a training ground and arena of experimentation for the feature film.

We declare our right to create the new German feature film.

This new film needs new freedoms. Freedom from the usual conventions of the industry. Freedom from the influence of commercial partners. Freedom from the tutelage of other groups with vested interests.

We have concrete ideas about the production of the new German film with regard to its intellectual, formal and economic aspects. We are collectively prepared to take economic risks.

The old film is dead. We believe in the new one.

Less than two months later, in April 1962, the BMI announced plans to launch a new scheme to provide grants for feature film projects, scripts and script outlines. Nearly three years passed, however, before the first film subsidy agency was actually founded, the *Kuratorium junger deutscher Film* (Board of Young German Film). In the interim Alexander Kluge and Detten Schleiermacher persuaded a private college, the *Hochschule für Gestaltung* in Ulm, to establish a department of filmmaking. In the autumn of 1962, under the direction of Kluge and Edgar Reitz, the department started to develop the demands of the Oberhausen Manifesto into a programme for a new cinema, offering a four-year course to train a new generation of filmmakers, or *Filmautoren* as they were termed. Restructured as an autonomous institute (*Institut für Filmgestaltung*) in 1965–66, this avenue of training was the first of its kind in the Federal Republic. Art colleges had not yet introduced film departments, and although a German Institute for Film and Television had been set up in Munich in the fifties, it was so chronically underfunded that practical training to a professional level was never feasible.

Founded in February 1965, the *Kuratorium junger deutscher Film* commenced its work in October 1965 with a brief to promote the kind of filmmaking propounded by the Oberhausen Manifesto and to 'stimulate a renewal of the German film in a manner exclusively and directly beneficial to the community'.[13] The source of funding was the BMI, which granted DM5 million to finance the *Kuratorium*'s first three years of operation. A selection committee, composed largely of film critics and journalists, was elected to allocate money. This took the form of interest-free production loans of up to DM300,000 for a first feature film, which were to be repayable from box-office receipts. The money repaid would then be used to fund more first features by other new directors.

The *Kuratorium* was a very direct response to the demands made by the Oberhausen signatories, and it was initially highly successful in fulfilling its brief. The contracts drawn up between the *Kuratorium* and the recipients of its loans were designed to enable filmmakers to retain total artistic and financial control over their work. This in turn made it beneficial for directors to become their own producers. In its first two years of operation twenty-five films were produced with *Kuratorium* funding. Four of these were the first features of Oberhausen signatories Alexander Kluge (*Abschied von gestern / Yesterday Girl*, 1965–66), Hans Jürgen Pohland (*Katz und Maus / Cat and Mouse*, 1966), Edgar Reitz (*Mahlzeiten / Mealtimes*, 1966), and Haro Senft (*Der sanfte Lauf / The Gentle Course*, 1967). A further two – *Professor Columbus* by Rainer Erler (1967) and *Tätowierung / Tattooing* by Johannes Schaaf (1967) – were produced by signatory Rob Houwer. These first films did indeed appear to be the beginnings of a new cinema. As Ingrid Scheib-Rothbart and Ruth McCormick observe, they 'swept away old cinematic stereotypes, challenging audiences to give up outmoded habits of identifications and to accept new kinds of forms, character development, narrative, and imagery'.[14]

Some of these films also received much critical acclaim. Kluge's *Yesterday Girl* won several awards including the Silver Lion at the 1966 Venice Film Festival and thereby became the first West German film to win a Venice prize, while the following year Reitz's *Mealtimes* took the Best First Feature Award. This success also seemed to mark the beginning of an upturn in the fortunes of West German cinema generally. Non-*Kuratorium* financed films by other new directors were also favourably received at Cannes in 1966, especially Ulrich Schamoni's *Es / It* (1965), Volker Schlöndorff's *Der junge Törless / Young Törless* (1966) which received the International Critics Prize, and Jean-Marie Straub and Danièle Huillet's *Nicht Versöhnt / Not Reconciled* (1965). In Germany Peter Schamoni's *Schonzeit für Füchse / Close Season for Foxes* (1966) also won a Silver Bear at the Berlin Film Festival. Edgar Reitz recalls,

> The press was unbelievably positive. And when the first films came out, there was a degree of public interest which has never been matched since. Films like *Abschied von gestern*, or my own *Mahlzeiten*, attracted audiences of over a million.[15]

This critical acclaim was accompanied by financial rewards. Nine of the *Kuratorium*'s first films received the top quality rating entitling the producer to relief from entertainment tax. Between 1967 and 1969 three *Kuratorium* films also picked up DM1.1 million in Federal Film Prize money,[16] while three more films by new young directors received a further DM1.05 million.[17]

However, this initial stage of euphoria did not last. Having made their first feature films, the new directors were faced with limited funding possibilities for their second films. If they were not lucky enough to win one of the Federal Film Prize awards they had to turn to the diminishing commercial sources. Moreover, while their first films had indeed been well received, they did not do well enough at the box office to repay their production loans. Consequently the *Kuratorium* had rapidly dwindling funds with which to continue its work.

At the same time, the *Kuratorium* funding had given rise to what the commercial sector viewed as unfair competition. As Joe Hembus commented in January 1966:

> In this same German cinema where the emergence of a *single* new film-maker used to create quite a sensation, the first works of no fewer than six filmmakers have made their debut since October 1965. In the upcoming months there will be at least six more. If that continues, we'll see more films by new filmmakers than by the old in 1966.[18]

In a bid to win a share of the subsidies for themselves, the film industry started to lobby Bonn during the *Kuratorium*'s first year of operation, calling for a more commercially orientated revision of subsidy policy.

Although the new directors set up their own organization in 1966, the Syndicate of New German Feature Film Producers, they were unable to counteract the commercial lobby. On 22 December 1967 a new Film Development Act (FFG) was passed, formulated largely according to economic rather than cultural criteria. The act raised a levy on every cinema ticket sold in the Federal Republic and West Berlin to provide funding for film production (estimated to amount to around DM15 million), and the Film Development Board (FFA) was set up to administer these funds. The funding was awarded on the basis of the financial success of the producer's previous film; as long as it had grossed DM500,000, or DM300,000 if it had been given a quality rating, (criteria which were later changed to minimum audience attendance figures) during its first two years of release, a production subsidy for the producer's next film was automatically awarded.

Consequently, first-time directors were not eligible for FFA funding. Reitz moreover maintains that films by new directors like himself were deliberately withdrawn from cinemas by distributors and replaced with industry products, so that the commercial sector could monopolize the new subsidy money. After the FFG had been passed the BMI also ceased funding the *Kuratorium* and handed responsibility over to the *Länder* (states). In June 1969 the *Länder* agreed to provide the agency with an annual budget of DM750,000, which represented a reduction in its resources of over 50 per cent and produced a similar reduction in the number of films financed.

By the beginning of the seventies, therefore, Germany's promising new cinema appeared to have been virtually squeezed out of existence, while the commercial industry cashed in on the new source of film subsidy. Although designed to encourage the economic revival of the industry, the retroactive nature of the FFA funding in fact proved detrimental. It encouraged the production of tried and tested formula films which gave rise to what one observer has described as a cinema of 'unparalleled mediocrity'.[19] This consisted primarily of sex films and low-brow classroom comedies, driving the more intellectually demanding segments of the cinema audience away and resulting in further cinema closures.

Almost as soon as the FFG was passed its shortcomings had become apparent. As early as 1968, parliament resolved that:

> Renewal and improvement of the German film on a purely commercial basis would remain incomplete without a simultaneous raising of quality standards, vigorously promoting research, development and education in the area of film culture, and planned and continuing support for new young filmmakers, as well as the strengthening of existing impulses for reform. The act ... for developing the German film should therefore be supplemented as soon as possible by increased cultural funding via federal and state sources.[20]

Ironically, it was television, the advent of which had contributed so significantly to the decline in cinema audiences, that initially secured the continuing existence of the new German film. Described by Elsaesser as 'the patron saint of the new independent feature',[21] the medium was to assume a crucial role within West German cinema: by the 1980s very few films were produced without television funding of some kind. The structure of West German television was such that there were ten broadcasting companies: nine regional ones which constituted the national network of the first channel (ARD) and the regional networks of the third channel, and *Zweites Deutsches Fernsehen* (ZDF) which broadcast the second national channel. All of these were public corporations and produced relatively few programmes themselves, commissioning commercial companies or freelance independents to produce the rest. Television therefore represented a potentially enormous source of funding that could be tapped by the new directors. West German television moreover had a constitutional commitment to promoting cultural 'quality' and thus provided a more sympathetic producer for the new directors than they were likely to find in the commercial film industry.

During the late 1960s and early 1970s, however, the television companies were commissioning work on a fairly arbitrary basis and the contracts broadcasters made with filmmakers were of a highly ad hoc nature. Being premiered on television also severely diminishes a film's theatrical distribution prospects, since it does not usually do well at the box office and commercial distributors tend not to be interested in such films. After a television screening a new director's film could effectively 'disappear'; with no distributor it could simply become buried in the archives of the broadcasting corporations.

The role of television within West German cinema was therefore formalized and regulated in 1974 by the Film and Television Agreement, drawn up between the FFA and the ARD and ZDF television networks. Whilst they also continued to commission other work, the television corporations agreed to provide DM34 million over a five-year period for film production. Productions funded by this scheme would be guaranteed a theatrical release before being broadcast, with a time lapse of anything from six months to five years. Further funds were put at the disposal of the FFA for the purpose of film project development, with no guarantee that television would eventually be a co-producer in the realization of such projects.

As the seventies progressed, the funding options available gradually began to improve still further. Successive revisions to the FFG ensured, for instance, that pornographic or low-quality films could not automatically qualify for subsidies, and empowered the FFA to make discretionary cash awards to 'good entertainment films' which fulfilled a minimum audience attendance requirement. In 1974 the FFA also introduced project funding awarded on the basis that a project seemed likely 'to improve the quality and profitability of the German film'[22] rather than being dependent on the box office success of a producer's previous film.

In 1977 the *Länder* agreed to increase funds for the *Kuratorium* and Berlin pioneered the idea of regional funding. Although Berlin's scheme was primarily economically motivated, the city was also empowered to finance productions of 'particular cultural and political interest to Berlin'.[23] In the next three to four years Bavaria, Hamburg and North Rhine–Westphalia followed suit and introduced their own regional funding schemes. While the Bavarian scheme is largely based on economic criteria, those of Hamburg and North Rhine–Westphalia have an explicit cultural orientation and are moreover administered largely by the filmmakers themselves.

Although television increasingly functioned as exhibitor, distributor, and often as co-producer for the new German film, it became apparent very early on that in order for a national cinema to develop, the distribution and exhibition sectors of the film industry also needed subsidy. With the distribution sector largely under American control – according to Elsaesser, by the early 1970s there was not a single commercial distributor which was not American controlled[24] – the new directors had no guarantee that their films would go into distribution. As Reitz explains, 'right from the start, half the films produced with public money were left on the shelf. No one making a film could know whether his picture had any chance with ... the distributors or anywhere else.'[25] According to Rentschler, 'in April 1970 it was reported that nineteen Young German films could not find a distributor'.[26] As the film subsidy system developed therefore, increasing attention was paid to these areas. As early as April 1970 the BMI started awarding cash prizes to cinemas which had programmed what was termed a 'suitable quota' of 'good' German films; and from December 1976 it introduced awards for companies that had distributed quality rated or state subsidized German films. From 1971 the

Kuratorium also diverted some of its funds into distribution and exhibition.

In 1971 a group of thirteen filmmakers also took their own initiative, among them Wenders, Fassbinder and Thomas Schamoni, and founded *Filmverlag der Autoren* (Film Publishing House of the Auteurs). Originally set up as a production collective, the *Filmverlag* quickly moved into and prioritized distribution. A second independent distributor, *Basis-Film Verleih*, was also set up at the beginning of the seventies with the aim of acting as both a theatrical and a non-theatrical distributor. These initiatives coincided with the building up of an alternative exhibition circuit. At the beginning of the seventies the Senator for Cultural Affairs in Frankfurt had campaigned for the setting up of cinemas which would be funded by local authorities. This resulted in *Kommunale Kinos* or municipal cinemas being opened in a number of West German cities, which were both able and willing to show the new German films.

As revisions of the film subsidy system began to improve the production, distribution and exhibition opportunities for new German films during the seventies, the New German Cinema began to reassert itself. During 1977–8 half of the feature films being made belonged to the new cinema. Although few of them achieved box-office success, and although the New German Cinema directors were not without their critics at home,[27] the new cinema won renewed international acclaim. Successful films from this period include Schlöndorff and Margarethe von Trotta's *Die verlorene Ehre der Katherina Blum / The lost Honour of Katherina Blum* (1975), Wim Wenders's *Im Lauf der Zeit / Kings of the Road* (1976), von Trotta's *Das zweite Erwachen der Christa Klages / The Second Awakening of Christa Klages* (1977), Fassbinder's *Die Ehe der Maria Braun / The Marriage of Maria Braun* (1978), and Schlöndorff's *Die Blechtrommel / The Tin Drum* (1979). When *The Tin Drum* won the highly coveted American Oscar for the best foreign film in 1980, one critic appeared to be wholly justified in describing the New German Cinema as 'one of the most remarkable, enduring, and promising developments in the cinema of the 1970s'.[28]

As the film subsidy system developed, however, it had become apparent that the 'freedom' from vested interests demanded by the Oberhausen signatories had not been and indeed could not be achieved. As one academic has observed, the New German Cinema was 'almost totally dependent on public money for its existence'.[29] Although a cinema of cultural and artistic 'quality' had emerged, it had been at the cost of political and artistic censorship. Such censorship was of course not new and had already occurred in the fifties when tax concessions had first been tied into quality ratings. But as the new cinema became increasingly dependent on state support, it was increasingly difficult for projects that did not meet certain funding criteria to obtain support. A tendency to tailor funding applications to meet those criteria consequently became virtually unavoidable.

Although there was a concern, for instance, to promote cultural 'quality', the economic rationale underlying the guidelines of many of the funding sources often determined the final decision. Commenting on his work with the FFA project commission, freelance journalist Wilhelm Roth asserted in 1978 that: 'The main discussion that takes place in the project commission is always about whether or not the film will be successful at the box office.'[30] In its early days, the new cinema had incorporated documentary and formally experimental work alongside episodic narratives and more conventional feature films. The early films of a number of directors have, for example, been characterized by their complete rejection of narrative cinema:

> Young German films ... often bore little reference explicitly or implicitly to national or international film culture. The early films of Syberberg or Herzog, for instance, were to a remarkable degree objects *sui generis*, outside any recognizable tradition of filmmaking either commercial or avant garde. Kluge's essays on celluloid, and even Jean-Marie Straub's or Vlado Kristl's films seemed ... inspired by what one might call 'cinephobia', a revulsion against the commercial film industry and its standard product, the fictional narrative film.[31]

However, as subsidy policy became more commercially orientated, filmmakers shunning traditional narrative forms began to experience difficulty in securing subsidies. Eventually such difficulties mitigated against them even applying for funding. Consequently, formally experimental work played a diminishing role in the new cinema, which started to become predominantly a cinema of narrative-based feature films.

Projects that were socially critical or addressed politically sensitive issues similarly risked being turned down for funding. In 1975, for instance, Fassbinder submitted a proposal to the FFA for a film entitled *Der Müll, die Stadt und der Tod/Garbage, The City and Death*. Based on Gerhard Zwerenz's novel *Die Erde ist unbewohnbar wie der Mond/The Earth is as Uninhabitable as the Moon*, which examines some of the negative aspects of capitalism, Fassbinder had originally written it as a play to be performed at the *Theater am Tor* in Frankfurt. However, a charge of anti-semitism had been levelled at the play and it was not staged. The FFA felt that the racist implications persisted in the film project and refused funding.

Even if a project was awarded funding this did not necessarily guarantee that the director or the resulting film would be free from censorship. A quality rating could be withheld which meant not only that a producer was not entitled to tax relief, but also that his or her film was required to gross a higher amount before he or she could qualify for an automatic FFA subsidy for their next project. Both these factors diminished a producer's chances of financing a new film. Kluge was even informed that he would have to repay the subsidy with which he made *Gelegenheitsarbeit einer Sklavin/Occasional Work of a Female Slave* (1973) when discrepancies between his submitted script and the finished film were noticed. Rentschler has interpreted this as 'an official attempt to censure Kluge for the critical stance he expressed in the film toward existing abortion statutes'.[32]

In West Germany representatives of the various political parties sat on the administrative councils of all the television corporations. Politicians from the right-wing CDU/CSU in particular have not been reticent in voicing their disapproval of various productions. In 1980, for instance, they blacklisted *Der Kandidat/The Candidate*, a film about the CSU politician Franz-Josef Strauss during his electoral campaign of that year, made by a group of directors who included Kluge and Schlöndorff. The following year Helga Reidemeister reported that she had received rejections from nine different television companies when trying to raise funding for a feature-length film about Karola Bloch. Bloch was a Jewish political activist who joined the German Communist Party in the thirties and lived in East Germany after the war with her philosopher husband Ernst Bloch, until in 1956 the couple were forced to leave because of Karola's unorthodox Marxist views. According to Reidemeister, 'The problem is Karola's past as a CP member, something I can't and don't want to conceal.'[33] She eventually received one quarter of her projected budget and could only make a much condensed version of her original project.

Such censorship reached an unprecedented peak in the mid to late seventies. The Great Coalition formed in 1966 between the CDU/CSU and the left-wing SPD had possessed an overwhelming majority in parliament.[34] This situation precipitated the growth of an extra-parliamentary opposition movement (APO). The movement crystallized among left-wing students of the immediate post-war generation, who were disenchanted with the lack of social change that had come about since the end of the war. Amongst other things, they found the toleration of ex-Nazis in prominent positions difficult to accept. This opposition movement was of course not confined to Germany; student protests swept across Europe and America, opposing in particular America's involvement in Vietnam. As the sixties came to a close and the student movement collapsed, however, a small number of left-wing extremists in Germany turned to violence.

There had been sporadic terrorist acts such as bombings since 1968, with a first peak in 1972. In that year a ruling, the so-called *Berufsverbot*, was introduced to prevent political extremists from taking up posts within the civil service. In Germany this includes not only senior staff of government departments, but also teachers, judges, post-office workers, engine drivers, dustmen and gravediggers, who together comprised 16 per cent of the labour force. Continuing terrorist activity, including killings and kidnappings, during the seventies resulted in increasing intolerance of dissident viewpoints and the introduction of measures prohibiting certain acts: for instance, advocating criminal deeds in a manner hostile to the constitution, or approving of criminal deeds in public. Leftist bookshops, printers and news services were also subjected to continual harassment in the form of investigations, searches, arrests and confiscation of books.

By 1977 West Germany appeared to many to be well on the way to becoming a police state. According to Margit Mayer:

> Any part of the media that does not cooperate is intimidated by the force of the law. The effect is a public arena, a public opinion, in which no positions deviant from that of the state can exist.[35]

Film funding agencies predictably became even more conservative in their selections, avoiding any projects that could be construed as politically radical, controversial or socially critical. By 1977 the situation was such that filmmakers were beginning to voice their protest, and some threatened to leave the country to work abroad. Fassbinder, for instance, asserted: 'If things get any worse, I'd rather be a streetsweeper in Mexico than a filmmaker in Germany.'[36] The choices left to filmmakers in the Federal Republic were singularly unpromising. If they attempted to address politically sensitive issues such as terrorism they effectively risked 'professional suicide'.[37] Of over twenty scripts addressing the issue of violence in West Germany that had been submitted to the BMI for consideration in 1977, only a handful received any funding.[38] As a member of the reconstituted German Communist Party associated with the overtly political 'Berlin School' of filmmaking, Erika Runge simply gave up seeking work with Bavarian television in the seventies since her film projects were unlikely to be favourably received in this traditionally right-wing area of Germany.

Alternatively filmmakers could either exercise a cautious self-censorship or seek other sources of funding – which, however, tended to be limited. The two films which did overtly address the issue of terrorism during this period, the collectively-made *Deutschland im Herbst/ Germany in Autumn* (1978) and Fassbinder's *Die dritte Generation/ The Third Generation* (1979), were both made through private investment.

The effects of this political climate on state-subsidized filmmaking were twofold. Firstly, it exacerbated the traditional tendency for German cinema to draw on literary sources. Already compounded by funding agencies demanding that applications be accompanied by finished scripts, political conservatism resulted in what was perceived to be a *Literaturverfilmungskrise* (literature adaptation crisis) in the years 1976–77. Not only was there a significantly large number of literature adaptations, but most were based on nineteenth-century classics often lacking in 'creative ingenuity or critical life'.[39]

On the other hand, censorship gave rise to what one critic has described as a 'passion ... for oblique approaches and microcosmic case histories'.[40] This is particularly evident in films such as Margarethe von Trotta's *Das zweite Erwachen der Christa Klages/ The Second Awakening of Christa Klages* (1977) and *Die bleierne Zeit/ The German Sisters* (1981), both of which allude to terrorism, but do not overtly examine terrorist activities or politics. Some critics have suggested that the approaches of such films are so oblique that they are as lacking in contemporary relevance as many literature adaptations. Of the latter film (which is discussed in further detail in chapter five), Charlotte Delorme maintains that 'if *The German Sisters* were really what it purports to be, it would not have received any support, distribution or exhibition'.[41] Others, however, have argued that the film subtly explores contemporary social problems and their connections to Germany's past through the experiences of individual protagonists.[42]

Developments in the seventies appeared to threaten the existence of Germany's new cinema for a second time. By 1979, however, terrorist activity was on the wane; the *Literaturverfilmungskrise* appeared to have passed (only fifteen out of eighty-one films produced in 1979 were based on literary sources);[43] and an air of optimism was developing amongst the country's new generation of directors. In September sixty filmmakers attending a film festival in Hamburg published the following manifesto, the so-called Hamburg Declaration:

> On the occasion of the Hamburg Film Festival we German filmmakers have come together. Seventeen years after Oberhausen we have taken stock.
>
> The strength of the German film is its variety. In three months the eighties will begin.
>
> Imagination does not allow itself to be governed. Committee heads cannot decide what the productive film should do. The German film of the eighties can no longer be governed by outside forces like committees, institutions, and interest groups as it has been in the past.
>
> Above all:
> We will not let ourselves be divided
>   – the feature film from the documentary film
>   – experienced filmmakers from newcomers
>   – films that reflect on the medium (in a practical way as experiments) from the narrative and commercial film
>
> We have proved our professionalism. That does not mean we have to see ourselves as a guild. We have learned that our only allies can be the spectators:
>
> That means the people who work, who have wishes, dreams, and desires, that means the people who go to the movies and who do not, and that also means people who can imagine a totally different kind of film.
>
> We must get going.

The manifesto represents a celebration of difficulties overcome during the years since the signing of the Oberhausen Manifesto in 1962. It was as if its authors wished to assert, even to reassure themselves, that a new national cinema had indeed finally emerged, one that was marked by diversity and encompassed the whole spectrum of possible filmmaking styles and formats. Despite their assertions, however, the New German Cinema had become predominantly a cinema of narrative-based feature films, while all other styles of filmmaking had become increasingly peripheral activities. It is also apparent that the authors wished to express a feeling of mutual solidarity, which suggests that their difficulties and experiences had been shared. However, their attempt to unite the feature film with other areas of filmmaking under a single banner of 'German film' conceals another very real division – that which existed between what Rentschler has termed 'the male mainstream and the extremely active feminist film culture'.[44]

Fassbinder, Herzog, Kluge, Reitz, Schlöndorff and Wenders already had several feature films to their credit by the early seventies and had thereby been able to establish themselves relatively quickly as promising new directors. Most of their female counterparts, however, found that restrictive social conditions and institutional sexism frequently denied them access to the production facilities that would have enabled them to do likewise. For instance, out of the forty-six films produced with *Kuratorium* funding from its inception up to the end of 1973, only eight were directed by women and only one of these was a feature-length film.[45] Although many women filmmakers, like their male colleagues, had worked in the film and television sectors since the late sixties and early seventies, most did not make their first feature films until 1976–77 or later.

The disparity between the experiences of male and female New German Cinema directors goes unacknowledged in the Hamburg Declaration. This is symptomatic of the sexist attitudes which several women have maintained were prevalent among male filmmakers. Writing in 1980, Claudia Lenssen stresses that 'whenever male German filmmakers discuss their work, they speak in terms of … themselves. Only when the women have registered their protest do they condescendingly admit to having meant women as well.'[46] Indeed, such was the feeling of dissatisfaction with the representation of their interests during the discussions at the 1979 Hamburg Film Festival that a group of women filmmakers set up an Association of Women Film-workers (*Verband der Filmarbeiterinnen*) to actively promote the interests of all women working in film and television.

In the early seventies women not only had to contend with the fact that film directing was a male-dominated profession, but also with a general refusal even to acknowledge the fact that women filmmakers existed. Claudia von Alemann, for instance, recalls: 'When I was asked about my profession and I said, "I make films", I regularly met with the reply, "oh yes, being an editor must be an interesting job."'[47] Ula Stöckl relates how for her 'it got to the point where part of me felt that I really didn't exist, not that I was just misunderstood, but that I simply wasn't there at all.' Stöckl is exceptional among her female colleagues in that she directed her first feature, *Neun Leben hat die Katze / The Cat has Nine Lives*, in 1968 and continued directing features throughout the seventies. Yet she was not included in a book of interviews with a number of the new cinema's directors, all of whom were male, that appeared in 1973 under the title *Die Filmemacher – zur neuen deutschen Produktion nach Oberhausen/ The Filmmakers – New German Production after Oberhausen*.[48] This was despite the fact that, according to Stöckl, many of those included 'made their first feature film long after me'.[49]

The dominant perception of women as 'absent' from filmmaking effectively tended to render those who were in fact working as directors 'invisible'. Consequently, women interested in film directing lacked role models. As late as 1977 Helke Sander maintained that 'Until now, with a few exceptions in the silent era, film has been a *purely* male domain'. (my emphasis)[50]

Sander is one of a number of women filmmakers – who include Helma Sanders-Brahms, Margarethe von Trotta, Doris Dörrie, Elfi Mikesch, May Spils, Dorothea Neunkirchen and Marianne Lüdcke – who originally wanted to become, or worked as, actresses before taking up directing. In contrast, their male colleagues have a whole tradition of well-known 'great' German directors to draw on, including Fritz Lang, Ernst Lubitsch, F.W. Murnau, G.W. Pabst and Richard Siodmak (several of whom had successfully pursued careers in Hollywood). Indeed, Kluge, Reitz and Schleiermacher attempted to recruit Lang for the Ulm Film Institute. For women filmmakers, this link did not exist; even after the critical and box-office success of *Männer/Men*

(1985), its director, Doris Dörrie, asserted that most women have difficulty relating to such directors as role models.[51]

Women also came up against the assumption that they did not need to pursue a career in the same way as their male colleagues. In 1974 Sander explained how she was once asked, 'Do you absolutely have to be a director to do what you want to do? Couldn't you achieve it by another means?' She also cited the case of a woman journalist who was passed over for a job on the editorial staff of a news programme in favour of a man, despite the fact that she was better qualified. The argument offered to support this decision was that 'the man they had decided to employ had a family to support.'[52]

As a parent, Sander also drew attention to the particular difficulties faced by women filmmakers with children. According to Sander's experiences and those of her female colleagues, even if a woman had a male partner who was agreeable to sharing domestic chores, childcare tended to remain a female responsibility. Thus some women film-makers did not have the same freedom to pursue their professions as their male colleagues, who were either single or could rely on the support of partners. Moreover, given the male-dominated nature of the profession, a woman's role as a parent was generally not acknowledged and therefore not allowed to interfere with her work. As women with children could not necessarily guarantee this, motherhood was a further possible source of discrimination, especially when seeking commissions from television. If a woman was a single parent the situation was exacerbated still further, as Heidi Genée explains:

> Nobody cares that you have three children and are alone with them. I may know how much work is involved, but if the film does not turn out the way it should, I cannot apologize because I had my three children with me during the shoot. You have to pretend to behave like your male colleagues. Yet, when they wake up in the morning, their women bring breakfast and pay them compliments. When I wake up in the morning, I think of the new pair of pants I should buy my son Daniel or if I should not send him to a therapist after all or what's going on at school.[53]

Such experiences are not of course unique to women directors in West Germany. For this reason, and through the influence of the contemporary women's movement, some women filmmakers came to view their work as having more in common with that of their female counterparts abroad than with that of Fassbinder and the rest. Consequently, they were often more interested in identifying and promoting a feminist film culture than in a new national cinema.[54] At the same time, the institutional structures that supported the New German Cinema also played a crucial role in severely restricting their participation in that national cinema. Although the New German Cinema's reliance on public money certainly limited the scope of male directors' work, it virtually excluded women directors from feature film production during its first ten years.

At an institutional level women were frequently confronted with lack of confidence in their technical abilities. Even though none of the Oberhausen Manifesto signatories, all of whom were male, had previously directed a feature film, their ability to fulfil the promises of their manifesto – to create a new cinema – was accepted without question. Most had acquired some film experience through making shorts, but for women filmmakers actual experience often carried little weight since, as von Alemann observed, 'a woman has to first overcome the distrust that she even "can".'[55] Even after several years experience of working as a director Erika Runge still maintained that she met with 'a fundamental mistrust of women' in media institutions.[56] She and other women directors stressed that they had to work harder and achieve more than men in order to be recognized and accepted as filmmakers. Even women who feel they encountered fewer difficulties than most of their female colleagues have echoed this view. Heidi Genée established herself as an editor in the sixties and found the transition to directing relatively easy, but still asserts that 'With we women, of course, we have to be twice as good. That's the way it is.'[57]

This lack of confidence was not confined simply to directing. Camerawomen were frequently assumed to be not only technically incompetent, but also physically incapable of operating a 35mm camera.[58] When Jutta Brückner chose to use camerawoman Hille Sagel on her film *Laufen lernen / Learning to Run* (1980), for instance, the producers felt her decision jeopardized the project; they assumed her choice was ideologically motivated rather than based on Sagel's technical expertise.[59]

Such attitudes towards women filmmakers and workers had tangible effects during the seventies and effectively produced an additional level of censorship for their work. A number of women film-makers were (and remain) interested in combining fiction and docu-mentary filmmaking styles in feature-length films. As Sander explained, for instance, she 'would prefer to work more essayistically, filming very slowly ... somewhere between fiction and documentary ... where fictional people enter documentary films.'[60] But she and her colleagues found it difficult to attract funding for mixed-format projects. According to Helga Reidemeister, this was partly due to the privileging of the 'pure' documentary work propounded in West Germany by filmmaker and Berlin film school teacher Klaus Wilden-hahn.[61] This gave rise to a general resistance to film projects which introduced fictional elements into documentary filmmaking. However, like feature film production, this is also a much more ambitious style of filmmaking than 'pure' documentary and requires a substantially higher level of funding.

During the seventies funding agencies and commissioning bodies, such as the FFA and television, proved distinctly reluctant to invest large sums in women's film projects. The greater the financial invest-ment, the greater the degree of confidence required in a director's capabilities and commitment. This was compounded in Germany by the structures of funding agencies such as the *Kuratorium* and the FFA. Since these encouraged directors to be their own producers, and since many women filmmakers also wrote their own screenplays (some even acted in their own films), the 'success' of a project might rest on the capabilities of a single person. As Claudia Lenssen has stressed, this meant that filmmakers 'have to convince people with their personal prestige in order to find backers'.[62] This frequently proved difficult for women filmmakers, who tended to be judged on the basis of their gender rather than their artistic and technical capabilities. In 1976, for instance, Helma Sanders-Brahms, who had by then directed a number of productions, observed:

> Whenever I turn up anywhere as a director, the first thing to be estab-lished is that I am a woman. That is more important than anything else that I have done. It is rarely or never the case that my films are judged without the viewpoint 'she is a woman' coming into it.[63]

The funding agencies and commissioning bodies proved more

willing to award small budgets to women's projects. Indeed, with regard to the work of the FFA project committee on which she sat for three years at the end of the decade, Gesine Strempel observed that 'As long as it's about small amounts of money, then women have equal rights.'[64] Women therefore found it less difficult to break into documentary filmmaking, shorts and television work.

Even the women who did succeed in getting more ambitious projects funded were forced to work with a much smaller budget than is usual for such projects. When the *Kuratorium* first started its work, it awarded up to DM300,000 for a first feature film. Although a male director complained that such a sum was totally inadequate to promote a 'quality' national cinema and necessitated the use of friends and non-professionals to realize a project,[65] ten years later Ulrike Ottinger was given only DM80,000 to make her first full-length feature film, *Madame X – eine absolute Herrscherin / Madame X – An Absolute Ruler* (1977). For her film *Die Macht der Männer ist die Geduld der Frauen / The Power of Men is the Patience of Women* (1978) Cristina Perincioli reported that she 'received only one-fifth of the money that a network normally invests in this length TV film'.[66] Not only did this mean much work went unpaid, but it brought additional pressures to bear on those involved. Dagmar Beiersdorf highlighted these pressures when discussing the filming of *Die Wolfsbraut / The Wolf Girl* (1985):

> We were a small team of six people. No production manager, no extra people for make-up or costume. So, one is, of course, responsible for the bulk of the work oneself. For instance, I needed a piano for three days, but had no properties manager. So during filming I had to keep running to the phone in order to organize a van and a piano. Everywhere I was getting refusals because I couldn't pay the prices. And when I eventually got something agreed, it was 'but you have to collect and load yourself'. So at five o'clock in the morning – filming the piano scene was supposed to begin at nine – I set off, collected the van, picked up two sleepy friends, we drove out to Gatow and heaved the monster into the bus. When we unloaded the thing again where we were filming shortly before nine o'clock, we were of course completely worn out. Nevertheless, we did the filming. And several days were like that. If I hadn't had such a helpful and patient team, several days' filming would have fallen through.[67]

According to Sander this additional level of censorship was compounded in the early seventies by a resistance, particularly from commissioning editors of television corporations, to the topics that many women filmmakers wanted to address. Although there were exceptions, many women who wanted to make films dealing with what were identified as specifically 'women's issues' found it difficult to find funding (the reasons for this are explored in chapter three). Of her own film project about menstruation (to be called *Rote Tage/Red Period*) Sander recalls

> the funding commissions ... were so disgusted ... they didn't even want to deal with the topic. It was meant to be neither an educational nor a documentary film, but a film about myths; for it, I was advised to try for ten minutes on the weekly TV health program![68]

Once again, even if such a project did get funding the filmmaker was rarely free from further censorship. Jutta Brückner, for instance, complained of intolerable levels of editorial interference when she was commissioned to make one of a series of films about women in mid-life crisis:

> The producer and TV editor – both men – had their own ideas about how a film about a woman, written and directed by a woman, should look. Their interference began with the script and became ever worse. You face such censorship in almost all productions that institutions commission: censorship of how one approaches the theme, of the dramatic structure which must not be 'boring', and generally a narrowing of topics, because the private sphere is to remain private.[69]

Although exercising cautious self-censorship could increase a filmmaker's chances of working, it could not combat all levels of institutional sexism. One avenue open to male directors that women were less able to exploit – in view of the male-dominated nature of the film industry – was 'going commercial'. Some of the Oberhausen signatories, such as Peter Schamoni, Hans-Jürgen Pohland and Rob Houwer, made commercially orientated films in order to trigger the automatic subsidy of the FFA to get funding for projects of more personal interest. According to Elsaesser, Schamoni and Houwer headed production companies which invested in sexploitation films, as well as in the work of New German Cinema directors.[70]

While many women filmmakers would not necessarily have pursued such an option, institutional sexism did result in a narrowing of options available to them. As a result women filmmakers have been more prone to periods of unemployment than their male colleagues. In an article on sexism in the mass media Sander highlighted the fact that unemployment was not only demoralizing for many women film-makers, but also denied them the opportunities to improve their skills, while decreasing their confidence in existing ones.[71] The case of Ula Stöckl confirms Sander's analysis. Even though Stöckl worked exten-sively during the seventies, by November 1979 she reported to Renate Möhrmann that 'I haven't had any commissions in ages and also haven't received any loans or subsidy monies.' For this reason Stöckl denied there was any truth in Möhrmann's assessment of her as 'one of the most prolific women directors' – Möhrmann reports that it in fact moved Stöckl to tears – and saw herself instead as 'just vegetating. I've simply been forgotten.'[72]

Women's ghettoization within low-budget areas of filmmaking and their frequent unemployment meant that, to a far greater extent than their male colleagues, they had to rely on the help of friends rather than paid professionals to get film projects realized. But as von Alemann stresses, 'This method of working is no solution, if one can only practise one's profession virtually as a "hobby"'[73] and has to earn a living by other means. Some women turned instead to the experi-mental or avant-garde film sector, where they could be less dependent on funding agencies and the goodwill of friends by working with cheaper, more manageable mediums such as super-8, video and 16mm. Reidemeister was even advised by a television editor that she should work with video because it was cheaper.[74] This functioned, however, to compound the prevailing scepticism regarding women's technical capabilities. As von Alemann explained:

> It is difficult to continually produce so cheaply. The films often look 'shabbier'. For instance, women use black/white more frequently than colour, as is the norm practically everywhere today. The means of expression are limited and that has a boomerang effect on women. They are accused of simply not being capable of making 'better' films.[75]

During the seventies therefore women filmmakers experienced additional difficulties to those faced by their male colleagues when trying to realize film projects and pursue careers as directors. These additional difficulties had the effect of largely limiting them to the areas of documentary filmmaking, shorts and television work, while feature film production remained the domain of male directors. By the end of the decade most studies of West Germany's new cinema were discussing women's contribution under the heading of 'Realists and Documentarists' or *Das andere Kino*, Germany's avant-garde or independent cinema,[76] both of which were viewed as peripheral to the mainstream of New German Cinema activity. Thus women were perceived to have made only a minimal and highly marginal contribution to that new cinema.

TWO

Critical Reception

Awareness in Britain and the USA of the existence of a new German cinema started to grow during the mid seventies, approximately ten years after the first batch of *Kuratorium*-financed films had been produced. In February 1976, for instance, the US magazine *Newsweek* ran an article entitled 'The German Film Renaissance'; a few months later the BBC featured the new cinema in an *Omnibus* report entitled 'Vigorous Signs of Life'; and by 1978 *Time* magazine described it as 'the liveliest in Europe'.[1] Although more recent discussions have emphasized the social, political and economic factors that helped shape the New German Cinema,[2] these early accounts tended to suggest that the 'renaissance' had been brought about almost entirely by a small number of talented and dedicated young directors. Typical of the descriptions of German cinema's rebirth was that offered by *Time*:

> With little encouragement, less money and no older hands to guide them, a few extraordinary young directors have given birth to a phoenix – the brilliant German cinema of Fritz Lang and Ernst Lubitsch that Hitler had consigned to the ashes forty-five years ago.[3]

Fassbinder, Herzog and Wenders were singled out for particular praise, especially in the US, and eventually came to enjoy the status of international stars.

In keeping with this approach, many observers focused on the personalities of the new directors, discussing them as creative geniuses, 'artists with something to say'.[4] The emphasis on individuals was reinforced by the particularly colourful and forceful personalities of directors such as Herzog and Fassbinder, which undoubtedly served as evidence of an artistic temperament. Tales of Herzog's eccentric and often demonic behaviour during filming have repeatedly been reported, while Fassbinder was dubbed *Wunderkind* because of his obsessive approach to work and prolific output. Indeed, it is possible that these and other directors deliberately cultivated public personas that promoted a personality cult.[5]

New German Cinema films were consequently discussed, in mainstream film criticism at least, almost exclusively in terms of their directors' personal visions. Charles Eidsvik's description of Herzog is typical:

> A brooding, often mystifying director concerned with the borders between normal behaviour and insanity, Herzog links dream and reality, the grotesque and the normal, the bizarre and the everyday ... Herzog puts extreme subjects into extreme situations in narratives structured like dreams ... Perhaps excepting Bergman and Murnau, no film-maker has ever created visions as intense and disturbing as Herzog's.[6]

In classic auteurist fashion, such critics tend to identify recurring stylistic and thematic elements in a director's work. Biographical information is also frequently introduced and distinct developmental stages in their filmmaking careers noted. This information is then used to construct a coherent authorial vision that informs a director's *oeuvre*.

This approach to film criticism stems from *la politique des auteurs*, a polemic launched by the French film journal *Cahiers du Cinéma* during the fifties, the origins of which date back to an article written by New Wave director François Truffaut in 1953.[7] Truffaut and other contributors to the *Cahiers* journal were committed to the idea that film was an art form, just like music and painting, which could offer an individual – in this case, the director – the freedom of personal expression. They believed that, even in commercial cinema with its industrial constraints, a director could make personal statements through (usually) his films.

According to Truffaut, however, there was a certain tendency in French cinema to produce lifeless filmed literature, as exemplified by the films of directors such as Jean Delannoy, Yves Allegret and Claude Autant-Lara. Although such films were popularly thought of at the time as constituting a quality cinema, Truffaut argued that these directors were not really 'men of the cinema' but *metteurs-en-scène*, that is, they merely added 'pictures' to scenarios and dialogue taken from novels, failing to be truly cinematic or original. He contrasted them to directors like Jean Renoir, Jacques Tati and Abel Gance, whom he felt brought something genuinely personal to their subjects. For Truffaut, their ability to do this meant they could be regarded as *auteurs*, as the 'authors' of their films, and that their films could be distinguished as works of real artistic merit. Ed Buscombe has succinctly characterized the distinction: 'Instead of merely transferring someone else's work faithfully and self-effacingly, the *auteur* transforms the material into an expression of his own personality.'[8]

The idea that some filmmakers managed to make personal statements through their films was in fact not new.[9] But the *Cahiers* writers went further and tried to develop it into a new basis for the evaluative critical analysis of films. Their *politique*

> attempted to be a critical method, to provide a way of reading films and uncovering the thematic and stylistic unities and motifs that functioned within a text, and with discerning the preoccupations of a director across the range of their work no matter what project they had been given.[10]

This approach was taken up and developed by various critics and theorists,[11] which has resulted in some broad degree of acceptance within film criticism of the idea of a director as the 'author' of his or her film. Hence we talk about Francis Ford Coppola's *The Godfather* (1972) as well as Wim Wenders's *Im Lauf der Zeit/ Kings of the Road* (1976) and generally regard the director as responsible for whatever the viewer finds of structural, stylistic or thematic interest in a film. It is hardly surprising therefore that the New German Cinema was first discussed in terms of its 'talented' and 'extraordinary' young directors.

However, this is not to suggest that all film directors are now regarded as *auteurs*. Critics still differentiate between *metteurs-en-scène* and *auteurs*, and only a relatively small number of directors are critically acclaimed as the latter. Yet in the case of the New German Cinema there seems to have been complete agreement from the outset amongst British and American critics that this was a '*cinéma des auteurs*', since 'each film, in content and technique, bears the distinctive stamp of its director.'[12] In the eyes of at least one critic this rendered the application of an auteurist critical methodology 'uniquely appropriate'.[13] However, a number of other factors contributed significantly to the unanimous discussion of Germany's new directors as *auteurs*.

Firstly, there was a deliberate and self-conscious promotion of the new German films as an *Autorenkino* (cinema of *auteurs*) by the filmmakers themselves. Although the German concept of *Autor* differs from the French *auteur*, both identify the director as a film's creator and regard a film as an expression of that creator's personality.

The notion of an *Autorenkino* was certainly implicit in the Oberhausen Manifesto. By categorically stressing that the new German film needed freedom from economic and vested interests, the signatories effectively set themselves in opposition to industrial modes of production and demanded the freedom of expression normally associated with 'artistic' production. Echoing Truffaut's *auteur/metteur-en-scène* distinction, Alexander Kluge reinforced the notion of a director as *Autor* when he subsequently contrasted the new German film with what he termed a *Zutatenfilm* (recipe film). A typical industry product, the *Zutatenfilm* is a film made up of ingredients, for which 'a producer buys up stars, material, ideas, directors, specialists, scriptwriters, etc.'[14] Such a comparison suggested that the new German film would be more than just the sum of its parts, and therefore implied that the new directors would bring something personal to their films. Thus unlike the classic use of *auteur*, which is applied to a director on the evidence of a pre-existing body of work, the new directors conceived of themselves as *Autoren* even before the first new films were made.

During the sixties these ideas were developed by Kluge and Reitz into a coherent education programme at the Ulm Film Institute. This had the express purpose of training a new generation of filmmakers for an *Autorenkino*. Eschewing industrial production methods, these filmmakers would receive an all-round film education (in a manner which echoed the Bauhaus approach to art education in the twenties) and become familiar with all areas of production, rather than training as specialists in areas such as camera, scriptwriting, production or direction.[15] Students would thus become *Filmautoren*, directors who exercised a far greater degree of authorial control than was traditionally the case in an industrial context. They would also differ from specialists in conceiving of film as a 'medium of expression of intelligence and human experience'[16] rather than as a consumer product. Although the Ulm Institute ceased practical training in 1970 and the Munich film school (HFF) favoured vocational specialization, when the Berlin film school (DFFB) opened in 1966 it followed Kluge and Reitz's lead. It stated that its training goal was (and still is)

> to provide future filmmakers who want to work independently with a theoretical and practical basis for their later professional activity. It is not divided into specialist areas, but offers a unified training programme.[17]

As a consequence of the lobbying of Kluge and others, the demands of the Oberhausen Manifesto and the concept of an *Autorenkino* also informed the institutional framework of the first film subsidy agency, the *Kuratorium junger deutscher Film*. In his account of the development of the work of the *Kuratorium*, Norbert Kückelmann, founder member and inaugurator of the agency, explains how,

> according to the fundamental Oberhausen principle the filmmaker was to have autonomy in giving shape to his film idea ... he was to retain control over the direction and entire production process.... This concept was clear.[18]

Thus the *Kuratorium* clearly identified the director as the originator or author of a film, and sought to protect his or her independence. Implicit in this principle moreover was the notion of filmmaking as an act of personal expression and hence of film as an art form. Indeed, the *Kuratorium* was modelled on forms of patronage and commission that had traditionally supported the fine arts.[19]

Therefore, not only did the new directors conceive of themselves as *Autoren*, this self-designation was also officially sanctioned. This was not, however, due solely to the lobbying efforts of Kluge and his colleagues. The initiative of the Oberhausen signatories coincided with 'a political will to see film acquire the status of "Kultur"'.[20] Film was identified by the West German government as an important medium for promoting and exporting German culture as a 'manifestation of national identity'.[21] The film subsidy system that evolved, although shaped by economic objectives, was 'motivated, above all, by the argument that film along with literature, theatre, music and the fine arts, constitutes an autonomous art form'.[22] Hence, much of the subsidy system, following the *Kuratorium*'s example, identified the director as the author or creator of a film.

In practical terms, the notion of *Autorenkino* and the structuring of contractual arrangements between the funding bodies and the directors resulted in filmmakers frequently being their own scriptwriters and producers. Once the new directors started making films, they were therefore also easily identifiable from a critic's viewpoint as author figures, the creative geniuses behind the 'vision'.

Over the years the new directors continued to promote film as an art form and themselves as *Autoren*: when thirteen of them set up their own production and distribution company in 1971 they called it the *Filmverlag der Autoren*. Literally, this means Film Publishing House of the *Auteurs*, and implies a similarity between producing for the cinema and publishing literary works. The statements of these frequently interviewed filmmakers also served to reinforce, at least in Britain and the US, their public image as creative geniuses. In 1978, for instance, *Time* quoted Fassbinder as asserting: 'We had nothing, and we started with nothing ... For a generation nobody made important films in Germany. Until us.'[23] That Fassbinder and the others were likely to push for as much authorial legitimation as possible is not surprising since this strategy would increase their personal prestige and institutional power. In fact, they did so to such a degree that more than one critic was moved to comment on the self-serving nature of many of their statements.[24]

Basis Film, another independent producer and distributor of new German films set up in the seventies, also contributed enormously to the active promotion of an *Autorenkino*. They identified the *Autorenfilm* as essential to the survival of a national film culture and stressed the need to 'fight for the recognition of film as cultural property ... with an author whose rights must be protected and whose artistic freedom is inalienable'.[25] Their production and distribution policies have therefore been specifically structured to support and maintain the existence of an *Autorenkino*. According to the company's long-time director, Clara Burckner:

> The filmmaker is responsible for the ultimate version of his screenplay, for the casting and the employment of his most important members of staff, for the shoot, how long the shoot would take and the final length of the film i.e. the final cut, etc. So, all essential decisions are the responsibility . . . exclusively of the filmmaker.[26]

When commercial companies showed little interest in distributing such films, *Basis* developed a non-commercial distribution network and exhibition strategy in order to deliver them to audiences. This included supplying background material to accompany the film and inform post-screening discussions, as well as arranging for directors to attend screenings.

Thus, by the time the New German Cinema started attracting critical attention in Britain and the US, a conceptual and institutional framework was already in place which located and promoted it as a cinema of personal expression. The tendency among the new German filmmakers to draw on literary sources offered a further reason for discussing them as *auteurs*. This tendency was so prevalent that it caused one critic to observe that 'Literature is the backbone of German cinema. Remove the backbone from the history of the New German Cinema, and it appears to be a jellyfish.'[27] Although a reliance on literature might be viewed as incompatible with a cinema of personal expression, this predilection for adaptations in fact opened up a space for filmmakers to demonstrate their creative abilities and for critics to identify a personal input.

As Truffaut had observed, adaptations can result in dull and lifeless filmed literature, with segments of dialogue simply reproduced verbatim and settings lovingly recreated with extreme faithfulness to an author's description. A number of New German Cinema adapters, however, transformed their literary sources into specifically cinematic products through a rather more imaginative use of the medium. Just as some directors have been viewed as capable of transcending the constraints of commercial cinema to make personal statements, the New German Cinema directors were frequently regarded as having brought something personal to their films by transcending the letter of the written text. Although the *Literaturverfilmungskrise* of 1976 to 1977 produced a number of less creative film adaptations – described by one critic as 'devoid of artistic invention, much less personal involvement'[28] – critics have repeatedly stressed how the new directors 'might have borrowed the story, but it is *their* film'.[29]

For instance, in his article on the film of Heinrich Böll's novel *Die verlorene Ehre der Katherina Blum/ The Lost Honour of Katherina Blum* (1975) Lester Friedman stresses how directors Schlöndorff and von Trotta 'successfully translate Böll's novel to the screen, capturing the mood, spirit, and important themes of his work ... by employing devices unique to the medium of film instead of relying on those simply borrowed from literature'.[30] One of the themes structuring Böll's novel is the individual's loss of privacy and rights to privacy when the needs of the individual conflict with those of the police and press. Friedman describes how Schlöndorff and von Trotta visually represent this invasion of privacy in their film through a pattern of image development and the use of visual symbolism. He notes, for example, how a shift from colour to black-and-white is used to signify police surveillance of the framed image. This is set up in the opening sequence of the film and also occurs later in the film when Katherina and her lover embrace in the lobby of her apartment block unaware that they are being observed. Extensive use is also made of glass and mirror images, with Katherina, her lover and friends frequently framed in or next to windows, reflecting in or standing by mirrors. They are thus constantly represented as 'encased in glass'[31] and appear exposed, unable to protect themselves from the gaze of others, leading 'a kind of fish-bowl existence'.[32] For Friedman, this ability to represent cinematically the spirit and meaning of a literary text means that 'a director becomes not merely an illustrator of the written text, but an artist in his own right, one who draws inspiration from original sources'.[33]

Eric Rentschler has likewise highlighted ways in which 'directors have transcended their textual starting points so as to add a personal dimension' to literature adaptations, and in doing so have produced films with 'their own narrative, structural, thematic, and topical integrity'.[34] In Schlöndorff's *Die Blechtrommel/ The Tin Drum* (1979) he argues that – albeit for practical reasons – the first person narrative of Günter Grass's novel has been replaced with a more 'objective and encompassing' positioning of the camera to offer a third-person viewpoint. In the case of Herzog's *Lebenszeichen/Signs of Life* (1967), based on Achim von Arnim's *The Mad Invalid in Fort Rattoneau*, he maintains that the director introduces his own personal style through the motif of a circle, which Rentschler maintains correlates with Herzog's own vision of 'trapped human existence'.[35] Other directors, such as Jean-Marie Straub and Danièle Huillet, have gone still further and infused a project with their own personalities to the point of rendering their literary sources almost unrecognizable. According to Franklin:

> Attempts were made to prevent the screening and distribution of *Not Reconciled* and *History Lessons* by the publishers of Heinrich Böll's *Billiards at Nine-Thirty* and of Brecht's *The Affairs of Mr Julius Caesar* – the literary sources for the two films – on the grounds that the Straubs had unconscionably butchered the originals.[36]

Thus the application of an auteurist critical methodology to discussions of the New German Cinema is more than simply 'uniquely appropriate'. Rather, it is possible to argue that Germany's new cinema has been overdetermined as a *cinéma des auteurs* which has resulted in an overwhelming and unquestioning tendency to discuss and assess it as such.

However, the concept of *auteur* or notion of individual creative authorship is both relatively recent and privileged in western culture. Its origins can be traced back to the period of the rise of early capitalism in the second half of the sixteenth century. Before this period:

> [most] cultural objects were authorless in the modern sense partly for religious reasons and partly because such a system of categorization had no meaning or value. With the Renaissance, the rise of capitalism and of a bourgeois class, artists began to express personal visions and ideas from a more autonomous position.... Furthermore, whilst artefacts had, for a long time, been marketable commodities, they now also became differentiable objects, i.e. some were 'better' than others and hence more valuable.[37]

Since the concept of *auteur* makes it possible to differentiate between cultural artefacts, its application to cinematic production has encouraged the 'grading' of directors. Usually, a small number of directors are identified and valued as exceptional talents, against whom others are then judged and assessed. The privileging of individual authorship moreover renders it difficult for discussions of cinema to address areas of filmmaking where films cannot be so easily evaluated or understood as expressions of their directors' personalities or where, for some reason, it is difficult to identify a single author figure. This results in a tendency for critical attention to be focused on a small number of directors and for the work of a great many others to be marginalized or excluded from discussions.

In discussions of the New German Cinema this tendency has been exacerbated by its overwhelming characterization as a *cinéma des auteurs*. In Britain and the US a small number of directors – Fassbinder, Herzog, Kluge, Schlöndorff, Straub, Syberberg and Wenders – were singled out and became the main focus of attention to such an extent that for a number of years they effectively came to constitute the New German Cinema. Critical attention tended to be deflected away from other factors that shape film culture and all other filmmakers were represented as working on the peripheries of the new cinema. The degree to which this occurred is evident in the way that recent studies, such as Rentschler's *West German Film in the Course of Time*[38] and Thomas Elsaesser's *New German Cinema: A History*[39] have consciously rejected an auteurist approach and are informed by a desire to, as it were, set the record straight.

In order to fully understand the films of some German filmmakers, for instance, viewers require knowledge of the sociopolitical, economic or institutional factors that informed and helped shape them: they cannot be fully understood if discussed solely as acts of personal expression. Such films tend either to be ignored, discussed as part of a marginal genre, or explained away as less accomplished than those of Fassbinder and his colleagues. Consequently, the work of a predominantly Berlin-based group of filmmakers which focused on the lives and experiences of the contemporary German working classes, and was very much a product of specific historical and institutional factors, is always discussed as a genre, the so-called *Arbeiterfilme* (worker films). Although these films are distributed by *Basis* and are identified as part of the New German Cinema, they are less easily discussed purely in terms of an authorial version.[40]

The work of Peter Lilienthal has also been largely ignored until relatively recently, even though his first feature film, *Malatesta* (1969), was included in the 1972 programme at the Museum of Modern Art in the US and his *David* (1978–79) won first prize at the 1979 Berlin Film Festival. In her discussion of Lilienthal, American academic Lynne Layton stresses that at first glance his films 'hardly seem personal', since his camera adopts the perspective of his characters and his recent films deal with political struggles which focus on groups rather than on individuals.[41] According to Layton, Lilienthal has also not promoted himself as an *Autor*, but prefers 'to work collectively and enjoys confrontation with minds active in other media'.[42] Moreover, he has worked extensively in television, a medium not traditionally associated with the notion of personal expression or individual authorship. Lilienthal's *oeuvre*, working methods and work history in consequence mitigated against his being discussed as an auteur. Nevertheless, because of the way the New German Cinema has been overdetermined as a *cinéma des auteurs*, Layton finds it necessary to elevate him to *auteur* status in order to rescue him from critical neglect. She does this by drawing on Lilienthal's experiences as an exile during the Third Reich to identify a personal vision in his more politically orientated films.

One area of filmmaking that has been particularly marginalized in, even excluded from, discussions of the New German Cinema has been women's film production. This is not to suggest that women film directors cannot be discussed as *auteurs* nor elevated to *auteur* status. Directors such as Ulrike Ottinger, Elfi Mikesch, Claudia von Alemann, Ula Stöckl and Jutta Brückner, who frequently write, direct and produce their films, exercise a large degree of control over their work and have on occasion been discussed as author figures. Others, such as Margarethe von Trotta and Helma Sanders-Brahms, who have attained a position of some international prominence, have also at times been discussed in this way. Many of these women, when interviewed, also stress that they have a clear idea of what they want to present on screen and of the difficulties they may have in achieving it or the disappointment they experience if they do not succeed.[43] Others have pursued authorial legitimation as much as their male colleagues, often in the face of adverse criticism from female colleagues.[44]

However, the auteurist critical methodology privileges the notion of individual creative authorship. This value system, reinforced through the New German Cinema's overwhelming characterization as a *cinéma des auteurs,* has served to inhibit any sustained, in-depth analysis of women's filmmaking in studies of the New German Cinema. In its privileging of the *creative* genius, for instance, auteurism is a methodology that has been applied primarily to feature film production. Women's ghettoization within low-budget areas of filmmaking during the sixties and seventies, confining them largely to documentary filmmaking, shorts and television work, therefore mitigated against women filmmakers receiving extensive critical attention. Their association with documentary filmmaking has been particularly detrimental, since it is predominantly viewed as involving – at least at some level – the recording of 'reality', an area of cultural production that has rarely been associated with notable creativity.[45]

Women's virtual absence from the field of feature film production in the early years of the New German Cinema also reinforced the age-old view that women are not creative. In the past this has elicited such assertions as that made by Karl Scheffler in 1908: 'In an Amazon society there could be neither culture nor history nor art, since art is not essential to woman.'[46] According to this myth, women can only 'adapt', 'interpret', or provide the inspiration for someone else's work and thus their role in art is that of stage performer or represented object, never 'originator'. Indeed John Berger has argued that the tradition of western art evinces an acceptance of the concept that 'Men act and women appear. Men look at women. Women watch themselves being looked at.'[47]

Consequently, when women began to break through into feature film production towards the end of the seventies, their achievements were often accounted for in terms other than individual creative authorship. Implicit in some accounts is the suggestion that rather than becoming 'originators' when they stepped behind the camera, they were merely continuing to 'adapt' the work of their male colleagues and thus to all intents and purposes remained 'performers'. John Sandford, for instances, asserts that 'Feminist implications have been discernible in the New German Cinema from the outset, initially in the work of male directors, and latterly in the films of the growing number of women directors.'[48] Although this is not necessarily a denial of women's creative abilities, it does tend to suggest that women directors were simply following the lead given by their male colleagues. Moreover, he discusses the work of women directors in conjunction with films by male colleagues which focused on female protagonists under the all-encompassing heading of 'women'. This suggests that the role women assume behind the camera is indistinguishable from their role as 'performers' in front of the camera for a male director. This collapsing of the two roles into one reinforces the perception of women as being capable only of 'adapting' the work of others.

Even when critics were ostensibly trying to rescue women film-makers from critical oblivion, the notion of 'woman as adapter' often underlay their arguments. In a discussion of 'German Feminist Cinema' Robert Acker asserts that films made by women 'account for some of the finest cinematic creations this country has to offer'.[49] After a discussion of thematics, he highlights formal devices which recur in this feminist cinema, such as the insertion of documentary material in fiction films, voice-over narration, intertitles and the making of a film within a film. However, he identifies a male 'originator' of these techniques, arguing that:

> The heavy use of these devices by women directors can probably be traced to the influence of Alexander Kluge, who was a teacher in the film section at the Ulmer Hochschule für Gestaltung in the late 1960s, a film school which many of these women attended.[50]

Acker's assertion, like Sandford's, does not of course necessarily deny women's creative capacity. As discussed earlier, adaptation of someone else's work opened up the possibility of personal input and fuelled the discussion of New German Cinema directors as *auteurs*. Moreover, Acker makes a point of acknowledging the 'quality' of the films made by women directors. But in this context, the reference to Kluge does not throw light on how a director has transformed someone else's work into her own. Indeed, of the fifteen women directors that Acker mentions in his article, only four studied under Kluge at Ulm. Instead, the discussion of formal devices is used to help establish what these films have in common with one another, to help define the category 'feminist cinema'. Rather than signalling individual 'talent', the use of these devices therefore denotes similarity. This in turn suggests that women directors failed to infuse their films with something genuinely personal and were thus simply adapting Kluge's ideas.

In the case of some women directors, critics emphasized their connections with male colleagues in the film sector as a means of accounting for their entry into feature film production. The English edition of a book by Hans Pflaum and Hans Prinzler, for instance, describes Margarethe von Trotta, Heidi Genée and Christel Buschmann as 'in a comparatively favourable position' or 'well placed'[51] to start directing features, since von Trotta was married to Volker Schlöndorff, Genée to film producer Peter Genée and Christel Buschmann to filmmaker Reinhard Hauff. The implication is that their 'cinematic creations' could not have been achieved without male assistance and thus that they result – at least to some degree – from a male input.

Other women who have managed to make debuts as feature film directors apparently unaided by the 'helping hand' of a male colleague have on occasion been accounted for in terms that suggest their work is less accomplished than that of more 'established' directors. Helke Sander, for instance, is described by James Franklin as 'one of the most *promising* feminist directors'.[52] (my emphasis) Such a description implies that she manages less successfully to articulate a coherent authorial vision in her films than the star *auteurs*. Yet her first feature, *Die allseitig reduzierte Persönlichkeit/The All-Round Reduced Personality* (1977), was highly acclaimed both at home and abroad and nominated film of the year in Hanser's Film Yearbook 1978–79.[53]

This is not to suggest that these arguments are entirely without foundation. In a 1976 interview, for instance, after having made *The Lost Honour of Katherina Blum* (1975) with Schlöndorff, von Trotta acknowledged that her husband was playing a significant role in launching her career as a director:

> When Volker says that in Germany we first have to sell the film and sell it under his name because the name of Schlöndorff and not von Trotta is the product, it is sad but true. For certain projects I'd get absolutely no funding or support. And the realization that that could mean that another collaboration with Volker as co-director is unavoidable ... which is not in Volker's interest but primarily in mine ... is also very painful.[54]

However, the foregrounding of such arguments to 'explain away' women's breakthrough into feature film production has tended to devalue and hence limit discussion of their contribution to what has been perceived predominantly as a *cinéma des auteurs*.

It is also noteworthy that very few women directors have undertaken literature adaptations,[55] an area of filmmaking that had helped define the new cinema as one of personal expression. Rather, women's cinema in West Germany has been based to a considerable degree on autobiographical material. Films such as Helma Sanders-Brahms's *Deutschland, bleiche Mutter / Germany, Pale Mother* (1979–80), Jutta Brückner's *Hungerjahre / Years of Hunger* (1980), Marianne Rosenbaum's *Peppermint Frieden / Peppermint Freedom* (1983) and Helke Sander's *Die allseitig reduzierte Persönlichkeit / The All-round Reduced Personality* (1977) drew extensively on the filmmaker's personal histories. Many more films that are not explicitly autobiographical are concerned with representing women's experiences in a patriarchal society in general and are frequently based on the lives of actual women.

Many critics have consequently regarded women's filmmaking in West Germany as a cinema of personal experience. Although drawing on one's own experiences, especially autobiographical material, would tend to identify the filmmaker as a film's author, the representation of personal experiences can be viewed as diametrically opposed to a cinema of self-expression. The former is rooted in real events and can thus be viewed as constituting a representation of 'reality' rather than as an act of creative self-expression. Consequently, when women directors began working in feature film production the content of their films appeared to some to have little to do with individual creative authorship and in fact permitted discussion of their work to continue under the heading of 'Realists and Documentarists'.[56]

Auteurism also privileges the notion of *individual* authorship, which calls for the identification of a single 'originator' to whom whatever the critic finds of interest in a film can be attributed. Women who have collaborated with male colleagues have therefore frequently been viewed at best as little more than helpmates to their male partners, with little if any creative input of their own. Birgit Hein, for instance, has been working with her husband Wilhelm since 1966 and they have always been equally responsible for their joint film work. Although the Heins' work is more associated with Germany's *das andere Kino*, its avant-garde cinema, Birgit's comments are indicative of a general attitude towards the female half of a female/male team. In the late sixties and early seventies, she asserts, 'People simply ignored me – naturally only one person, and of course that was the man, could be the artist.'[57]

In her 1976 interview Margarethe von Trotta, who not only co-directed with Schlöndorff but worked with him as actress and co-writer for a number of years, went on to say that her decision to go into solo directing was partly motivated by the fact that 'the public by and large only acknowledged Volker.... I'm always regarded as an appendage by the public.'[58] This singling out of Schlöndorff was, according to von Trotta, exacerbated by their public image. Although they wrote as a team, when appearing together on location or at press conferences Schlöndorff assumed a position of authority and control. 'As soon as a journalist walked through the door, it immediately put things on a new level, with new behaviour. Volker talked and I sat alongside.'[59]

Von Trotta's experience is, however, far from exceptional. In interviews, Danièle Huillet has taken a far less active role in discussing her joint film work than her collaborator and partner, Jean-Marie Straub. She has maintained – contrary to von Trotta – that this has happened with her blessing. However, her argument that Straub is 'better' at such discussions and that she does not 'like relating things so much and answering questions',[60] seems more of a justification for dominant patterns of social behaviour than an explanation.

The need to identify an individual author has also rendered it difficult for discussions of the New German Cinema to address films made by women who have, for one reason or another, adopted collective working methods.[61] A number of women, such as Cristina Perincioli and Jutta Brückner, have simply expressed a preference for working collectively with other women. Others, like Helga Reidemeister, have consciously rejected claims to authorship of the films they have been involved in because they have attempted to involve the subjects of their films in the filmmaking process as much as possible. Reidemeister's film *Der gekaufte Traum / The Purchased Dream* (1974–77), which focuses on the lives of a family of unskilled workers in Berlin, was made in direct response to the complaints of the Bruder family who disliked the Berlin *Arbeiterfilme* because 'They never show us the way we want to be shown'.[62] Rather than assuming authorial control, Reidemeister was concerned that the family should do some of the filming themselves and gave them a camera to use. Through lack of access to fully funded means of production some women have also had to pool their resources and work collectively with other filmmakers and friends in order to realize a project. Of her film *Madame X – Eine absolute Herr-*

scherin / Madame X – An Absolute Ruler (1977), Ulrike Ottinger maintains, 'I had so little money ... that I was forced to work collectively from the start.'[63]

Collective working methods were of course privileged within the women's movement. Although not all women filmmakers adopted this mode of production, feminism has been an enormous influence on women's film production in Germany. Not all women filmmakers would describe themselves as feminist directors, but with relatively few exceptions women filmmakers have focused on female protagonists and much of their work in some way addresses issues raised by the women's movement. Also, when women filmmakers have been interviewed or their work discussed, this has largely been in specialist journals or anthologies devoted to feminist film criticism or in publications sympathetic to feminist politics. The highly limited discussion of women's filmmaking which has taken place in mainstream studies of the New German Cinema has therefore been framed within the context of an emerging feminist film culture.[64]

Although feminism is obviously an important context, the term has been used virtually to subsume all women's filmmaking in West Germany. Consequently, women filmmakers tend to be referred to as 'feminist directors' (as Franklin does with Sander) and their work viewed more as a genre, with the term *Frauenfilm* (women's film) being applied to films as diverse as those by Ottinger, Sander and von Trotta. However, when films are identified as belonging to a genre, structural, stylistic and thematic elements are usually discussed in relation to other films in the genre (as Robert Acker does), and critical attention is focused far less on individual directors.

For the *Cahiers* writers and subsequent *auteur* critics, working within a genre did not necessarily prevent a director from being elevated to *auteur* status. In some cases, it has even resulted in the reappraisal of hitherto critically despised film genres. For instance, at the end of the sixties and during the early seventies a number of New German Cinema directors produced films that were hailed as reworkings of the *Heimatfilm* (homeland film), one such hitherto critically despised film genre which has persisted throughout the history of German cinema. This trend, combined with Edgar Reitz's recent epic *Heimat / Homeland* (1984), has begun to precipitate a critical re-evaluation of this enduring genre.[65] However, in the case of women's filmmaking in West

Germany, when combined with the marked focus on personal experience and the dominant perception of women as incapable of creative authorship, the tendency to view the work of women directors as a genre places it in a position fundamentally at odds with any *cinéma des auteurs*.

The dominant perception of women as 'uncreative' has also deflected attention from their documentary filmmaking, shorts and television work. Although auteurism is a methodology primarily applied to feature film production, a number of the star *auteurs* did also make shorts and documentaries. Once directors are elevated to *auteur* status their non-feature film work is often retrospectively identified as 'interesting' and a suitable object of critical attention. In his discussion of Herzog, for instance, Sandford refers to two documentaries the director made in 1976, *How Much Wood Would a Woodchuck Chuck?* and *La Soufrière*. They are of 'interest' because, according to Sandford:

> each in its way is *a classic example of Herzog's approach to film-making*: on the one hand a film that observes some bizarre people who ... hover on the verge of making fools of themselves, on the other hand the most apocalyptic of Herzog's grandiose landscapes, a volcano in the fury of imminent eruption.[66](my emphasis)

Since women, on the other hand, have on the whole not been discussed as *auteurs* their non-feature film work has tended to be dismissed. For instance, when Franklin wants to give an example of how difficult it can be for a 'newcomer' to find funding for film projects in the Federal Republic, he chooses the case of Helke Sander. He cites the difficulties she experienced in trying to raise funding for her second feature film after the critical success of her first, *The All-Round Reduced Personality* (1977).[67] Yet Sander had been directing shorts and documentaries with television funding for over ten years by the time she made her first feature.

The overwhelming tendency to characterize the New German Cinema as a *cinéma des auteurs* has thus functioned at a number of different levels to inhibit serious consideration of the work of women filmmakers. Although the existence of women directors is at least now acknowledged – in contrast to Alemann's and Stöckl's experiences in the early seventies – the dominant perception of their contribution to the new cinema as minimal and highly marginal persists. While most cinema enthusiasts, especially followers of the European art movie circuit, have heard of Fassbinder, Herzog and Wenders and are relatively familiar with their work, very few can name a single West German woman film director.

PART TWO

Other Histories

THREE

The Women's Movement

The women's movement which developed in West Germany in the late sixties and early seventies had a powerful effect on the lives and conditions of a significant number of German women — and thereby on society as a whole. Its agenda went beyond campaigns for equal rights and opportunities, embracing approaches such as separatism and radical lesbianism. It had a profound effect on a variety of cultural practices, such as art, photography, drama, music, theatre and, of course, film. Yet the relationship between the women's movement and those women involved in cultural production has often been oversimplified. In the case of cinema, two popular myths have emerged. The first is that all women directors came from the movement and are feminists. The second is that the influence of the movement has given rise to a single film genre, the so-called *Frauenfilm* (women's film).

The main impetus for the contemporary women's movement came from within the student protest movement which emerged in Germany and other western countries during the sixties. With the Socialist German Students Union (SDS) as its intellectual spearhead, the student movement drew on Marxist political thought and was committed to anti-authoritarianism, human autonomy and the elimination of oppression. Although involved in the movement, women in West Germany as elsewhere found they were expected to perform support roles for their male colleagues, such as typing leaflets, looking after the children and making coffee, and that they were valued primarily for their role as man's helpmate.

During a SDS conference in September 1968 Helke Sander made a speech in which she drew attention to this oppression of women and the fact that there was not a single level within the student movement at which women's interests were represented. She went on to inform her male colleagues that:

> women make up more than half of the general population; and we believe it is high time that we express our concomitant expectations and demand that they be included in future plans. If the SDS is not able to make the leap forward to this insight, we would be forced into a power struggle which we would rather prevent.[1]

Sander's speech, however, fell on deaf ears. There was an unwillingness on the part of the SDS men to acknowledge the oppression of women and thus a refusal to concern themselves with their situation in society. Infuriated at the indifference that Sander's speech met with from her male comrades, another woman delegate, Sigrid Rüger, threw three tomatoes at the board of executives, successfully hitting SDS theoretician Hans-Jürgen Krahl, whom she denounced as a 'counter-revolutionary'.[2]

Sander maintains that their feelings were not shared by the majority of SDS women: 'on the contrary: most SDS women found our presence rather embarrassing'.[3] However, her speech is generally taken to mark the birth of the new women's movement in West Germany. Yet women had actually begun to organize prior to this. As one of only two women in the Berlin film school's first intake of thirty students in 1966, Sander had rapidly become aware of the imbalance between her own position and that of her fellow male students:

> At that time I was working exclusively with men who were much younger than I. Despite our common work and political goals, I began to sense more and more the contradiction between their situation and mine as a single mother. For the first time in my life I began to seek women, their opinions, their discussions.[4]

In January 1968 Sander and others set up an Action Council for Women's Liberation (*Aktionsrat zur Befreiung der Frauen*) in Berlin where women could meet and talk. The initiative did not have a particularly visible public profile, publicized as it was only through word of mouth and leafleting. Nevertheless, as Sander recalls, they had identified a need: 'Hundreds of women came and went. There was such pleasure in talking, in exchanging experiences with one another. We could never tear ourselves away, and chatted together well into the night.'[5]

A significant number of these women were, like Sander, mothers. With childcare still very much a female responsibility, one of their first priorities was to found alternative, anti-authoritarian day-care or play-group centres. This childcare initiative, the so-called *Kinderladen-Bewegung*, was picked up by the women's movement as it began to emerge, and gave the movement an initial cohesion. Indeed, in her SDS speech Sander had stressed that 'the group most easily politicized are women with children. It is they who are the most aggressive and the least speechless.'[6] It was in the wake of her speech that women's groups started to be set up throughout the country and began to campaign for women's rights.

By the beginning of the seventies, however, feminist activity had dwindled considerably, especially in comparison with Holland and the US. The women's magazine *Brigitte* drew attention to the fact that German women were not 'burning their bras ... not disrupting beauty contests ... not demanding the abolition of marriage ... there are no enraged pamphlets, no campaigning magazine. There's no rage.'[7] Out of the initial flurry of activity only four women's groups remained and the impetus for further action eventually came from France.

In the spring of 1971 the Paris women's movement initiated a campaign to demonstrate against French anti-abortion laws in which over three hundred women publicly declared that they had had abortions. Alice Schwarzer, a journalist working at that time in Paris and active in the movement there, imported the idea into Germany. With the help of three women's groups she launched a similar campaign, known as the Paragraph 218 campaign, for the legalization of abortion in West Germany. Many women approached by Schwarzer, especially those from the SPD, the communist party and trade unions, refused to participate for fear of the consequences. Some felt it would only harm the cause of women's emancipation, others feared they might face criminal proceedings or lose their jobs, and others were not prepared to face the reactions of family and friends.

Eventually, however, 374 women, among them secretaries, factory workers, office workers, actresses, students and a large number of housewives, signed a petition in which they admitted to having had an abortion. The petition called for the deletion of Paragraph 218 (from which the campaign took its name) from the Basic Law which criminalized abortion. It also demanded the right to have pregnancy terminated within the provisions of the state health service, and free access to contraception. The petition, together with names and photos, was published in *Stern* magazine in June 1971 and had the effect of rallying women throughout the country in support of the campaign. In direct contrast, the response from the male establishment was generally one of outrage: doctors declared that they would not perform abortions even if the law was reformed. It took several more years of campaigning before the *Fristenlösung*, a law which allows the termination of pregnancy within the first three months for 'social' as well as purely medical reasons, was passed.

In the meantime other issues were raised and further organizational initiatives followed. The abortion issue led to a concern with methods of contraception and with the mystification of medical practices. The first self-help groups were set up to enable women to examine and learn about their own bodies. The first Federal Women's Congress was held in March 1972 and links began to be forged with women overseas. A proliferation of feminist leaflets and pamphlets appeared and the first women's yearbook was published. Campaigns were arranged to highlight the exploitation of women in the workplace for a lower wage than men, and in the home as unpaid labour. By spring 1974 around a dozen women's centres had been set up, all of which were self-financed and self-run, to operate as organizational bases, discussion groups and advice centres. The movement soon numbered a couple of hundred women's groups and several thousand activists.

In the mid seventies the question of violence against women also began to be addressed. Discussions and initiatives covered not only the problem of domestic violence and rape, but also the practices women have been subjected to by the male-dominated medical profession, by the media and on the street. The first house for battered women was opened in November 1976, and within its first three months 193 women had sought refuge there with their children. Self-defence groups were organized and the first rape crisis line, together with the first public demonstration against rape, followed in spring 1977. Under the slogan 'our bodies belong to us', self-help groups had spread throughout the country, and in October 1977 the first women's health centre opened in Berlin.

Amid this campaigning activity a women's counter-culture also began to emerge. The need for women to organize separately had been identified early on in the existence of the movement. Most women agreed that such a strategy was necessary if they were to analyse the workings of their own oppression, learn to represent their own interests, and if the power relations that come into play when men are present were to be avoided. Although such work was not viewed as just a transitional process, the women who attended the first Federal Women's Congress also stressed that 'we are not refusing to work together with men in other organizations and on necessary occasions.'[8]

Gradually, however, traditional forms of social organization – especially marriage and the family – also began to be questioned. In Germany as elsewhere, these were identified as patriarchal institutions which had significantly contributed to women's oppression. Where possible women tried to replace such hierarchical structures with collective, participatory methods of organization. For segments of the movement the demands for equality began to be superseded by a more fundamental questioning of 'whether we even accept these male domains in their structures, whether we even want to participate in male politics, male science, etc.'[9]

As the seventies progressed, women increasingly undertook social, educational and domestic activities in the company of other women. In 1974 a women's festival comprising information stands, market stalls and various entertainments was organized in Berlin. That summer women from Germany went to the Danish island of Femø where a group of women from Copenhagen had organized an international women's holiday camp. In the same year large numbers of women began to come out as lesbians. During the mid seventies an increasing number of so-called 'alternative' women's projects were also set up. Among these were women-only pubs, all-female bands, women's bookshops and publishers, feminist magazines (most notably *Emma* and *Courage*), women's studies courses and women-only communal households. The focus of the movement had started to shift: 'What had begun as a fight against men became a fight for women.'[10]

As in other countries, throughout the first decade of the women's movement there was a concern amongst feminist activists and film-makers to make films at a grassroots level. These were primarily campaigning films intended to 'support the women's movement in such a way as to have an immediate effect'.[11] As elsewhere the majority of these were documentaries, and among the earliest were two made by Helke Sander. The first was *Kinder sind keine Rinder / Children aren't Cattle* (1968–69) about the first alternative day-care centre. Made with the children from her son's own group, it argues for the right to self-determination for children and shows the work done to both win support for such centres as well as encourage people to set up new ones. At the same time she also made *Kindergärtnerin was nun? / What now, Nursery School Teacher?* (1969), a short campaign film in support of a strike by women nursery school teachers for better working conditions and smaller play groups.

Other films addressed the Paragraph 218 campaign, contraception and the problems arising from unwanted children. These included Helke Sander's and Sarah Schumann's *Macht die Pille Frei? / Does the Pill Liberate?* (1972), Ingrid Oppermann and Gardi Deppe's *Kinder für dieses System – Paragraph 218 / Children for this System — Paragraph 218* (1973) and Sabine Eckhard's *Paragraph 218 und was wir dagegen haben / Paragraph 218 and What We Have Against it* (1976–77). A number of films also examined the situation of women in the workplace. These usually focused on women's protests against low wages, but some also addressed the question of training, the role of trade unions or related the work situation to women's position in the home. Among these were Barbara Kasper's *Gleicher Lohn für Mann und Frau / Equal Wages for Men and Women* (1971), Valeska Schöttle's *Wer braucht wen? / Who Needs Whom?* (1972), Claudia von Alemann's *Es kommt drauf an, sie zu verändern / The Point is to Change it* (1972–73) and Oppermann's *Frauen – Schlußlichter der Gewerkschaft? / Women – At the Tail End of Trade Unions?* (1975).

One of the key films to come out of this grassroots activity was Cristina Perincioli's *Die Macht der Männer ist die Geduld der Frauen / The Power of Men is the Patience of Women* (1978). This highly compelling film addressed the issue of domestic violence: the number of battered women in the Federal Republic during the mid seventies was estimated to be around four million.[12] According to Perincioli, 'We, women from the women's movement and socially committed women journalists, began to make the public aware of this problem, through the radio and television and the book *Violence in Marriage*.'[13] After helping found Germany's first women's refuge, she and women at the refuge made *The Power of Men is the Patience of Women* for television to publicize the issue further.

Using a low-key realist style, the film constructs a dramatized account of one woman's real-life experiences. Repeatedly beaten (and on one occasion requiring hospitalization) by her husband, Max, Addi attempts to leave. Taking her young son with her she finds it difficult to find both accommodation and work, and eventually has to return to the family home. One day, however, she sees a news item on television about the Berlin women's house, packs her bags and heads there with her son. At the refuge she finds support and strength among other battered women who help her through the legal and bureaucratic processes involved in instigating divorce proceedings and securing custody of her child. Eventually, Addi, two other women and their children move into an apartment together and establish a collectively run household.

The film does more, however, than merely draw attention to the existence of the problem of domestic violence. *The Power of Men* also highlights the enormous difficulties women face in dealing with it and conveys important information about the role that women's refuges can play. Although the film's format is primarily that of a feature film, an intermittent voice-over commentary is used to provide statistics and further information on social attitudes towards the problem. This device foregrounds the subject as a social problem rather than a personal one, and this is reinforced by the film's visual style. Much of the film is comprised of medium and medium-long shots, with relatively few close-ups. Although a static camera is often used to underline Addi's despair, its distance discourages viewer identification with her as an individual and focuses attention on her situation.

An important aspect of such films was the way in which they communicated that social change with regard to such oppression was possible. As Perincioli explains with regard to her own work:

> My films' upbeat endings represent the collective wish of those involved
> to show that things can work out.... If you want a housewife to wake up
> and say, 'What the hell am I doing?', you first have to give her a glimpse

of the possibility of change. Only then can a woman afford to realize how shitty her own position is. If you just show once more how boring her day is, then she will tune out.[14]

The importance attached to communicating the possibility of social change led some filmmakers to travel with their films to participate in post-screening discussions. It also resulted in an increasing number wanting to move into feature film production, or at least to combine documentary and narrative conventions as Perincioli did.

For many feminist activists documentary had initially seemed the most appropriate medium for drawing attention to women's experience of oppression. This is because it is one that purports to record 'reality' or reveal a pre-existing 'truth'. However, some women filmmakers started to feel that the documentary aesthetic had a limited capacity for communicating with an audience. According to Erika Runge, 'it neglects the utopian elements ... I find other possibilities arise from the play of emotions in fiction; fiction offers a different kind of appeal to the audience and other possibilities of making contact.'[15] Although the documentary voice-over plays an important role in Perincioli's *The Power of Men*, the choice of a dramatic structure for the film was also a deliberate one: 'we portrayed the issue in an easily understandable, conventional way so that people would still want to watch something about it after a day at work.'[16]

On occasions a documentary aesthetic actually proved counterproductive to the filmmaker's intentions. In the case of Helga Reidemeister's powerful film *Von wegen 'Schicksal' / Who says 'Destiny'* (1978–79), for instance, attention was deflected away from its 'optimistic' conclusion precisely because of its documentary techniques. The film is about Irene Rakowitz, a working-class dressmaker in her forties, partially disabled and divorced after twenty-two years of marriage. It revolves around her problems, disappointments and hopes as the mother of four. While her former husband dismisses the problems of everyday life as 'destiny', Irene recognizes the social conditions that construct her situation, and realizes the importance of participating in political initiatives if she wants to change that situation. The film suggests that Irene's hopes for change will be realized in her youngest daughter and ends with Irene reaffirming her belief in the possibility of emancipation.

Although filmed in classic *cinéma-vérité* style, Reidemeister often acts as an off-screen interviewer during the film. Her questions can be heard on the soundtrack, but she herself does not appear in the frame. She therefore structures the direction of discussions, effectively participating in and even precipitating the filmed situations. Family arguments and painful emotions of a highly disturbing nature are moreover uncompromisingly subjected to the camera's gaze. In one scene the extreme distress of Irene's eight-year-old son is unrelentingly filmed during a domestic confrontation. These techniques tended to focus critical attention on Reidemeister. She won the 1979 Federal Film Prize for best documentary direction, on the one hand. But less sympathetic critics described the film as exploitative and voyeuristic, and were prompted to question Reidemeister's integrity as a filmmaker.[17]

Some women also began to realize that the use of 'fiction' increased the possibility of reaching a wider audience, which was of crucial importance to those trying to raise awareness of women's oppression and campaign for women's rights. Once again, as Perincioli explains: 'I think it's important to create a dramatic film if we choose a socially controversial issue. Otherwise an in-group watches it and not those people for whom considering that issue is really new.'[18] Echoing this viewpoint Heidi Genée has stressed that she would rather forego awards and good reviews in favour of a large audience: 'I'd rather communicate and ... reach people.'[19]

In addition to making films which campaigned for social change and women's rights, some women also used film to document the initiatives undertaken and 'alternative' projects set up by the movement. During the seventies a group of women in Frankfurt set up the *Mond / Film / Frauen* film group with the specific aim of working with women's houses, theatre groups and self-help groups. Edith Schmidt, together with the *Frauenkollektiv Frankfurt*, made the documentary *Das hat mich sehr verändert / It's Changed me Greatly* (1976) about the origins and work of the Frankfurt women's centre. In 1979 Birgit Durbahn and Petra Wybieralski made *Walpurgisnacht / Walpurgis Night* to provide a filmic record of the third annual women's demonstration against rape and outline its history. The following year Durbahn, together with Andrea van Straeten, went on to make the video *Unter Rock* about a lesbian rock band of the same name on the occasion of their last live performance in Hanover. In the two years the band were performing together, they regarded themselves not just as the rock band but as a lesbian project. The video is intended as a documentation of both their work as musicians and the internal structures and problems that developed within the group.

Such films were usually less concerned with reaching wider audiences than films such as Perincioli's *The Power of Men.* Instead, they were intended mainly as resources for women within the movement. Some, however, were also produced in order to provide future generations of women with a historical record of the second wave of feminism. By the mid seventies the women's movement in Germany had begun to discover the writings of feminist activists from the nineteenth century. Although encouraging, the discovery that their initiatives were not without precedent also proved cause for concern. Not only had women's rights been fought for before with apparently little success, but the history of this earlier fight had been lost. As Helke Sander asserted: 'None of us knew that there had already been a women's movement in the nineteenth century.'[20] Such films were regarded as a means of helping ensure that the contemporary women's movement would not 'vanish' without trace as well. According to Sander, this had become a very real possibility by the end of the decade:

> Young women now hardly know any more out of which questions, and from which women, the beginning of the new women's movement derives. There is hardly anything written about it, and the little there is, is extremely questionable. It is as if you had to make the same invention over and over again.[21]

This concern was the motivation behind Sander's second feature film, *Der subjektive Faktor/ The Subjective Factor* (1981). Largely autobiographical, and intercutting news footage from the period, the film recounts the beginnings, in 1967 to 1970, of the new women's movement in West Germany. It not only shows the early campaigning initiatives undertaken by women in Germany, but also explores the sociopolitical context out of which these arose. It focuses on Anni, who moves into a student commune with her young son. There she becomes involved in the theoretical debates and political activities of the student Left. In the process, she starts to examine her own oppression and looks to her male colleagues for help and support. However, she (like Sander) meets with indifference and has to turn to other women.

As the work of the women's movement began to raise awareness of the way in which women have been virtually excluded from historical discourses, a number of films were also made that explored other aspects of women's history. Many of these were documentaries made for television at the end of the seventies and during the early eighties. Hannelore Schäfer's *Zwei Frauen erleben das dritte Reich/Two Women's Experiences of the Third Reich* (1979), for instance, is about the experiences and work of two women who opposed the Nazi regime. Luisa Francia's *Hexen/Witches* (1980) and Anke Wolf-Graaf's *Hebammen/Midwives* (1982) focus on the work and persecution of those women thought to be witches in the middle ages because of their knowledge and practices, while Christa von Braun's *Verfremt verfälscht vergessen/Ostracized, Falsified, Forgotten* (1982) looks at the role of women in the French Revolution and their feminist demands. Claudia von Alemann, however, returned to the feature film for her project about nineteenth-century socialist and feminist Flora Tristan (which is discussed further in chapter five), *Reise nach Lyon/Blind Spot* (1980).

However, like other 'national' women's movements, the German movement was not a unified or coherent one. Rather, it encompassed a number of viewpoints that had initially found common ground in the childcare initiative and the Paragraph 218 campaign. These issues succeeded in politicizing a large segment of the female population; but by 1973 a broad polarization was evident within the movement between a socialist-feminist faction on the one hand and a more radical anarcho-feminist one on the other.

Splits in the movement also occurred over specific issues, such as women's exploitation in the home as unpaid labour. One faction launched a 'wages for housework' campaign. This was a concept which found support among right-wing politicians since it was identified as a means of helping keep women in the home. Others, however, argued against the classification of housework as women's work, stressing women's right to pursue professional activity and the need for housework and childcare to be shared responsibilities. As the seventies progressed, a further conflict developed in Germany as elsewhere between separatist lesbians and so-called 'hetero-women'.[22]

According to Hilke Schlaeger, by the late seventies the women's movement had 'used up its revolutionary strength in quarrelling'.[23] The plethora of 'alternative' women's projects and an emerging separatist mentality compounded the dissipation of its initial political impetus. As segments of the movement also turned to a glorification of motherhood and the female body, a distinct anti-intellectualism pervaded the movement. Although the women's movement had originally been clearly identified as a political movement – a women's congress in 1972 had, for instance, been held under the slogan 'No socialism without feminism, no feminism without socialism' – Sander asserts that by the late seventies a large part of the movement was far more interested in promoting a women's culture than in pursuing political aims.[24]

Despite this factional fragmentation, the work undertaken by the women's movement was highly successful in bringing the question of women's rights into the public arena. Even among women who had not actively participated in the movement or knew little of its origins there was a growing consciousness of the way in which women had been oppressed. As Sander asserted in 1977:

> Women have just begun to *dare* to see themselves, others and society, with their own eyes; to compare alien opinions and theories to their own experiences; to formulate first concepts with the help of which we can begin to comprehend the nature of past feminine oppression, contemporary social contradictions, and our expectations for a different human future.... We must first learn to see with our own eyes and not through the mediation of others.[25]

Within the movement there was an emphasis on encouraging women to acknowledge their own experiences. In feminist journals and magazines so-called self-experience reports occupied a prominent position. Some feminist activists also regarded it as the duty of women engaged in or concerned with cultural production to help women with this consciousness-raising process. Given the role that the audio-visual media has played in propagating male-determined images of women, women involved in film were deemed to have a particularly important role to play. The editors of *Frauen und Film*, a feminist film journal founded by Sander, declared:

We want to speak to women viewers who are constantly exposed to film images and subject matter which, if not produced by the dominant culture, certainly reproduce it and thereby renew and strengthen it. *Frauen und Film* should give women the courage to escape such brainwashing and admit their own experiences. This is also true for women who work in or with the medium of film.[26]

Despite the journal's 'call to arms', relatively few women filmmakers did actively participate in the women's movement. Ula Stöckl, for instance, found herself very much as odds with it:

The women's movement developed parallel to me. I was already making films when it began to organize and formulate goals. I considered radical separatism absurd. Moreover, the leaders of the organized women's movement in West Germany completely ignored my work. Indeed the fact that I had already achieved what they were still struggling for was counted against me. For them I was a 'man's woman'.[27]

Some directors even had their work criticized by feminist activists who felt it was not sufficiently supportive of the movement's aims. Stöckl's films were criticized for focusing on women who do not fully achieve emancipation. Ingemo Engström's *Kampf um ein Kind/Fight for a Child* (1974–75) also came under attack for examining the difficulties professional women face if they want to have children. At the time, the women's movement was still campaigning to get abortion decriminalized, and Engström's film was deemed to do little to help the movement achieve that goal.

However, the movement's success in its consciousness-raising aims did result in a women's cinema that was concerned with representing and foregrounding the authentic experiences of women. Consequently it has been characterized as a cinema of personal experience. Some films inevitably thematized women's oppression, but this work equally stemmed from a recognition of the fact that women's own lives are, as Lisa Katzman expresses it, 'adequate to comprise the central concern of and reason for making a film'.[28]

As the terms 'authentic' and 'personal experience' suggest, the majority of films comprising this cinema explored or were based on the lives of actual women. Several filmmakers simply turned their cameras on women in their own circle of friends and acquaintances. In her film *Ein gar und ganz verwahrlostes Mädchen/A Thoroughly Demoralized Girl* (1977) Jutta Brückner documents a day in the life of her friend Rita Rischak. Using a combination of staged scenes in which Rita plays herself and interviews, the film shows how the young woman's attempts to improve her life all come to nothing.

Elfi Mikesch made *Ich denke oft an Hawaii/I Often Think of Hawaii* (1978) about her neighbours, forty-two year old Ruth Rossol and her two teenage children, Carmen and Tito. The film highlights the isolation and monotony that has come to characterize Ruth's life since her husband deserted her, and focuses on the daydream strategies Carmen employs to cope with the emptiness of family life. Like Brückner's film, it is not an explicit documentation but rather, according to Mikesch, 'tries to be authentic with the aid of imagination'.[29]

Several films were based on the documented lives of actual women. Ula Stöckl's *Eine Frau mit Verantwortung/A Woman with Responsibility* (1978) draws on a clinical case study of a young woman who eventually became neurotic due to her inability to assert her own desires against the wishes first of her father and then of her husband. Petra Haffter's film *Wahnsinn, das ganze Leben ist Wahnsinn/Madness, Life is Total Madness* (1979) and Helma Sanders-Brahms's *Die Berührte/No Mercy No Future* (1981) are both based on the diaries of real women. The former uses the published diary of sixteen-year-old Karin Q, who escapes into daydreams of marriage and motherhood to cope with the struggle of growing up. Sanders-Brahms's film draws on a diary kept by a schizophrenic young woman who searches for a reincarnated Christ in the men she encounters among society's outcasts.

Two of the internationally best-known films in this style are *Das zweite Erwachen der Christa Klages/The Second Awakening of Christa Klages* (1977) and *Die bleierne Zeit/The German Sisters* (1981) by Margarethe von Trotta. The first film dramatizes the story of nursery-school teacher Margit Czenki, who robbed a bank in Munich in order to obtain money to finance a children's day-care centre. The second (which is discussed in further detail in chapter five) came about when von Trotta met Christiane Ensslin after her sister Gudrun, a member of the Baader-Meinhof group, and two other terrorists had been found dead in Stammheim prison in October 1977. The film focuses on the relationship between two sisters, one of whom, Juliane, is a feminist activist, while the other, Marianne, has left her husband and child and turned to terrorism.

A number of directors, however, turned to their own experiences and produced overtly autobiographical or semi-autobiographical feature films. Among these are Helma Sanders-Brahms's *Deutschland, bleiche Mutter / Germany, Pale Mother* (1979–80) which is discussed further in chapter five, Recha Jungmann's *Etwas tut weh / Something Hurts* (1979), Jutta Brückner's *Hungerjahre / Years of Hunger* (1980), Jeanine Meerapfel's *Malou* (1980) and Marianne Rosenbaum's *Peppermint Frieden/Peppermint Freedom* (1983). Although other issues are also raised in these films, the directors all look back to their own childhoods, their experiences of growing up in the fifties and the lives of their parents. Even Heidi Genée's more commercially successful comedy *1 + 1 = 3* (1979) is autobiographical. The story of a young single actress, Katharina, who decides to have her baby after a half-hearted attempt to have it aborted, the film was criticized for its apparently rose-tinted representation of the situation. Genée responded by revealing: 'It happened exactly as I showed it. Katharina is my mother, and the baby – that's me. And my mother never regretted her actions. And I had a wonderful childhood.'[30]

Equally autobiographical, but more contemporary in its subject matter, is Helke Sander's *Die allseitig reduzierte Persönlichkeit/The Allround Reduced Personality* (1977) – *Redupers* for short. Made in black and white, the film focuses on Edda Chiemnyjewski, a single mother and freelance photographer living in West Berlin. It revolves around her attempts to balance her commitments as a mother and a member of a women's photography collective with her need to earn a living. The parallels with Sander's own well-documented experiences of trying to combine her role as a single mother with her professional activity as a filmmaker are unmistakable.[31] Moreover, as if to underline the autobiographical nature of the film, Sander herself plays the central protagonist.

Within these films there is a specific concern to foreground particular aspects of women's reality that have traditionally been excluded from the public sphere. As Brückner asserted: 'We are confronted with images of women everywhere: mother, rosy lovers, or deceived wives. But a large part of female reality ... is not shown.'[32] Sander has argued, for instance, that 'the ousting of children is a fundamental reason for the distorted image of reality offered by the mass media'.[33] Since child-care remained primarily a female responsibility during the seventies, this affected the image of women's reality in particular.

In *Redupers*, therefore, Sander foregrounds Edda's role as a mother. In the opening scenes Edda is shown getting ready to leave for work, picking up her young daughter as she does so to say goodbye. She hands the child over to her flatmate, but the girl clings on to Edda's scarf and refuses to let go. In despair Edda takes the scarf off and leaves it dangling in her daughter's hand as she rushes out of the door. The position of this scene means that one of the first things we find out about Edda is that she is a mother. Its composition – mother and child in a 'tug-of-war' – also emphasizes how Edda's role as wage-earner conflicts with that of mother. This combination makes the scene very powerful and creates a lasting impression. Although the child is subsequently absent during whole sections of the film, it is impossible as a viewer to forget what employers so frequently want to ignore – that women are frequently mothers as well as workers.

In *Years of Hunger* Brückner graphically depicts the moment a young girl gets her first period and contextualizes it as part of the female experience of adolescence. At the beginning of the film the young female protagonist is shown sitting on a toilet in the family bathroom. As she goes to pull up her pants, she notices a blood stain on them. She gets a towel, wipes herself and then goes to her mother in a state of confusion, thinking she is ill. Such aspects of women's reality have not been totally excluded from the public sphere: a girl's discovery of her first menstrual blood forms the opening sequence to Brian de Palma's film *Carrie* (1976), for example. However, in the context of de Palma's horror film Carrie's blood takes on symbolic and mythic meaning. Rather than being represented as part of women's authentic experience, menstruation serves as evidence of woman's 'impurity' and ultimately leads to the destruction of a whole community.

This concern to foreground the authentic experiences of women produced a cinema which offered women viewers a recognizable representation of themselves and their lives. Individual experiences obviously can and do differ according to race, age, class, religion, and so on. Yet the response that these films met with demonstrates that some experiences do transcend such boundaries.

Jutta Brückner, for instance, was surprised at the response *Years of*

Hunger elicited outside Germany, since she felt the film was culturally specific. It focuses on a teenage girl, Ursula, growing up in the fifties in a divided Germany. She becomes totally alienated from her own body, due to the restrictive values espoused by those around her, and finally attempts suicide. When a twenty-four-year old British interviewer told Brückner that the film reminded her of her own adolescence and that she identified with its protagonist, the filmmaker asserted:

> I didn't think that ... it would appeal to so many women – not just women from other countries, but from totally different societies. Egyptian women, for instance, have said the same thing to me as you just did.... They must have a completely different lifestyle, how *can* they identify with it? ... I'm forty now and I always thought the film would appeal to a particular generation.[34]

Brückner has theorized this response to her film using a concept she has termed 'collective gestures'. As she explains:

> There are certain ways of hiding one's feelings, certain types of inhibition ... for instance, in the scene where the daughter comes home after her accordion class, and a boy has asked her out. The daughter pulls her nightdress over her head before she undresses, just like her mother does, because right at that moment she's ashamed to undress in front of her mother. And then when the mother sits by her daughter's bed and strokes her hand over the quilt because she can't stroke the child itself any more, and doesn't want to, because suddenly a barrier has grown up between them. Obviously these are gestures which every woman knows: even if they didn't happen *exactly* like that, women can still remember how it *did* happen for them.[35]

Thus these films function as implicit explorations of women's *collective* experiences. Although they have been termed *Frauenfilme* or women's films, this particular aspect of women's film production also attracted the attention of male viewers. Of *Redupers*, a male critic observed:

> Helke Sander has not only succeeded in offering an impressively characterized portrait of the reduced city of Berlin, she has also managed to frame her own situation as author, *the situation of many professional women,*

in images and scenes against which men currently have shamefully little to say.[36] (my emphasis)

In some cases, male viewers have even identified with the situation of the female protagonist.[37] This ability to represent contemporary collective experiences through an individual protagonist was singled out as the specific strength of women's filmmaking in West Germany. In 1978, for instance, Gottfried Knapp commented:

> While the male protagonists of the latest generation of directors ... are becoming increasingly entangled in their own private pet neuroses and the feigned artificialities of madness ... *a new, intimate, productive relationship to the present* is being heralded on the women's side.[38] (my emphasis)

Working methods were also influenced by the women's movement. The movement's privileging of collective, participatory methods of organization led a number of women filmmakers to attempt to employ such methods in their work. Indeed, according to Claudia Lenssen, the first generation of women film directors in West Germany 'put much time and energy into trying to work collectively'.[39] Perincioli, for instance, stressed that in her work 'the most important factor is ... the group cohesion and solidarity as a creative basis from which to work'.[40]

The collective ideal was pursued with those in front of the camera as well as those behind it. Although she drew up the final script for *The Power of Men*, Perincioli stresses that it evolved through extensive input from the women in the film: 'I did not know how the women talked to each other in the shelter, for example. They acted it out for me, and I wrote the best parts into the script.'[41] This process continued during the actual filming:

> We rehearsed almost every scene in front of the video cameras. Then we watched the scene together and talked about it and made any necessary changes. It is a method that I like to use because we can all learn together.... If you work with amateur actors, you are likely to find out very quickly where the script is inadequate. Professional actors do everything, even the most absurd antics, but amateurs cannot do everything. They act well only when they feel comfortable with the text. That is how we determined if the script needed changes.[42]

Even directors not so actively engaged in the women's movement as Perincioli have adopted such working methods. When making her film *Dark Spring* (1970) about women's concepts of utopia and attitudes towards relationships, for instance, Ingemo Engström based her script on extensive conversations she had with the actresses involved:

> I wrote it according to their own statements, and then when we were filming they played themselves. So it wasn't pure documentary, it documented the fictional situation that we'd constructed together.[43]

The preference for working collectively also led some directors to favour working with all-female crews as they found women tended to be more willing to work in this manner than men. As Perincioli explains:

> I prefer to work together with women, even if less professional than men. The film team's atmosphere and the support that it develops is of prime importance. Not all women can or will participate in this way, but it's more likely so in a women's group than with individual men who are so proud of their craftsmanship and are actually very isolated.[44]

Despite Perincioli's assertion, the concepts of collective work and 'teams' have not in fact been confined to women's projects. The degree of collectivity and precise form of collaboration obviously varies according to the degree of authorial control exercised by the director and the original concept behind the project. However, several male directors have gone on record as expressing an interest in or preference for collectively-based work.[45] Joint projects have also emerged within the 'male mainstream', such as the frequently referenced *Deutschland im Herbst / Germany in Autumn* (1978), followed by *Der Kandidat / The Candidate* (1980) and *Krieg und Frieden / War and Peace* (1982).[46] Furthermore, as Charles Eidsvik has observed, 'teamwork' was one of the New German Cinema's major characteristics:

> The first thing one must understand about the Germans is that they create in small 'family' groups. Though we prefer to identify films by their directors, the Germans learned quickly that one-man-one-film does not work. Even Herzog and Fassbinder, who write their own scripts, have tightly-knit, utterly loyal film 'families'. The core of each

team ... is a writer and a director/producer. With a couple of exceptions, even Wenders has never worked without Peter Handke as
screenwriter; on even Wenders's own scripts, Handke advises. Thus one
must usually identify films by both writer and director: Schlöndorff/
Von Trotta (who co-write and co-direct); Brustellin (writer)/Sinkel
(director); Steinbuch/Reitz. Those who both direct and write usually
work with the same small team comprised of a cameraman, an editor,
and a production manager.[47]

Although such teamwork was organized on a hierarchical basis, it is
precisely as members of such teams that many women have made a
substantial, if usually unacknowledged, contribution to the New
German Cinema. As editors, for instance, women have played an
enormous role. Beate Mainka-Jellinghaus has edited virtually all of
Herzog's films and has also worked extensively with Kluge, while
Fassbinder used either Thea Eymesz or Juliane Lorenz to edit most of
his films.[48]

Women's contribution to the New German Cinema has been at its
most visible in front of the camera as actresses, 'family' members that
Eidsvik overlooks. Fassbinder not only repeatedly used Eva Mattes and
Irm Hermann, but worked with Hanna Schygulla so frequently that
after his death German journalists prophesied the demise of her
career.[49] Kluge has frequently worked with Hannelore Hoger and his
sister Alexandra, while Schlöndorff and von Trotta have often worked
with Jutta Lampe, Barbara Sukowa, Angela Winkler, Hanna
Schygulla, Katherina Thalbach and Tina Engel. These actresses have
also appeared in innumerable films by other New German Cinema
directors and have thereby played an important role in constructing a
recognizable identity for Germany's new cinema.[50]

A preference for 'team' work and an interest in more collectively
based work has therefore not been unique to women directors.
Fassbinder, Herzog and other male directors, however, actively
promoted themselves as the heads of their 'families', as *Autoren*. In
contrast, the influence of the women's movement led many women
directors to reject such rigid hierarchy. But this is not to suggest that
they have pursued what Erika Runge has termed 'blind collectivism'.[51]

By the beginning of the eighties, the problems inherent in the
feminist ideal of collectivity had become apparent. Some filmmakers
complained about the endless discussions involved,[52] others that

differing interests often led to conflict.[53] Indeed, Lenssen asserted that when she talked to some women directors about their future plans they maintained that 'they want to have better control of their films, to work primarily as directors and to have other people follow their instructions'.[54]

Nevertheless, women filmmakers have proved to be more willing than their male counterparts both to invite and to acknowledge the contribution of others involved in their projects. Actresses and crew members have, for instance, commented on the way in which many women directors encourage people to work *with* them rather than *for* them. Actress Hanna Schygulla succinctly characterized this method of working after having made *Heller Wahn / Friends and Husbands* (1982–83) with Margarethe von Trotta. She observed that male directors are usually 'like a father or a lover' whereas von Trotta 'likes to be a sister'.[55] Even a more commercial director such as Doris Dörrie shares this tendency:

> I've worked with the same crew on all my features. We've set up a fragile system of no hierarchy, of everybody being encouraged to come up with ideas and contribute to the story.[56]

Rather than foregrounding their own role as originators of a project, they have also stressed the productive nature and pleasurable aspects of collaborative and participatory work methods. With regard to her film *Die Wolfsbraut / The Wolf Girl* (1985), for instance, Dagmar Beiersdorf emphasized that credit for the powerful musical sequence which ends the film had to go to actress Martine Felton who performed it:

> When I get to know my actors during rehearsals, I will happily incorporate their idiosyncrasies and strengths into the script. Or take out things which don't suit them. For example, it's thanks to Martine that Dennis sings in the film. She has a fantastic voice, which simply had to be in the film. It wasn't in my original story.[57]

Indeed, some women directors have gone so far as to complain about the way in which the media identify the director as the sole originator of a film. Helga Reidemeister, for example, stressed that her film *Who Says 'Destiny'* evolved out of a relationship based on mutual trust. Afterwards, however, she found that 'one person, myself, was singled out as the filmmaker, as the "careerist". That was a bitter and disruptive experience.'[58] After the phenomenal success of her film *Männer/Men* (1985) Doris Dörrie similarly complained about the way in which the media singled her out for attention, and stressed that she would have been unable to make the film without the creative input of her whole team.[59]

But the women's movement can be seen to have done almost as much to hinder and restrict women's filmmaking as to promote it. Involvement in or association with the movement during the seventies could actually result in unemployment for women filmmakers. Some, for instance, had supported the movement by helping to make campaigning films. Much of this work, however, was carried out in collaboration with non-professionals and with limited resources. As a result women filmmakers were not always able to work to particularly high technical standards. When subsequently applying to funding agencies or television for film finance, such films could be used as grounds for turning applications down: the low production values were taken as evidence of minimal technical skills.[60]

In certain circumstances, adopting the collective, participatory methods of working privileged by the women's movement could have similar consequences. Several filmmakers have stressed that if they tried to discuss their work with a television crew instead of assuming an authoritative attitude, this was interpreted as a sign of 'feminine weakness'.[61] This in turn reinforced the dominant perception of women as being incapable of making films.

During the early seventies there was also a frequent assumption amongst employers that women who could be termed feminists could not be 'objective' about issues relating to the women's movement. Sander maintains it provided broadcasters with ideal justification for institutionalized sexism, since it was possible to argue that by not employing women filmmakers they were protecting the public from a lack of 'objectivity'. She was given this as a reason by a department head at a television station in 1969 when he rejected her proposed project about the women's movement.[62] The same argument was later reiterated by funding commissions.[63]

Perincioli's project *Anna und Edith/Anna and Edith* (1975) suffered a similar fate. The film is about a group of women employees fighting for better working conditions, who are both frightened and encouraged by the growth of a lesbian relationship between two of them. Although ZDF accepted the script and Perincioli to direct, after filming began she was replaced by Gerit Neuhaus. As Perincioli explains: 'I was fired as director for my own script ... because the TV network thought I was too partisan and that a man could deal better with a lesbian relationship.'[64]

This attitude affected a significant number of women filmmakers. Women who addressed issues raised by the movement in their film work tended to be automatically categorized as feminists, irrespective of their actual connection (if any) with the women's movement, their politics, or how they viewed their work. The term was moreover used to describe women's initiatives as diverse as separatism and fighting the class system, and was of course subject to media distortion. According to Sander this led to a commonly-held thesis in the early seventies: 'All women filmmakers who are somehow committed form a group, somehow come from one party, the feminist one.'[65]

Consequently it tended to be male directors who made films about 'women's issues' during the early seventies. In 1971, for instance, Fassbinder made *Die bitteren Tränen der Petra von Kant / The Bitter Tears of Petra von Kant* about a lesbian relationship, while Kluge addressed the subject of abortion in his film *Gelegenheitsarbeit einer Sklavin / Occasional Work of a Female Slave* (1973). Indeed, some critics have made particular note of the 'feminist implications' in the work of the 'male mainstream'.[66] The apparent pro-feminist positions espoused in some of their films were, however, called into question by their female colleagues. Sander, for example, asserted that many male filmmakers 'simply exploit women's problems for the purpose of self-promotion under the pretext of accepting women's emancipation'.[67]

Women who avoided such issues could be relatively successful in getting work since, according to Sander, 'If you do not concern yourself with "women's issues" ... that proves you are not biased.'[68] However, she argues that for women filmmakers such as herself, who were actively involved in the women's movement, and for those who became implicitly associated with it, the prevailing attitude of media institutions effectively constituted a *Berufsverbot* for many women filmmakers (see chapter one). That is to say, they were prevented by employers or funders from pursuing their profession on grounds of their acknowledged or assumed feminism.

Sander's assertion may at first seem extreme, especially given that a number of women – such as Gloria Behrens, Gertrud Pinkus, Helma Sander-Brahms and Katrin Seybold – worked extensively in television during the early to mid seventies. However, much of their work was not focusing on 'women's issues'. Of Sanders-Brahms's early films, for instance, *Gewalt/ Violence* (1970) is about a couple's descent into criminal activity, *Die industrielle Reservearmee/ The Industrial Reserve Army* (1971) deals with Germany's Turkish *Gastarbeiter* (guest workers), *Der Angestellte/ The Employee* (1972) and *Die Maschine/ The Machine* (1973) both focus on workers, *Die letzten Tage von Gomorrha/ The Last Days of Gomorrah* (1974) is a science fiction film, and *Erdbeben in Chile/ Earthquake in Chile* (1974) is based on a novella by Heinrich von Kleist.

Prior to her involvement with the student Left and the women's movement, however, Sander had had no difficulty working in television. In the mid sixties she had been in permanent employment as a director in Finland, where she had been able to choose her own material. She stresses that 'I always had work and recognition when I was still a bourgeois artist; things went downhill when I became a socialist; but I have only got into a fix since I have actively concerned myself with the interests of women.'[69] Sander has not been alone in appropriating the term *Berufsverbot* to describe employment discrimination against women based on factors other than political affiliation. Other feminist activists have used it to

> point to the secretary who was fired for having sunburn and thus didn't appear attractive enough for office representation; or to the publisher's representative fired because of the birth of her child (her director anticipated that motherhood would be incommensurate with her professional obligations).[70]

From the outset the women's movement had also elicited a negative reaction from the male 'establishment' for its challenging of patriarchal authority. This reaction had been compounded by the large percentage of women terrorists who were being sought by the police during the seventies.[71] Writing for *Der Spiegel* in 1977, for instance, Günther Nollau had expressed the opinion that female terrorists were an 'excess in the liberation of women', while the *Bayern Kurier* reported that the movement was regarded 'as an essential reason for the recent change of sex roles on the terror front'.[72] Monica Jacobs has argued that once this connection had been made, women who were perceived to be 'liberated', and could therefore be described as feminist, entered the realm of the politically suspect.[73]

That Sander's assertion was not without foundation is particularly evident in connection with the Paragraph 218 campaign. Although a number of films were made within the women's movement about the abortion issue, according to the campaign's initiator Alice Schwarzer, media institutions prevented their female employees from addressing the campaign. The reason given was apparently the one cited above by Sander and Perincioli: that women could not be 'objective' about such an issue.[74]

Schwarzer's assertion, like Sander's, also appears extreme at first. However, adopting a pro-abortion stance, which a significant number of women did, *could* be interpreted as contravening the programming guidelines laid down in the constitutions of the television corporations. Those of ZDF, for instance, state:

> The channel is watched primarily within the family environment and by people of different ages and sex, possessing various levels of education and at different stages of maturity. Programme planners therefore have a particular responsibility towards the family.... Marriage and the family may not be questioned, belittled or derided as institutions. Within this framework analytical and critical examinations of marital and family problems are permitted if ... the destruction of marriage and the family are not shown to be the norm.[75]

Since the legalization of abortion gave women the right to choose not to participate in the family unit, it potentially undermined the family as the 'norm'. As this 'norm' had contributed significantly to women's oppression, the threat posed to it by a pro-abortion argument could also be viewed as a fundamental challenging of patriarchal authority. Actions taken by the police against pro-abortion campaigners certainly appeared indicative of a perceived threat. In Frankfurt the police attempted to criminalize the city's women's centre for its participation in the campaign,[76] while Helke Sander had film of an anti-Paragraph 218 demonstration confiscated by the Berlin police.[77] Renate Möhrmann has asserted that the Berlin incident resulted in Sander receiving no further funding for the project on which she was then engaged.[78]

Schwarzer's own attempt to publicize the Paragraph 218 campaign on television also met with censorship. A parliamentary debate on the abortion issue had been planned for spring 1974. Since the Church, most of the political parties and a majority of doctors had continued to maintain an anti-abortion position, the chances of achieving the abolition of Paragraph 218 looked slender. With limited but invaluable support from the medical profession, a final bid for reform was made which involved publicizing an actual abortion. As a journalist for the *Panorama* magazine programme Schwarzer did a report about this 'final attempt'. However, in a dramatic last-minute consultation the directors of ARD banned it. As Schwarzer maintains: 'The media men had realized the explosive nature of the issue.'[79] In protest the *Panorama* team withdrew the whole programme, and for forty-five minutes during prime-time viewing, pictures of an empty studio were broadcast in its place.

By the mid seventies, however, the work of the women's movement had succeeded in winning a degree of acceptance for the principle of equal rights for women, even if the rights themselves had not been fully achieved. Consequently, as the decade progressed many women film-makers started to find it easier to obtain funding for their projects and employment with television companies. WDR, for instance, co-produced Edith Schmidt's film about the Frankfurt women's centre mentioned earlier, *It Has Changed Me Greatly* (1976). She also made two further 'women's issues' documentaries for ZDF, *Wir Frauen sehen uns an / Let's Look at Ourselves* (1977), highlighting experiences from the women's movement and *Wir Frauen sind unbezahlbar / We Women are Priceless* (1978), about the wages for housework issue.

A small workshop department at ZDF played a particularly important role in enabling women filmmakers to develop their careers. Called *Das kleine Fernsehspiel* (The Little Television Play), the department was charged with developing new forms of television, promoting aesthetic experiment and encouraging personal expression. To achieve these ends the department was prepared not only to extend a high degree of creative freedom but also to 'sponsor total amateurs'.[80] They were responsible, for instance, for commissioning Jutta Brückner's first film, *Tue recht und scheue niemand / Do Right and Fear Nobody* (1975), about her mother. Brückner described her experiences of working for the department as follows:

It's an excellent department, they're very, very good people to work with. They really let you do things the way that you want to.... They're useful to talk to – they'll say what they think, but if you say, 'No, I want to do it this way', they'll leave you in peace. And they've got a wonderful arrangement known as 'Kamerafilm'; you get a very small sum of money, but it's put entirely at your disposal. The only thing you ever have to do is deliver a film on the date agreed.[81]

Although they did not adopt a conscious policy of positive discrimination, the department did commission a far higher proportion of women directors than was normal.[82] In fact, they commissioned or co-financed many of the films discussed in this chapter, including Jutta Brückner's subsequent films, *A Thoroughly Demoralized Girl* (1977) and *Years of Hunger* (1980), Helke Sander's *Redupers* (1977) and *The Subjective Factor* (1980), Elfi Mikesch's *I Often Think of Hawaii* (1978), Perincioli's *The Power of Men* (1978), Reidemeister's *Who Says 'Destiny'* (1978–79), Petra Haffter's *Madness, Life is Total Madness* (1979) and Luisa Francia's *Witches* (1980).

Its late-night programming slot and relatively small air-time allocation meant, however, that the television audience for such work was correspondingly small. Yet the department's investment in women directors undoubtedly helped promote awareness and acceptance of women's filmmaking. During the late seventies the films made by women consistently achieved well above average viewing figures when they were broadcast. Many of these films, once made, were subsequently screened at foreign film festivals and thus reached an international audience as well.

The process also worked in reverse, since the department also purchased completed productions from time to time. This enabled films such as Valie Export's *Unsichtbare Gegner / Invisible Adversaries* (1976), Reidemeister's earlier film *Der gekaufte Traum / The Purchased Dream* (1977) and Ulrike Ottinger's film (discussed further in chapter five) *Bildnis einer Trinkerin / Ticket of No Return* (1979) to reach a larger domestic audience than was possible through a theatrical release alone. For instance, Export's *Invisible Adversaries* enjoyed only a six-week cinema run in Berlin, after which it was impossible to see the film until it was broadcast by ZDF in January 1978.

By the late seventies 'women's issues' had become 'fashionable' with media institutions, resulting in a new form of censorship for women directors. They were now expected to deal exclusively with such issues. Projects by women that attempted to address subjects not popularly considered 'women's issues' continued to meet with funding difficulties. Perincioli's experiences were not untypical:

> Recently, for my Three Mile Island film project, I wrote to fourteen German and foreign TV studios, studios which knew me or had purchased my earlier films. Two responded affirmatively, but their offers then evaporated.... We've struggled so long to be able to make films about women's issues. Now we have done that for a while, and we women are becoming interested in issues such as nuclear power and the military. Helke Sander and I have found, however, that TV producers will not accept our script suggestions on these 'male' themes. It will take a long time to overcome that prejudice.[83]

The responses of critics to two first features made by women directors, one from 1968 and one from 1984, succinctly highlight the shift in attitudes towards women's filmmaking achieved by the women's movement. In 1968 Ula Stöckl made *Neun Leben hat die Katze / The Cat has Nine Lives* about the lives of four women friends. Male critics reacted negatively to the film 'mainly because there were "too many women" in it'.[84] Sixteen years later, Maria Knilli made *Lieber Karl / Dear Carl* (1984) about a boy who becomes ill through trying to conform to his parents' expectations. Although the film was highly praised, Knilli was asked why she had made a film about 'Carl' rather than 'Carla'.[85]

The influence of the women's movement did also result in the emergence of the 'women's film'. However, the work of women directors can also be characterized – like the rest of the New German Cinema – by thematic and formal diversity. Gudrun Lukasz-Aden and Christel Strobel's reference book *Der Frauenfilm / The Women's Film* reveals an enormous breadth of issues addressed in films by women,[86] from personal relationships and the family, through issues of work, politics, and the environment. Formally this work ranges from documentary films, through experimental narratives and arthouse realism, to commercial features.

What the women's movement did was to precipitate a number of filmmaking initiatives and areas of activity – of which the new 'women's film' is only one. These areas of activity were not entirely discrete, as they all focused on women and were all broadly supportive of the aims of the movement. Nevertheless, they constitute significant trends rather than a single genre. Furthermore, although some initiatives did come from within the movement, others emerged as a result of a more general awareness of women's oppression and of the supportive environment fostered by the work of the movement.

FOUR

Institutional Initiatives

The so-called 'female wonder' of German film ... did not fall from
heaven, but was the product of long and arduous work by committed
women.[1]

Although the women's movement substantially improved the general
position of women in West Germany, women working in film and television found it necessary to undertake their own initiatives in order to
address their specific situation. These initiatives were numerous and
varied. Not only did they campaign for equal access to the means of
production, they also tried to promote awareness and discussion of
women's work, as well as ensure opportunities existed to see films
made by women. Some endeavours met with more success than others,
but an alternative institutional framework gradually emerged which
played an enormous role in the development of West Germany's
feminist film culture.

One of the first initiatives was the Seminar on Women's Films held
in Berlin in November 1973. Organized by Helke Sander and Claudia
von Alemann, the seminar screened forty-five films and videos by
women from seven different countries. Although there had already
been women's film festivals in other countries, this was the first such
event to take place in the Federal Republic and, in keeping with its
groundbreaking role, it adopted an approach different to that of
previous overseas festivals, which had simply screened available films
made by women in an attempt to celebrate women's frequently over-

looked contribution to the cinema. By contrast, Sander and Alemann structured the Berlin seminar around an explicit educational goal, selecting only films which 'convey[ed] facts about and analyses of the discrimination against and oppression of women in various areas of society'.[2] The films were then programmed to focus attention on four particular areas: women in the workers' struggle; representation of women in the media; women and Paragraph 218, sexuality and role behaviour; and the women's movement in Europe and the US. Discussions were held after screenings in order to help viewers both to analyse the issues raised by the films and also to relate them to their own lives.

Among the films shown by German women were several of the campaigning films made in support of the women's movement: Helke Sander's and Sarah Schumann's *Macht die Pille frei?/Does the Pill Liberate?* (1972), which looks at the conditions under which women have sexual relations with men and the role of the pill as a method of contraception; Claudia von Alemann's *Es kommt drauf an, sie zu verändern/The Point is to Change It* (1972–73) which looks at women's role and exploitation in the workplace; and Gardi Deppe and Ingrid Oppermann's *Kinder für dieses System – Paragraph 218/Children for this System – Paragraph 218* (1973), which examines the social implications of the anti-abortion law. Other German films included were Marianne Lüdcke's and Ingo Kratisch's *Akkord/Piecework* (1971), about a group of women factory workers who fight against the lowering of their piecework rate; Ingrid and Detlef Langer's *Lebenshilfe auf Glanzpapier/ Counselling on Glossy Paper* (1972), which offers a critical analysis of the images of women in women's magazines; and Elsa Rassbach's *His-story* (1972), which examines socialist theory with regard to women's emancipation.

In addition to its educational role, the seminar also performed two other important functions. Firstly, it provided a rare chance to see the work of contemporary women filmmakers; and secondly, it offered the first opportunity in Germany for women filmmakers to meet each other and discuss their work. Up until then, most women had worked in relative isolation and were themselves unaware of the extent of women's filmmaking activities. As Sander stressed: 'for most of us it was surprising that there were already enough of us to be able to fill a whole festival with our films.'[3]

The level of interest in the work was also sufficient for further seminars to be arranged elsewhere in Germany. In December 1973 Angela Haardt of the International Forum of Avant-Garde Film organized a similar event in Munich. While Haardt programmed far fewer films, she shared the educational goals of the Berlin organizers. Discussions were arranged to use the films – among them Sander's and Schumann's *Does the Pill Liberate?* (1972) and Alemann's *The Point is to Change It* (1972–73) – to explore women's position in society. Other women's film seminars followed in Erlangen, Frankfurt and Tutzing.

In the early seventies these seminars provided the only forum for a discussion of such films. On the whole, and in direct contrast to the media attention that the first *Kuratorium*-funded films received,[4] the work of feminist filmmakers met with very little interest from the press in the Federal Republic. Although films like Sander's *Eine Prämie für Irene/A Bonus for Irene* (1971), Cristina Perincioli's *Für Frauen – 1 Kapitel/For Women – Chapter 1* (1971–72) and Valeska Schöttle's *Wer braucht wen?/ Who Needs Whom?* (1972) received an odd mention, none of the larger papers reviewed them in any detail. The few films that did receive coverage were usually reviewed by male critics who, given the prevailing attitudes towards the women's movement, tended to respond negatively or, at best, ambivalently.

Despite the pioneering aspect of the Berlin film seminar, it also received very little attention from the press: the organizers issued a number of invitations, but none of the invited film critics attended. Indeed, many observers regarded it as more of an 'emancipation meeting' than as anything to do with film. Author Karin Struck, for instance, was scathingly critical of all the 'Noras, who want to leave their dolls' houses', of their 'abortion films' and of what she considered to be a rebellion against motherhood.[5]

In order both to provide a permanent discussion forum for women's film work and to promote its informed analysis, Helke Sander set up a film journal in 1974. Named *Frauen und Film* (Women and Film), the journal was conceived of as a feminist project operating within the film sector. Sander and her co-editors drew up an ambitious programme of work, the main aims of which were to examine the ways in which patriarchal ideology informed existing film culture and to explore the emerging feminist culture. The first task was to involve the critical analysis of films, an examination of film policy and the economics of the industry, together with a discussion of dominant film aesthetics. The second would deal with the work of the women's movement and how it had informed filmmaking both directly and indirectly, the question of feminist aesthetics, the contribution of women to cinema in its early years, the work and situation of contemporary women film-makers, as well as that of women working in technical and other roles in the film sector.

Articles that appeared in early issues included an analysis of the sexist attitudes that prevailed in media establishments, a discussion of porno-film culture, and reviews of von Alemann's *The Point is to Change It* (1972–73), Ingemo Engström's *Kampf um ein Kind / Fight for a Child* (1974–75), Fassbinder's *Fontane Effi Briest / Effi Briest* (1974) and Kluge's *Gelegenheitsarbeit einer Sklavin / Occasional Work of a Female Slave* (1973). Interviews with various filmmakers – among them Claudia von Alemann, Valie Export, Margarethe von Trotta, Erika Runge and Ula Stöckl – were also published, and special issues were compiled devoted to specific areas of study, such as sexuality in film, or to particular areas of film work, such as editing.

The journal's commitment to the women's movement was evident not only in its content but also in its presentation: it adopted the practice of not using capital letters. As some feminist theorists had identified the language of patriarchal society as a male discourse – as literally 'man-made' – many women explored ways of appropriating language for themselves. Although other theorists have since argued that it is the context in which language is used and which gives it its meaning that is 'man-made' rather than language itself, in the English language this gave rise to the coining of new terms such as 'herstory' as an alternative to the word 'history'. In German, capital letters are used not only at the beginning of sentences, but for all nouns as well. Although there is nothing inherently male about this characteristic of the German language, the non-use of capital letters – so-called *Kleinschreibung* (writing with small letters) – nevertheless has a significant impact on the appearance of written German, rendering it distinctly 'different'. This practice developed within the German women's movement and initially all texts in *Frauen und Film* (FUF) were printed in this manner.

Although the FUF editors succeeded in maintaining continuous publication, numerous difficulties continually threatened the journal's existence during its early years. The first issue was published by a women's group, Brot und Rosen (Bread and Roses), after which publication was transferred to a newly founded women's publisher based in Berlin, *Verlag Frauen*. Owing to a lack of financial resources, all work on the journal was undertaken on a voluntary basis and usually in the editors' own homes. For the first few issues the editors carried out not only the editorial work but also much of the design and production as well as some of the actual writing and transcribing. In reply to the inevitable criticisms of their production standards, they stressed 'we are not many, nor are we brilliant, nor even well educated'.[6] They also pointed out that they had to endure working conditions 'which would give our male colleagues nervous breakdowns. Children playing under a journalist's feet as she's translating a theoretical article on film, a baby on the back of a graphic designer as she puts together the cover design.'[7]

After a year, however, the editors decided it was impossible to continue under such intolerable conditions. Helke Sander approached the Rotbuch publishing house in Berlin, who agreed to take over technical and financial responsibility for printing, advertising and distribution. Sander and her co-editors chose Rotbuch because it was run by a collective that enjoyed virtual gender parity and because the publishing house acknowledged the value of FUF's work.

Nevertheless, the decision to use the publishing house elicited considerable criticism: for more radical feminists it represented an unacceptable level of collaboration with the male establishment. In defence of their actions, the FUF editors not only stressed the fact that Rotbuch exercised no editorial control over the journal, but also argued that such an extreme separatist mentality did little to secure women's emancipation. They emphasized the importance of working with men in order to achieve acceptance of feminist politics in the public sphere. Their arguments were, however, of little avail. By the beginning of 1977 the editors observed with dismay that 'FUF is no longer regarded as a women's project by segments of the women's movement, it's not even mentioned in the women's year book, ... it is tolerated in *Courage* ... as the "little sisters" who are still within the "family circle", and described as a magazine in which men have a say.'[8]

In its early days, the journal also failed to attract many contributions from women journalists and other professional women. Lack of financial resources undoubtedly played a role, but it also resulted from 'the discrimination which women face if they engage intensively and consistently with women's issues'.[9] In order to establish themselves, women journalists and film critics were obliged to write for more mainstream publications. According to the editors, professional women offered to write for FUF only when they were particularly angered by the images of women served up by male directors and needed an editor sympathetic to a feminist analysis.

Because of these difficulties, FUF owes its continued existence to the commitment of a very small number of women who gradually became co-workers and regular contributors. However, its highly limited resources inevitably restricted the scope of the journal and meant that much women's filmmaking activity went unreported. This led Helma Sanders-Brahms in 1977 to accuse FUF of being 'a journal which exists primarily to carry out public relations for friends and acquaintances'.[10] Sanders-Brahms had become a relatively well known filmmaker in Germany by then, yet FUF had given no coverage to her or her films.

In retrospect, although the failure to address the work of Sanders-Brahms (an omission FUF subsequently rectified) would appear to be a serious oversight, the FUF editors did succeed in initiating an unprecedented level of discussion about women's filmmaking; in the process, they began to reveal the previously unacknowledged extent of women's involvement in film at all levels. This discussion was not restricted to women working only in film, but also included women in other areas of audio-visual production such as television and video. During the seventies FUF published interviews with ten or more German women filmmakers, as well as with women editors, film historians, producers and cinema programmers. Innumerable films were reviewed and several filmmakers also began writing about their own work. Further special issues were produced on contemporary filmmakers, on Leni Riefenstahl, film policy, film theory, collective work, documentary film and on women viewers. The journal also performed an important newsletter and resource function. Details of women's film groups, reports on festivals and conferences, and news of lobbying initiatives were included, as well as directors' filmographies, film lists and contact addresses.

By not focusing exclusively on directors, but valuing all areas of film work, FUF also played an influential role in promoting the collaborative approach that came to characterize women's filmmaking in the

Federal Republic. Although its coverage may not have been exhaustive, the journal managed to draw together the beginnings of West Germany's feminist film culture and for a number of years came to act as its mouthpiece. As if in recognition of the importance of this work, the Federal Ministry of the Interior (BMI) awarded FUF partial funding in 1979.

During the late seventies, however, the journal and its role began to change. Helke Sander withdrew from the editorial board to concentrate on her film projects, leaving critics (like Claudia Lenssen and Gertrud Koch) and historians (such as Heide Schlüpmann and Uta Berg-Ganschow) to play an increasing part in determining FUF's direction. Although it retained a feminist identity, the journal's ties with the women's movement began to loosen and a move towards professionalism set in: from the end of 1980, for instance, the editors ceased the practice of *Kleinschreibung* (writing with small letters). During the early eighties the editorial work was also decentralized, with issues being compiled from bases in Berlin, Frankfurt, Cologne and Paris.

In 1982 the Berlin editors decided to withdraw from the project, arguing that 'with its feminist goals and practices, [FUF] had outlived its function'.[11] Although circulation figures had indeed declined, the Frankfurt group – which included Koch and Schlüpmann – undertook to continue the journal. These changes were announced in January 1983, in issue number 34, which looked back over the journal's work and outlined the form in which it would continue. Publication was to be reduced from four times a year to twice yearly, with each issue twice as long as before. Although it would retain some of its earlier features, such as reviews of film festivals, the new FUF would operate primarily as a forum for the discussion of film theory and film history.

By specializing, the journal attracted a different readership and consequently relinquished its central role within Germany's feminist film culture. In 1988 filmmaker Monika Treut asserted:

> It still is a good magazine. But for me it has changed – over the last two or three years it's become too specialized.... It used to be much more helpful because ... it was talking about festivals, talking about films, about filmmakers, about this and that, and now it is mostly only for students. It's more academic and that's a pity.[12]

As initiatives such as the film seminars and *Frauen und Film* started to give women the opportunity to discuss their work, they also began talking about the conditions under which they worked, repeatedly drawing attention to the lack of female representation at an institutional level and to how this could adversely affect women filmmakers. A petition drawn up during the 1975 Berlin Film Festival stressed:

> Men sit on the selection committees of festivals! – Men distribute the prizes at festivals! – Men write the film reviews! – Men are in charge of the means of production! – Men sit on the project commissions and the committees which award funding! – Men possess the information, the connections, the contacts.[13]

A similar situation prevailed within the television companies. At ZDF in the mid seventies, for example, all the company's directors and department heads were male, as were all the members of its administrative council. By the late seventies women had begun to secure a few committee seats, especially at the BMI. However, their number was so small, and so many committees were still exclusively composed of men, that filmmaker Christel Buschmann was moved to observe that 'one gets the impression "women" is a foreign word in film policy'.[14]

Many women felt that such a situation allowed sexist attitudes to go unchallenged, with the consequence of severely diminishing their career opportunities and infringing their right to the freedom of artistic expression. They therefore started to call for gender parity on all film funding and award selection committees: only if fifty per cent of all committee seats were occupied by women could women filmmakers be guaranteed equal access to production facilities. Both Helke Sander and Ulrike Ottinger have stressed that the presence of women at an institutional level played a crucial role in helping them realize their first feature film projects. Ottinger's *Madame X – eine absolute Herrscherin/ Madame X – An Absolute Ruler* (1977) was, for instance, rejected by the *Kuratorium*. She then submitted the script to ZDF and, after hearing nothing for a year, received funding only when a woman editor happened to see the script.[15]

However, it was also considered vital to achieve equal access to production facilities for another reason:

[its importance] lies in the fact that people spend 40 per cent of their leisure time, if not more, in front of the television.... It lies in the fact that to a large degree women learn their social roles via visual images. They learn to shape themselves mentally and physically according to these images.[16]

Unless women filmmakers had equal access to production facilities, women viewers would continue to internalize male-determined role models. Gender parity on all film and television committees could obviously not prevent films from being made which reinforced patriarchal images of women. But Helke Sander and others felt it could ensure the realization of a much higher proportion of women's projects offering not only alternative role models but also a more realistic representation of women's lives. They also believed that women's presence on committees would make it more difficult for projects which exhibited sexist attitudes to an extreme degree to receive funding. A male FFA project commission member confirmed that, 'during discussions about screenplays over the past few years men have never said, here are sexist elements. That is one aspect that plays absolutely no role whatsoever'.[17] As a result, films, such as Just Jaeckin's adaptation of Pauline Reage's sado-masochistic novel *L'Histoire d'O*, received funding with no questioning of their exploitation and degradation of women.

Jaeckin's film, *Die Geschichte der O/ The Story of O* (1975) is about a woman who agrees to undergo a series of sexual encounters and physical tortures as proof of her love for two men. Not only is the female protagonist 'forced' to participate in sado-masochistic practices and taken sexually against her will, but she is represented as coming to realize that she enjoys these activities. The film was released in Germany in 1976, when the women's movement had just started campaigning against violence against women. Although it has since been argued that the film actually poses the possibility of sexual pleasure for women,[18] at the time of its release the film precipitated massive and vehement protests by women's groups throughout the country.

The demand for gender parity on film selection committees met with considerable resistance. At the beginning of 1978 *Frauen und Film* conducted a series of interviews with a number of men who sat on the selection committees of the FFA, the BMI and the *Kuratorium* and/or were involved in the film sector in other institutional capacities.[19] Despite some exceptions, there was a general lack of awareness among the interviewees that the predominance of men at an institutional level could adversely affect women's prospects of enjoying equal opportunities. Yet by that time the FFA project commission, which had been in existence for four years, had funded only two films by women: Helma Sanders-Brahms's *Heinrich* (1976–77) and Heidi Genée's *Grete Minde* (1977). Furthermore, neither of the films dealt with contemporary feminist issues, both being based on nineteenth-century literary sources.

The interviewees did acknowledge that, because of their socialization and family responsibilities, women could experience greater difficulties in taking up or pursuing a career. The FFA project committee members also realized that the economic rationale underlying their selection criteria made it highly unlikely that projects expressing a feminist viewpoint would be awarded funding. They also understood that both these factors could result in fewer submissions being made by women. Yet there was also an implicit assumption that the funding agencies received very few applications from women simply because very few women wanted to develop film projects.

Consequently, the interviewees demonstrated a distinct resistance to the idea that gender parity on selection committees might improve the situation of women filmmakers. Klaus Eder, a film journalist and president of the film journalists' union, for instance, asserted: 'For me it's not a question of men and women, but of the viewpoints and qualities that are represented there.'[20] In a similar vein, Robert Backheuer of the FFA argued that even if his committee was composed exclusively of men, the selection process was nevertheless objective: 'A two-thirds majority is required to fund a project. Thus extreme, subjective opinions are neutralized and a sort of middle-ground objectivity results. Quantity turns into quality.'[21] As if to prove his point, Backheuer stressed that it was not only women's projects that were rejected.

These arguments are, however, also indicative of a reluctance to concede that they as individuals were supporting an institutional framework which discriminated against women. It is therefore hardly surprising that the interviewees also gave various reasons why they, as individuals, were not in a position to promote gender parity on selection committees. According to some, there were not enough women who were appropriately qualified. On the one hand, this meant the actual number of women working professionally in the film sector. Klaus Eder, for instance, excused the all-male executive of his own union with the argument that 'in this country there really are only very few women film journalists'.[22]

In contrast, however, Backheuer stressed that 'the proportion of women working in the area of film is already fairly large.'[23] For others therefore, simply working in the sector was not considered automatically to render someone suitable to sit on a selection committee. The essential prerequisite was rather to be 'well informed'. According to freelance journalist and FFA committee member Wilhelm Roth, this frequently meant having legal expertise rather than film knowledge. Sitting on the FFA committee, for instance, could require the ability to interpret the 'unclearly formulated law'[24] which governed their work. The law has, of course, traditionally been a male-dominated profession and such a requirement would tend to discriminate against women. Yet Roth also conceded the importance of having members who do not have a legal background on the committees – and even admitted to being one himself – to provide another perspective in the selection process.

Several committee members also drew attention to the fact that they were nominated to their seats as delegates from trade unions or as representatives of government departments. According to this argument, women would have first to achieve a greater presence within these organizations before they could secure gender parity on the selection committees. As a result Dr Günther Struve, film representative for the Berlin Senate, suggested that 'women might get on better if they were better acquainted with the instruments of the funding system.'[25]

In the face of such attitudes, and of the obvious reluctance to introduce change into the institutional apparatus, women working in all areas of the media started to organize themselves into support and lobbying groups. In Berlin, for instance, a group of women film workers began meeting once a month in a cinema to discuss their work and offer each other support. A ZDF women's group was also set up to discuss any problems experienced by women workers. They collaborated with other organizations, such as trade unions, to try and improve women's working conditions, achieving among other things the creation of more part-time jobs to assist working mothers. By 1978 there were a significant number of such groups and they organized their first 'media women' conference in Frankfurt. Attended by 130 delegates, the conference took as its agenda the questions of 'equality for women workers in the broadcasting companies' and 'realistic representation of women's concerns and living conditions in television programmes'.[26]

Despite such initiatives, men continued to occupy the majority of seats on film funding and award committees. Discontent with the status quo reached a peak during the 1979 Hamburg Film Festival when women filmmakers felt their interests were marginalized in the declaration of German filmmakers drawn up at the festival. In October 1979, immediately following the festival, Hildegard Westbeld, Christiane Kaltenbach and Petra Haffter arranged a meeting with a number of women filmmakers to formulate a clear set of demands and to initiate a campaign to lobby for their fulfilment. The result was the setting up of the Verband der Filmarbeiterinnen (Association of Women Filmworkers) during the last few weeks of the decade, and the issuing of the Manifesto of the Women Filmworkers:

The Association of Women Filmworkers takes the liberty of expanding the *Hamburg Declaration of the German Filmmakers* to address the demands of women filmworkers. We demand:

1. 50 per cent of all funds for films, production facilities and research projects;
2. 50 per cent of all jobs and training places;
3. 50 per cent of all committee seats;
4. Support for distribution, sale and exhibition of films by women.

Over eighty women filmworkers from the Federal Republic and West Berlin have signed.

Who we are – the women filmworkers – and why we have organized ourselves has been specified in the constitution of the *Association of Women Filmworkers*.

From the constitution of the Association:

1.1 Women filmworkers are all women who are or will be working in the film and audio-visual media sectors.

2.2   The goal of the Association is,
– to support, promote and distribute all films by women, which are committed to feminist, emancipatory and non-sexist forms of representation and goals;
– to keep records of, catalogue and, if possible, archive both old and new films by women;
– to contribute to and help out with the publication of reports, journals, books, leaflets and information sheets about women filmmakers and women in film;
– to support women filmmakers in the pursuit of their work by providing information and advice and by maintaining a constant exchange of information;
– to cooperate with both national and foreign institutions and groups with related objectives ...

The Association is committed to gender parity in all areas of film and the audio-visual media. It considers the demands of the women filmworkers of 3 October 1979 in connection with the *Hamburg Declaration of the German Filmmakers* as a definitive goal and is campaigning for their immediate realisation. The declaration of the women filmmakers on 3 October 1979 has been included in the constitution as the basic concept and forms the fundamental basis thereof.[27]

The decision to represent 'all women, who are or will be working in the film and audio-visual media sectors' followed the lead given by *Frauen und Film* (FUF). Like FUF, the Association acknowledged women's employment in all areas of film work and recognized their collective need for representation. Membership was therefore open not only to directors, but to producers, camerawomen, editors, make-up artists and scriptwriters, as well as film students. It was felt that unity and solidarity between women were also more likely to help the Association achieve its goals.

The Association commenced its work by holding regular meetings and setting up project groups, calling its first national meeting during the 1980 Berlin Film Festival. Although the organization rapidly achieved a highly visible public profile, like FUF it encountered several teething problems. To start with, their manifesto caused a storm of protest as soon as it was published. Its critics argued that the demand for gender parity was unreasonable in view of the relatively small number of women working in the film sector. Even after the Association had been in existence for over two years, co-founder Petra Haffter asserted that their most important task was simply 'to have our demands taken seriously'.[28]

Internal difficulties also arose due to the Association's very diverse membership. Initially viewed as a source of strength, Haffter subsequently admitted it also had its downside:

> It creates problems, for instance, with regard to deciding what position to adopt in questions of film policy. A member who is a producer will have a different position to an editor who belongs to a union. The difference arises from their different economic conditions. The fact that both are women should not hide the fact that differences exist.[29]

Haffter and her co-founders were also concerned that their campaigning work might simply precipitate a form of positive discrimination, with women being offered work because their gender rather than their professional expertise rendered them suitable. This was likely to restrict women to working on women's projects, however, instead of resulting in a real improvement in their professional opportunities. Haffter warned women against accepting work offered to them on this basis and, once again echoing FUF's approach, stressed:

> We must examine ... carefully, where we need to adopt a special position as women in order to further our 50 per cent demands and where, depending on the particular interests, we can ensure more effective policies by working together with our male colleagues in the respective trade associations.[30]

By adhering to this policy – for instance, the Association quickly joined the Federal Association of German Film, an umbrella organization representing the interests of a number of independent associations in the New German Cinema – the Association gradually became a recognized trade organization within the film sector. Although this trade bias has rendered it of less interest to some independent filmmakers, by October 1988 it had a membership of 117. It publishes a regular newsletter which has, to some extent, taken over the former newsletter function of *Frauen und Film*,[31] and which includes reports of the Association's work, dates of film festivals, information on meetings and conferences, news of appointments, the dates of submission deadlines for funding applications, articles and letters.

Alongside its campaigning activities, the Association also compiled a women's film handbook. Published in 1984, this reference work lists the biographical details and filmographies of nearly four hundred women filmmakers who have worked in West Germany since 1945. The book not only represents an enormous contribution to the history of women's film production in the Federal Republic, but is also an invaluable resource for cinema programmers. It is packaged in a loose-leaf binder so that revisions to the work could easily be made; but a lack of resources has meant that no revisions have been forthcoming, and the work has rapidly become out of date.

During the late eighties the Association concentrated on trying to secure one of its initial aims: 50 per cent of all committee seats. It has been particularly concerned with the FFA, a major source of funding for feature film production. When the FFG, the film promotion law administered by the FFA, was due for revision in 1986, the organization lobbied for gender parity to be made a mandatory requirement for all FFA committees. Since lobbying failed to produce results, the Association's members decided to instigate legal proceedings against the West German government in order to try and achieve their aim. Their case rested on the argument that the FFG violated the human rights guaranteed to all citizens in the country's constitution. Through its failure to legislate for gender parity on FFA committees, the complainants argued that the FFG denied women filmmakers 'their right to be treated equally, their right to equal access to the means of communication, their right to freedom of artistic expression, as well their right to practice their profession unhindered'.[32] After nearly twelve months of preparation, the case was taken to court in January 1988. Like all earlier efforts, however, it was unsuccessful.

This failure resulted largely from a misjudgement. In preparing the case, the Association had done what Petra Haffter had warned might not always be appropriate: 'adopt[ed] a special position as women in order to further our 50 per cent demands'. This was an area where collaboration with other organizations, particularly West Germany's Social Democratic Party, the SPD, might have been more productive. For a number of years the SPD had been promising to introduce 'equalities' into their party structure. In August 1988 they finally voted to give women at least 30 per cent of party jobs and undertook to increase this quota to 40 per cent by 1994. There was talk of a woman chancellor; Anke Fuchs, party manager, asserted, 'The public are ready for it.'[33] Although the SPD only introduced their quota after the Association members had brought their legal action, filmmaker Monika Treut maintains that the prevailing atmosphere could and should have been capitalized upon.[34] Failure to do so meant that, if anything, the Association's status as a trade organization was undermined and ghettoized as a women's project.

In view of the enormous amount of work required to prepare the court case, its failure was particularly demoralizing. Shortly after the ruling, the possibility of dissolving the Association was discussed, but a sufficient number of women remained committed to its work to continue. They took the decision to continue the legal battle for gender parity on committees by appealing to the European Law Courts.

In addition to the ongoing campaign for equal access to the means of production, there were also a number of more separatist-orientated initiatives aimed at ensuring opportunities existed to see the new feminist films. Until well into the seventies both the distribution and exhibition possibilities for most such films had been practically nonexistent:

> [they] are rejected ... because there is no money to be made out of them, because they are not easily consumable, because they depict the society in which we live as oppressive and criticize it.[35]

To start with, a number of women's cinemas and film groups were set up. One of the first was *Initiative Frauen im Kino* (Women's Initiatives in Cinema) in Berlin, set up by Hildegard Westbeld in September 1977. Westbeld rented a small cinema one night a week and screened films – these included documentaries and experimental work, as well as features – made by women to a women-only audience. She viewed the initiative as an 'offensive response' to the way in which 'women are largely excluded from the cinema, especially through the orientation of the cinema programme towards the entertainment and informational needs of men'.[36] Similar initiatives followed in Cologne, Munich, Saarbrücken and Hanover.

These exhibition projects were also concerned with creating a forum in which viewers (as opposed to critics) could discuss the work of women filmmakers. Although this was motivated partly out of a desire simply to exchange views with other women, it was also intended to promote a greater understanding of what women were trying to achieve in their films. Because many women filmmakers were attempting to challenge dominant representations of women and to put forward their own perception of reality, their work was often formally challenging and difficult to watch. In her documentary *Es kommt drauf an, sie zu verändern / The Point is to Change It* (1972–73), for instance, Claudia von Alemann undertakes an in-depth analysis of women's exploitation in the workplace. She attempts to demonstrate how women's work is not only structured differently to men's, but valued, paid, and documented differently, and how these differences make women a particularly profitable source of labour. Von Alemann makes excessive use of factual information and statistics via a voice-over commentary and frequent written inserts to help articulate her arguments. But when a seminar leader screened the film to her students she found:

> Many young people thought the film boring because so much 'theoretical stuff' was spoken. Consequently, many left the room during the screening. 'Theoretical' was used to mean that a lot was spoken, that there was little action in the film.[37]

As the cinemas and film groups were for women-only audiences, they elicited accusations of sexism and ghettoization from some feminist and leftist quarters. Westbeld responded by arguing that their separatist approach had in fact improved the situation of women filmmakers, by making cinema programmers, distributors and the public more aware of and interested in films made by women. Furthermore, these exhibition initiatives initially generated enormous interest among their intended audience. In its first few months the Berlin *Initiative*, for instance, attracted average audiences of eighty women per screening.[38]

However, some groups reported that after a while attendance figures began to fall off. Although various factors were involved, a crucial one was the limited choice of women's films available for hire. All too often, the films the groups wanted to screen were simply not in distribution. Some, like Ula Stöckl's film, *Neun Leben hat die Katze / The Cat has Nine Lives* (1968), simply failed to find a distributor. Stöckl had managed to

May Spils (centre) on the set of *Zur Sache Schätzchen / Go To It, Baby* (1967)

Helke Sander as Edda Chiemnyjewski in her *Die Allseitig reduzierte Persönlichkeit / The All-round Reduced Personality* (1977)

Addi (centre, played by Elisabeth Walinski) finds a new life among her women friends in Cristina Perincioli's *Die Macht der Männer ist die Geduld der Frauen/ The Power of Men is the Patience of Women* (1978)

Rebecca Pauly as Elisabeth Falusy in Claudia von Alemann's *Reise nach Lyon/ Blind Spot* (1980)

Tabea Blumenschein (bottom) as 'She' with Lutze, the bag-lady, in Ulrike Ottinger's *Bildnis einer Trinkerin – Aller jamais retour / Ticket of No Return* (1979)

Margarethe von Trotta's *Die bleierne Zeit / The German Sisters* (1981) – Juliane (Jutta Lampe, third from the left) visits sister Marianne (Barbara Sukowa, second from the right) in prison

Ulrike Ottinger

Elfi Mikesch

November (Gabriele Osburg) in a Nazi brothel in Alexandra von Grote's
Novembermond / November Moon (1985)

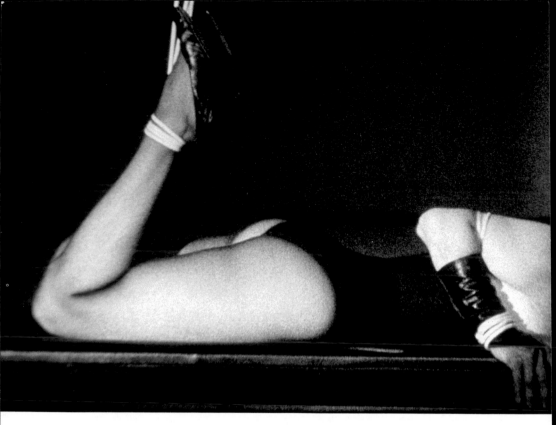

From Cleo Übelmann's *Mano Destra* (1985)

Stephan (left, played by Uwe Ochsenknecht), Paula (Ulrike Kriener) and
Julius (Heiner Lauterbach) in Doris Dörrie's *Männer/Men* (1985)

Doris Dörrie

Monika Treut

Susie Sexpert (right, played by Susie Bright) introduces Dorothee (Ina Blum) to her dildo collection in Monika Treut's *Die Jungfrauen Maschine/ The Virgin Machine* (1988)

From Wilhelm and Birgit Hein's *Die Kali-Filme/The Kali Films*
(1987–88)

Renée Felden interviews ARD correspondent Werner Sonne in Helke
Sander's *Die Deutschen und Ihre Männer/The Germans and Their Men* (1990)

interest a company in the film, but when it met with mixed reviews after being premiered at Mannheim, the distributor delayed the release date and subsequently went bankrupt. Then the director offered the film to Constantin who turned it down. Although her third choice, Ceres Film, expressed interest, it was on the condition that Stöckl added some 'good porn scenes'.[39] Other films, such as Erika Runge's critically acclaimed portrait of an elderly cleaning woman and miner's widow, *Warum ist Frau B. glücklich?/ Why is Mrs B. Happy?* (1968), had been television productions and were simply buried in the broadcasting companies' archives. As the Cologne group eventually observed, 'We really need a women's film distributor.'[40]

In 1979 Hildegard Westbeld obliged by setting up West Germany's first women's film distributor, Chaos. The name was intended both to reflect the situation of women filmmakers excluded from the official structures and to refer to Ernst Bloch's thesis that chaos provides a guarantee of freedom.[41] Westbeld launched the company with the release of Karen Arthur's *Legacy* (1975). Although Arthur's film had won the Josef von Sternberg prize at the 1975 Mannheim Film Week, it had never reached West German cinemas. *Legacy* ran for several weeks in the cinema, but Westbeld was unable to repeat this success. She rapidly accumulated significant debts and was forced to close Chaos after less than two years in operation. The women's cinemas also subsequently disappeared, but a number of other independent distributors – such as Basis Filmverleih, Freunde der deutschen Kinematik and the Zentral Filmverleih – did begin taking on the work of women filmmakers. Basis, for instance, now distribute films by Helga Reidemeister, Cristina Perincioli, Helma Sanders-Brahms, Helke Sander, Ulrike Ottinger, Heide Breitel and Marianne Rosenbaum.

Despite such initiatives, a significant number of women's films still fail to find a distributor and either remain inaccessible or disappear altogether. In the eighties a women's media centre in Hamburg, Bildwechsel, launched initiatives in an attempt to remedy this situation. Set up in 1979, the centre conceived of itself as a feminist project. Although it facilitates production work, the organization has always identified the distribution and exhibition of women's films as an important aspect of its work, and in 1982 set up a Women's Film Archive by transferring films onto video. Their primary aim was to ensure that a permanent collection of films by West German women exists and that this work will not 'disappear' should films fail to find, or be dropped by, a distributor. As the work was both expensive and time-consuming, they subsequently handed the archive over to Hamburg's Film House, where it continues to be housed. From the mid eighties Bildwechsel also started offering a nationwide information service to advise users where they could hire women's films, and began building up their own small video distribution library of women's movement films and shorts for use by women's groups. From time to time they also arrange screenings of women's work at their own premises.

The most recent initiatives have been the inauguration of two biennial women's film festivals, the *Feminale* in Cologne and *femme totale* in Dortmund. Both started out as regional initiatives, the former in 1984 and the latter in 1987, but both have now expanded to become major international events. The former, in particular, has become the country's main showcase for the latest work by European directors. With *Frauen und Film*'s change in direction and the disappearance of the women's cinema initiatives in the early eighties, these festivals were motivated by the desire to supply a (once again) much needed forum for the discussion of women's filmmaking. As at Sander's and von Alemann's 1973 seminar, workshop discussions play an important role at both festivals.

Since all these initiatives were set up in response to the inadequacies of existing institutional structures, they effectively constitute an alternative institutional framework. However, the aims of those involved have been primarily to *integrate* women's work into the film sector, rather than to ghettoize it as 'alternative' – that is, to secure women a place in the mainstream public sphere, rather than establish an 'alternative' public sphere. This is why, for instance, the Association of Women Filmworkers have consistently campaigned for mechanisms to guarantee women equal opportunities within existing institutions, and have not demanded special facilities for women or a special women's film budget. Although most of these initiatives have been beset with problems and are far from having achieved all their goals, they have succeeded at least in promoting awareness and understanding within Germany of women's film work, and in improving its availability. This, combined with the work of feminist activists in general, has in turn significantly improved the professional opportunities open to women filmmakers. The institutional initiatives undertaken by women have therefore underpinned the development of West Germany's feminist film culture. By bringing women together, they have also given rise to what can only be described as a women's filmmaking community – something greatly envied by women working in other countries.

FIVE

'Is There a Feminine
Aesthetic?'

Women depict different content from a different perspective, because as women they experience the world fundamentally differently. At all women's film festivals and women's film seminars the question consequently also arises of whether there is a feminine aesthetic.[1]

As a lively feminist film culture started to develop in West Germany during the late seventies, the emergent women's cinema began to win critical attention. In addition to the work of *Frauen und Film,* more mainstream publications and some overseas journals started to review and discuss the work of women directors. Although the specific concerns of these reports and interviews varied, they highlighted a number of recurring thematic concerns, such as mother-daughter relationships, women's history and female bonding. The overwhelming focus on such issues arose from a desire on the part of the directors, precipitated by the consciousness-raising work of the women's movement, to represent and foreground the experiences of women as discussed in chapter three.

However, a significant number of films from this period can also be characterized as much – if not more so – by their marked tendency to explore *how* their protagonists experience or perceive things as they can by the way they represent *what* those protagonists experience. Among such films are Helma Sanders-Brahms's *Deutschland, bleiche Mutter/ Germany, Pale Mother* (1979–80), Ulrike Ottinger's *Bildnis einer Trink-*

erin / Ticket of No Return (1979), Claudia von Alemann's *Die Reise nach Lyon / Blind Spot* (1980) and Margarethe von Trotta's *Die bleierne Zeit / The German Sisters* (1981). Although these films are narrative-based (and in fact very different from one another), they also undertake what Maya Deren has termed 'a "vertical" investigation of a situation'. That is, each film 'probes the ramifications of the moment, and is concerned in a sense not with what is occurring, but with what it feels like or what it means'.[2] In Germany, as elsewhere, the nature of women's artistic expression has been intensely debated – not least among women filmmakers and viewers. Certain aspects of this debate suggest that this 'way of looking' is in fact specifically feminine and may be regarded as constituting a feminine aesthetic.

Sanders-Brahms's film *Germany, Pale Mother* is autobiographical and, using the conventions of art-house realism, explores her parents' experiences during the Nazi era, the Second World War and the immediate post-war period. The opening scenes, which show how her parents, Lene and Hans, met during the 1930s at the height of Nazi fervour, fell in love and married, also foreground the way Lene is constrained and how she experiences her situation as oppressive. The film opens with a close-up of a Nazi flag reflected in a river. As the camera pulls back we see two men, Hans and his friend Ulrich, in a row-boat on the river in the foreground and a group of SA officers playing with a dog on the shore behind them. The dog attacks a young woman walking by who, without uttering a sound, tries to defend herself. The woman is Lene and in voice-over Sanders-Brahms explains that this is the first time Hans has ever seen her. He and Ulrich watch the incident from their boat. The fact that she does not scream or call out impresses both of them and even elicits praise from Ulrich. As the film starts at the precise moment when Hans sees Lene for the first time, it is as if Lene's life commences only when knowledge of her existence enters the consciousness of her future husband. The choice of this point to begin the film suggests that Lene is 'spoken more than speaking, enunciated more than enunciating'.[3] The construction of the scene reinforces this positioning by rendering Lene literally silent – even emphasizing the fact through Ulrich's valuing of it – and by making her an object of the male gaze.

When Lene first marries she appears happy, and their home together is clean, neat and tidy – a visitor even comments on the newly washed curtains. However, the well-ordered house lacks warmth and any evidence of being lived in. Lene moves around it in a stiff and careful manner; she is quiet and speaks relatively little within its confines. It is as if the house stifles and restricts her. This impression is powerfully underscored when, shortly after the couple move in, Lene pricks her finger on a needle which has been left in the curtains. This reference to Sleeping Beauty, the princess put to sleep for one hundred years when she pricks her finger on a spinning wheel, suggests that the house will have a similar effect on Lene.

With the outbreak of war, Hans – who is not a party member – is quickly shipped off to the front. When he returns on leave, Lene tells him she wants to have a child and subsequently becomes pregnant. Shortly after the child is born, the family house is completely destroyed in an air-raid. Rather than depicting the physical problems this creates, the film concentrates on the emotional effect it has on Lene. Although she has lost almost everything she owns and has nowhere to live, she experiences a sense of liberation. She becomes resourceful, independent and versatile, and Sanders-Brahms recalls in voice-over: 'With the end of the living room you became merry.'[4] Having salvaged what she can from the wreck of her home, Lene determinedly sets off on foot to seek shelter with her relatives in Berlin. We see her walking briskly and resolutely along a rubble-strewn street, wearing – as the narrator, Sanders-Brahms, points out – high heels and pushing her baby's pram in front of her.

For the rest of the war Lene and the infant Sanders-Brahms, who is called Anna in the film, go everywhere together and are always in one another's company. They constantly appear (with only rare exceptions) in frame together, usually in close physical contact. Lene is often holding Anna in her arms or on her lap, carrying her on her shoulders, or holding her hand. By the time Hans visits them on leave in Berlin an extremely close bond has developed between the mother and child, making them virtually inseparable. When Lene and Hans try to make love, Anna begins to scream. Lene gets up, brings the child into their bed and cuddles her. Hans can only watch enviously as Anna takes his place and receives the attention he was seeking. Lene also explains that she has had to continue breastfeeding Anna as there is nothing else to give her. For Anna, being with her mother has in fact become a prerequisite for life. It is as if they have never properly separated and are still joined by an invisible umbilical cord. Indeed, in her voice-over Sanders-Brahms rarely talks just about herself, but rather reminisces about 'Lene and I'.

Despite the parasitic nature of the relationship – which Lene admits drains her strength – both mother and daughter find pleasure in their bonding. Although the constant battle for survival is not without its strains and bleaker moments, Lene's pleasure is apparent time and again in her facial expressions as she holds, carries or touches Anna. In one scene, she smiles radiantly as she carries Anna on her shoulders. In another, she looks lovingly and contentedly at the child as they sit together in a makeshift bed in the house of their Berlin relatives. In voice-over Sanders-Brahms recalls this period in her life as if it were a wonderful secret adventure she and Lene shared together:

> Things really went well for us.... Hobos – Lene and I. And Lene and I loved each other in the bath tub and flew like witches over the rooftops. Lene and I. Me and Lene. In the middle of the war.[5]

As the war comes to an end, Sanders-Brahms summarizes this '"vertical" investigation' of her mother's situation by having Lene tell Anna a fairy tale. The tale is the Robber Bridegroom, the story of a young woman who is wooed by and agrees to marry a highly attractive suitor. When she visits his house which lies deep in the woods, however, she learns from an old woman that it is the house of robbers and murderers, who seduce, kill and then eat young women. Although the robbers return, bringing with them a girl who they kill and eat, the young woman manages to escape with the assistance of the old woman. She then exposes her bridegroom on their wedding day by producing the severed finger of the dead girl. The fairy tale is told while Lene and Anna aimlessly roam the German countryside and its telling takes approximately fifteen minutes. As it serves no narrative function within the film, Lene's telling of it implies that she sees it as an allegory for the way she perceives her own experience.

In a similar manner, Sanders-Brahms explores the effect war has on Hans rather than what he does or the role he plays as a soldier. When he is first sent off to the front, the director comments in voice-over: 'They sent you off to kill people, but you couldn't do that.'[6] In one of the very few scenes of Hans away at war he and a handful of other soldiers are sent into a field to kill a group of Polish peasants. Hans comes face to face with a woman who resembles his wife – she is in fact played by the same actress – and bursts into tears. Unable to perform what is expected of him on the battlefield, Hans longs for home. But when he returns on his first leave he finds himself rejected. Having remained faithful to Lene while he has been away, he is eager to sleep with her. In his excitement he starts to pull her clothes off, ripping the blouse she has lovingly embroidered in his absence. Hans's uncontrollable lust and disregard of her long hours of labour horrify Lene and make her withdraw from his advances. Confused and hurt, he strikes her and accuses her of having slept with another man. Although he learns to survive on the battlefield, by the end of the war Hans has become an old, broken and bitter man. When he and Lene are finally reunited at the end of the war, he is unable even to make love to her. When he also finds that former Nazis, like his friend Ulrich, prosper in the new post-war society while he fails to get promotion in his job, Hans's bitterness only increases.

In an attempt to compensate for his own feelings of failure and to gain recognition of some kind he ruthlessly reasserts his authority in the domestic sphere. As Sanders-Brahms observes in voice-over: 'The stones we cleared away were used to build houses which were worse than before. . . . That was the return of the living rooms. Then the war began inside, once there was peace outside.'[7] Hans becomes tyrannical towards Anna, not only shouting at her but also on occasions hitting and smacking her. When Lene develops a disfiguring facial paralysis he takes her to see a dentist who insists that the only course of action is to extract Lene's teeth. Disregarding her visible distress, Hans authorizes the dentist to go ahead with the operation. We then see shots of the dentist giving Lene an injection, inserting the pliers, pulling the teeth, putting the bloodstained molars neatly on to a tray, and of Lene spitting blood out of her mouth. The detail in which the operation is shown, combined with Hans's silent acquiescing presence in the background, suggests how Hans has been brutalized by his experiences, especially in his behaviour towards Lene.

This scene also clearly shows how Hans exercises control over Lene, and the final part of the film examines how Lene is once again constrained in the immediate post-war years. Her facial paralysis and the removal of her teeth affect both her ability and her inclination to speak. In order to conceal the disfiguring effects of the paralysis, she also starts to pin a scarf over the affected half of her face so that less of her is actually visible. Subsequently she simply retreats to her bed and spends more and more time hiding in her darkened bedroom. Finally, in a fit of despair, she locks herself in the bathroom and turns on the gas in the water heater in an attempt to commit suicide. Although she eventually responds to Anna's entreaties to open the door, Sanders-Brahms's voice-over explains: 'It was a long time before Lene opened the door, and sometimes I think she's still behind it, and I'm still outside, and she'll never come out, and I'll have to grow up and be alone.'[8] By showing how Lene effectively withdraws from life because of her disability and in the process breaks her bond with Anna, the film suggests that Lene has been 'silenced'. Again, Sanders-Brahms's voice-over functions to emphasize this: 'My mother. I learned to be silent, you said.'[9]

By exploring how Lene experiences war as a period of liberation and pleasure, and peacetime as a period of violence which 'silenced' her, the film suggests that the Second World War can also be understood as an event which disrupted the patriarchal order, while the return to peace brought about its violent reimposition. That is, it made women of Lene's generation aware of the patriarchal order and the way it oppresses women. Lene's telling of the fairy tale is therefore not only an allegory for her own experiences, but also her way of passing on to Anna her understanding of the workings of patriarchy. As if to confirm that she has learnt the lesson her mother taught her, Sanders-Brahms dedicates the film to Lene and states in voice-over that she herself has never married.

However, since this 'way of looking' foregrounds the effect historical events had on individuals rather than exploring how or why those events happened, Sanders-Brahms also appears to be suggesting that people like her parents were victims of history, simply caught up in the events of the time and in no way responsible for them. Although Sanders-Brahms has disputed this,[10] such an impression is reinforced by the role she constructs for Lene. Since the opening scene of the film positions Lene as 'spoken more than speaking' – that is, 'silent' – it implies that she does not possess the power to act and cannot therefore bear any responsibility for the rise of Nazism and the events that led to war. Similarly, the inseparability of mother and child during the war

can also be viewed as a denial of responsibility since Lene lacks autonomy, and as Angelika Bammer asserts, 'those who refuse to claim
their autonomy as historical subjects also cannot own their responsibility as agents of history.'[11] Sanders-Brahms has moreover argued that
the Robber Bridegroom also describes German history.[12] If this is the
case, it tends to suggest that she regards Nazism as an external evil
which invaded Germany and over which the country's population had
no control.

The question of who should bear responsibility for the atrocities
committed in the name of Nazism has, of course, been widely debated.
Since Nazism found immense support among large segments of the
population and since Lene's silence can in fact be viewed as a form of
collusion, most members of Sanders-Brahms's generation have taken a
far less sympathetic view of the issue. The film has consequently been
condemned by many critics as highly reactionary.

However, Sanders-Brahms also – paradoxically – appears to place
Lene outside of history. Several clips from archive newsreels of
bombings and devastated cityscapes are intercut at various points
during the film. The difference in film stock is very noticeable, func-
tioning to render the war alien to Lene. At one point, for instance,
Sanders-Brahms has edited old documentary footage of a young boy
looking for his parents amid the ruins of a city together with her own
filmed footage of Lene and Anna, to create the impression that Lene is
conversing with the boy. Despite skilful editing, the contrast in texture
and colouring clearly locates Lene in a space entirely different to that
of the 'real' war. This has the effect of transforming Lene into an
observer of history, a role which is particularly evident in the fairy-tale
sequence. As Lene tells the tale while she and Anna wander through
the countryside, she combines narrative drive with physical
movement and it is as if Lene is literally taking Anna on a journey
through German history. The fact that there are relatively few visual
references to wartorn Europe during the sequence emphasizes Lene's
outsider status.

In doing this, the film also suggests that Lene and, by implication,
others like her, perceived Nazism and the Second World War as a
backdrop to their own lives. Although they were aware that their
personal experiences were shaped by historical events, they did not
regard themselves as participating in them. This perception is evident

in Sanders-Brahms's use of the Nazi flag in the film's opening scene. Reflected in the river, the flag signals Nazism as a crucial context, but for people like the director's parents it existed in the background and was experienced only in a mediated form, not directly. This is not to suggest, however, that Sanders-Brahms actually does consider such people absolved of all responsibility. On the contrary, she counts her parents among the many people who 'elected Hitler. Or perhaps didn't vote, but also didn't protest, or go underground, or join the resistance, or end up in concentration camps or emigrate.'[13] But she does draw a distinction between actual lived reality and historical events. Although integrally related, the film shows how they are often perceived by those involved as quite separate.

Sanders-Brahms is not offering this as an excuse for people like her parents, but as a warning both to members of her own generation and, as she also dedicates the film to her own daughter, to those of her daughter's generation against assuming a morally superior position when standing in judgement on their parents. For, as she asserts: 'I don't live any differently to my parents, only in different times.'[14] The film therefore performs a similar function to the fairy tale within the film since it is Sanders-Brahms's way of passing on to her daughter her understanding of, her 'way of looking' at a particular situation.

Unlike *Germany, Pale Mother*, Ulrike Ottinger's film, *Ticket of No Return* is deliberately anti-realist, reflecting the director's background in fine arts. Through a highly episodic narrative it focuses on an exotically dressed, rich and eccentric young woman alcoholic – known only as 'She' – who launches herself into a self-destructive drinking binge across Berlin. In the course of her drinking sessions she meets and befriends the bag-lady Lutze, a well-known street character in Berlin, who then accompanies her on her tour of the city. Although Ottinger identifies the city and in fact shoots a great deal of the film on location, she makes no effort to clearly delineate spatial or temporal parameters. Instead, the film is more like a collage of bizarre outings across the city and into its bars. Following their trail are three women sociologists, all of them dressed in black-and-white dogtooth-checked suits. At various intervals throughout the film they comment – rather in the manner of a Greek chorus – on the problem of alcoholism in contemporary society. The film does not, however, show how or why the rich woman has become an alcoholic or the social consequences of her alcoholism, but rather explores what it feels like to be an alcoholic.

Although her drinking takes her among people, the protagonist's alcoholism continually results in her being rejected or ostracized by those around her. For one of her first drinking sessions, she goes into a crowded Möhring café, followed by the three sociologists who sit at a neighbouring table. 'She' spots Lutze outside in the street, beckons her to join her, and orders cognacs for herself and Lutze. After several drinks 'She' starts throwing the empty glasses at the window; Lutze does likewise. The people in the café watch silently until 'She' and Lutze are eventually thrown out. Subsequently we see 'She' seated alone in the middle of the auditorium of a lecture theatre where she is served wine by an old woman. Five other women are seated in the front row. As 'She' drinks her wine, they turn round and glare at her. Still later, she boards a pleasure cruiser on a lake and joins a small group of women. They all start drinking and smashing their glasses on the boat's deck, but their behaviour soon results in 'She' being thrown off. When 'She' finally collapses at the end of the film on the steps of a train station, not one of the horde of passengers who swarm past even bothers to stop.

In the middle of the film, 'She' also indulges in a series of daydreams. She fantasizes about being an actress and playing Hamlet, working as a secretary, being a tight-rope walker, and being a daredevil stunt artist. It is as if, finding herself a social outcast, she tries to imagine what it would be like to be properly integrated into society. However, even in her fantasies alcohol intervenes to deny her such a possibility. In the sequence where she imagines herself working as a secretary, for instance, her boss catches her drinking, berates her mercilessly for the crime, then sacks her since he sees her as posing a threat to his business. Ottinger emphasizes her inability to imagine a 'normal' scenario by using a low camera angle to make the company boss appear highly grotesque. When 'She' fantasizes about being a tight-rope walker we first see an older woman successfully complete a tight-rope walk. When 'She' in a drunken state has her go, however, she unsurprisingly falls off the rope halfway along and has to be carried away by two of the onlookers. The three sociologists are also present in each daydream, waiting for her to fail and condemning her for her alcohol abuse. Thus alcoholism not only forces 'She' into an isolated existence in reality but also renders her incapable of imagining anything else.

All of 'She's' costumes are highly elaborate and extravagant, providing a startling and artificial explosion of glamour and colour in the drab Berlin surroundings, and offering a dramatic contrast to the sombre (although very stylish) attire of the three sociologists. 'She' is also very wooden and mechanical in her movements, which gives her an inhuman, almost robot- or puppet-like quality. Furthermore, throughout the whole film 'She' does not speak a single word. Even when she appears to be attempting to communicate, she fails to actually do so. When she goes to the Möhring café, dressed in a bright yellow coat with matching sunglasses and hat, she sits at a table in the window and mouths words, but no sound comes out and her attempt is not directed towards anyone specific. In fact, it is as if 'She' is silently talking to herself in some imaginary world of her own and is totally unable to relate to other people.

This characterizes 'She' as 'other', and sets her apart from everyone around her. Although 'She' strikes up a friendship with Lutze, the contrast between them only serves to emphasize this difference. As one critic has observed, 'She' is constructed 'very much as an exotic, pleasurable object for us to look at'[15] and Ottinger emphasizes this positioning throughout the film. When 'She' and Lutze start throwing cognac at the window in the Möhring café, for example, two photographers suddenly appear out of nowhere and start to snap pictures of the two drunken women. In this scene the camera is positioned outside on the street and the scene shot through the window in which the two women are sitting: 'She' is framed as if in a photo or on a cinema screen. The photos subsequently appear in a tabloid newspaper as a sensational news item under the headline 'Rich Foreigner Goes Beserk in Möhring'.

Three of 'She's' fantasies are about being a performing artist, the role frequently allotted to women in mainstream cinema to legitimate their objectification. On other occasions Ottinger actually includes the audience in the film to foreground 'She' as an object to be looked at. In one scene, 'She' is sitting at a table with the three sociologists. The camera then cuts to show that they are sitting in a shop window and that a crowd has gathered outside to watch them.

This continual emphasis on 'She' as an object to be looked at suggests that 'She' has become isolated from herself and consequently has no sense of 'self'. Ottinger foregrounds this in one particular scene after the incident in the Möhring café. 'She' awakes the next morning to find that a tabloid newspaper has been pushed under her door; when she sees the photos of herself throwing cognac glasses at the café window, she takes the paper to a mirror and compares the photos with her reflection. Puzzled, she peers at both images several times as if trying, but failing, to find some evidence of herself in the images. Her isolation becomes complete at the end of the film when she eventually collapses unconscious. Although Lutze tries to help, she cannot revive her.

The film thus shows how an alcoholic becomes totally isolated, divorced from any sense of reality through addiction, incapable of social interaction, and ostracized by society. Yet, at the same time it is possible to argue that *Ticket of No Return* is not actually about alcoholism at all; the film only foregrounds 'society's failure to deal with the problems of alcoholism'.[16] Whenever 'She' drinks she is regarded as a nuisance, something everyone wants to get rid of, and proprietors repeatedly deal with the situation by throwing her out – at the end of the film she is even thrown out of a public lavatory. Although the three sociologists constantly recite facts and figures about alcoholics and drinking patterns, they never intervene to change the situation. Indeed, when given the opportunity actually to do something about the problem they only ignore or dismiss it. At the end of the film, for instance, a taxi drops them off at the station where 'She' has collapsed. As one of the sociologists passes her on the stairs, she simply observes: 'As you make your bed, so you must lie on it.'

Instead, the film can equally be viewed as exploring what it feels like to be a woman, foregrounding the way women are continually objectified within dominant culture and how many consequently have no sense of their 'true' selves. By making her protagonist an alcoholic, however, Ottinger also undermines that objectification. Although 'She' is 'an exotic, pleasurable object for us to look at', a drunk – and especially a female drunk – is not traditionally thought of as particularly attractive. Moreover, as an alcoholic 'She' is not simply there to be looked at, but has a will or desire of her own – to drink herself to death. When she finally collapses at the end of the film, she also disappears from view for a few moments amidst the train passengers, which suggests that by destroying herself 'She' has also destroyed her positioning as object. As if to suggest that this was her intention and the purpose of the film, the final sequence shows 'She' in high heels walking on mirror floor tiles. As she walks, slowly and deliberately, they crack under her heels, causing her image to break up as well.

Ottinger herself has asserted that she uses alcoholism as a metaphor – though not for the way in which women are objectified. By constructing the alcoholic as exotic 'other' and her existence on all levels as one of isolation, Ottinger is in fact also characterizing the contemporaneous situation of West Berlin, the location for the film. Like 'She', West Berlin appeared artificial – western in name and politics rather than geographical position; although part of the Federal Republic, it was also very different and isolated from the rest of West Germany; and as a walled-in western island amid East German territory, with road, rail and water connections dependent upon East German cooperation, it was also isolated and different from that which surrounded it. Consequently alcoholism is a means of representing the sense of isolation, of alienation from 'reality', that could arise from living in West Berlin. Of course, life in any big city can produce such feelings, and West Berlin, with its special situation (pre-1990), was simply a city whose political and physical isolation rendered other kinds of isolation more visible. According to Ottinger the film explores what it feels like to live in a big, modern city; and her use of anti-realist conventions skilfully renders such feelings tangible by presenting the viewer with a virtually unrecognizable image of Berlin.[17]

In her film *Blind Spot* Claudia von Alemann, like Ottinger, also employs an episodic narrative. Very gently paced, almost lyrical, the film focuses on contemporary historian Elisabeth Falusy, who is researching the life and work of Flora Tristan, the largely forgotten nineteenth-century socialist and feminist. Through reading Tristan's *Tour de France*, the diary of her travels around France, Elisabeth has developed an affinity for Tristan and wishes to find out more about her. However, all her library and archive research has left her dissatisfied, and she travels from her native Germany to Lyon, where Tristan spent some time, in order to try and find traces of her. Although Elisabeth's voice-over fills in a few details about Tristan's life – her idea of establishing a workers' union, her travels around France, how her socialist ideas predated those of Karl Marx, and how she became ill in Lyon and eventually died of typhus at the age of forty-one – the film does not offer a conventional historical reconstruction of Tristan's life.

In fact, *Blind Spot* provides very little information about Tristan and even less about Elisabeth. Instead, the first half of the film shows how Elisabeth tries a number of different ways to search for evidence of Tristan only to find that the past is in fact highly elusive.

On her first foray around Lyon after her arrival, Elisabeth looks for the street where a close friend of Tristan's had lived. Although she finds the street, its name has changed and no one can tell her where the house had been. Similarly she locates the hotel where Tristan stayed, but finds it is now a cinema showing karate movies. Adopting another tack, Elisabeth goes to an antiquarian bookshop and asks to see etchings of Lyon from the mid nineteenth century. The bookseller has, however, lost a folder of etchings and consequently only has very few to show Elisabeth. Of the few she has, several are of a particular square in Lyon, but they all show the same view because – so the bookseller explains – there was less to see in the opposite view. Others depict workshops from the period, which Elisabeth remarks seem relatively large. But according to the bookseller, etchings – especially from that period – are not very accurate.

In the evening Elisabeth goes to a café for some refreshment. On the wall outside the café there is a plaque which commemorates the arrest of eighty Jews from that street during the Nazi period of occupation. The owner of the café was a young girl at the time and remembers the incident. As she starts to tell Elisabeth about her past, it transpires that the Jews were not arrested but rounded up in the courtyard and shot. Although the owner remembers the shooting, she also explains that she did not actually see the incident as she was upstairs at the time, but maintains that she felt it and heard it. Although some evidence of the past can be found, the rest, as Elisabeth observes, fades, vanishes, melts and disappears. Several times in voice-over she remarks that although she is moving – both by travelling to Lyon and walking its streets – she is also motionless or immobile. It is as if she feels trapped in the present, unable to reach back into the past and bridge the 135 years that separate her and Tristan. Nevertheless, true to her historian training, she persists in reading Tristan's diary and typing up her thoughts about Tristan in her hotel room every night.

By foregrounding the way in which much of the past literally vanishes as time passes, the film calls into question the notion of historical truth and historical reconstruction. This is particularly evident in one scene where Elisabeth revisits the café with the plaque on the wall outside. She sits at a table next to a woman who is diligently cutting out clippings from many different newspapers and pasting them together to create a collage of news stories. Elisabeth asks the woman what she is doing and the woman explains that all the clippings are from the same day. By sticking them together she gets some idea of all that happened in the world on a given day. Elisabeth observes, however, that some stories have larger headlines than others and comments on how this shows that some events are considered more important than others. The other woman also admits that her collage is of course only a small part of what actually happened on the day in question.

Once day, however, Elisabeth eats her lunch while listening to some music on a portable tape recorder she has brought with her. The music reminds her of her own violin, made, as she informs us in voice-over, by a Viennese in 1792. Elisabeth suddenly realises that the violin therefore represents 'a sound that is history'. She starts to listen to her own footsteps and realizes it is a sound that Tristan would also have heard. Thus the sound of her own footsteps becomes, for Elisabeth, the sound of Tristan's 135 years later. Her typewriter is now replaced by her tape recorder which she carries everywhere, recording the sound of her footsteps, of street life, children playing, people arguing, of running water, and so on. By doing this and playing back the tape, listening to the recorded sounds, she feels she is remaking Tristan's own journey through the town. This intensifies her identification with Tristan to the point that, like Tristan, Elisabeth becomes ill. Through sound she has found her link with the past, a link which makes a particular aspect of the past tangible *for her* – that is, something she herself can experience in the present.

However, just after her arrival in Lyon Elisabeth also uses her tape recorder to listen to a tape of her partner and their young daughter talking. Von Alemann therefore identifies the tape recorder early on in the film as something which Elisabeth uses to recall her personal history – she remembers her own past through sound. Since, in contrast, the typewriter is where she initially records her thoughts about Tristan, the film suggests that to start with Elisabeth sees the remembering of her own past and her search for traces of Tristan, of history, as entirely separate. However, when she replaces her typewriter with her tape recorder in her historical research, Elisabeth is 'remembering' Tristan the same way she remembers her own past. This implies that she has come to see Tristan as part of her own history. That is, rather than being separate, Tristan and 'history' are as much part of her as her own personal past is. When we see Elisabeth playing her violin as the final credits appear, it is as if she is literally giving life to the past through herself, or actually living history.

Consequently, *The Blind Spot* is not about Flora Tristan – indeed Alemann has stressed that the film could equally have focused on another woman from the same era and she had in fact drafted portraits of Vera Figner and Emma Goldmann.[18] Rather it is a 'vertical investigation' of how we document history and the way we remember the past. After Elisabeth has started recording the sounds of Lyon, she visits a male colleague. He asks her what she has been doing and in response she plays him one of her tapes of street sounds. Baffled, he asks her what it means. When she explains, he thinks she has over-identified with Tristan and asserts that the historian's job is instead to efface herself and meticulously reconstruct the past. However, the film has shown how this is actually impossible since much of the past disappears; any process of documentation is inevitably selective. Hence the film shows how Flora Tristan – and by implication many others – has been relegated to a position of relative obscurity through the inadequacies of historical discourses.

The film suggests that if we are truly to 'remember' the past it is necessary to find a way of identifying or associating ourselves with it. That identification can then be translated into an action – in Elisabeth's case, the making of sound – which makes the past tangible in the present. As von Alemann has stressed that the film 'is based on my general sympathy for women of the nineteenth century',[18] her act of filmmaking can be viewed as her own attempt to 'remember' the past. Although we are given very few facts about Tristan, through the film we do 'experience' something of her life.

Using a more conventional narrative style Margarethe von Trotta's *The German Sisters* focuses on the relationship between two sisters, Marianne and Juliane, who are loosely based on Gudrun Ensslin, a member of the Baader-Meinhof terrorist group who died in Stammheim prison in 1977, and her sister Christiane. The first part of the film establishes the respective situations of the two sisters. Marianne has left her husband, Werner, and son, Jan, to join a terrorist group. Juliane lives with her boyfriend Wolfgang, is active in the women's movement and works for a feminist magazine. Unlike Marianne, she has chosen not to marry or have children. Although the fact that Marianne has become a terrorist is crucial to the film, nothing is actually shown of her terrorist activities. Instead, the film shows how Juliane experiences her sister's preferred method of effecting political change as an intrusion on her own life.

By turning terrorist Marianne has left Werner to cope as a single parent, a role he has found difficult to assume and is clearly incapable of fulfilling. Unkempt and agitated, he visits Juliane at the beginning of the film to ask her to look after Jan because he has taken a year's assignment abroad. Having consciously rejected motherhood herself, she refuses. When his insistent pleading fails to persuade her, he declares he is not prepared to play nursemaid for the next ten years and tries to make Juliane feel responsible for Jan by reminding her that she is Marianne's sister and that she in fact introduced them. Eventually Juliane agrees to take the boy for a few days until Werner can make alternative arrangements. Werner, however, commits suicide instead and in Marianne's absence Juliane is forced to assume the unwanted responsibility for Jan until she can find foster parents for him.

When Marianne subsequently meets her sister at a museum, she, like Werner, also begs Juliane to look after Jan. Although Juliane admits to sympathizing with some aspects of Marianne's politics, her angry response indicates how deeply she resents the way Marianne's actions rebound on her with unwelcome consequences. Von Trotta foregrounds this, rather than Jan's actual welfare, as the issue by positioning Jan in the background. When Werner arrives at Juliane's flat, for instance, Jan is asleep in Werner's arms and they put him straight to bed. The director makes no attempt to explore how Marianne's desertion or Werner's inadequacies as a father affect the child.

Juliane finds foster parents for Jan and Marianne goes to the Lebanon to work with Arab revolutionaries. One night, however, Juliane and Wolfgang are awoken in the early hours of the morning to the insistent ringing of their doorbell. Wolfgang answers the door to find it is Marianne, returned from her spell abroad, with two male friends. They barge into the flat, saying little, but the manner of all three is surly and brusque. Marianne goes to the kitchen and helps herself to coffee. Her two friends follow and sit down at the kitchen table. As they sense they are unwelcome their stay is very short, but as they leave Marianne dashes into Juliane's bedroom, pulls her clothes out of the wardrobe and, finding nothing that appeals to her, throws them on the floor. As the scene serves no narrative purpose other than to show Marianne is back in Germany, the terrorists' invasion of Juliane's private space functions primarily to further delineate Marianne and her terrorist politics as intruders in Juliane's life. Von Trotta emphasizes the sense of intrusion by frequently placing Marianne and her companions in centre frame and relegating Juliane and Wolfgang to the edge of frame. The fact that the visit takes place in the middle of the night also means that Juliane and Wolfgang appear highly vulnerable in their nightclothes alongside the jeans-clad and leather-jacketed terrorists.

Subsequently Marianne is arrested, but the film does not show how, when or where, nor does it show her being interrogated, charged or tried. Instead von Trotta focuses on how the prison system's treatment of Marianne becomes increasingly inhumane. Juliane visits her sister in prison a number of times, but with each visit the physical barrier between them increases. At first they sit on either side of a rectangular table, with only the width of the table between them. On Juliane's next visit they are made to sit at the two ends, with the whole length of the table separating them. Finally, when Marianne is moved to a new high-security prison, they are not even in the same room. They can only look at each other through a glass panel and have to speak through an intercom. Marianne cannot even hear Juliane's real voice. When the microphone breaks down and Juliane finds she also cannot see Marianne clearly because of her own reflection in the glass, it is as if imprisonment denies Marianne all possibility of meaningful human contact.

Juliane not only witnesses the way her sister is treated in prison, but to a certain extent experiences it for herself. On her first visit to see Marianne she is scrutinized by prison officers through a glass panel and intercom when she first arrives, escorted to a cloakroom, and ordered to loosen her clothing so that she can be thoroughly searched. When she is told to pull up her T-shirt she objects, but is informed she will not be allowed to see her sister if she does not comply. Marianne, however, remains rebellious and scornful throughout her imprisonment. Despite the fact that Juliane regards her sister as fanatical, arguing during one visit that Marianne would have been an ardent Hitler supporter if she had been born a generation earlier, she starts to develop some sympathy for her sister's situation and begins to help her by sending her clothing parcels.

Juliane's meetings with Marianne, both at the museum and in prison, are interspersed with a series of flashbacks to the sisters' childhood and teenage years. There are scenes of the sisters as young children during the forties being indoctrinated into the Christian ethic at the dinner table by their father and being woken up in the middle of the night to take cover from an air-raid. Other flashbacks show how as a teenager Juliane develops a sympathetic understanding with her mother, but comes into conflict with and rebels against her father, defying, for instance, his prohibition on her wearing black trousers to school. In contrast, we see Marianne avoiding conflict and playing instead at being 'daddy's girl' to get what she wants. In one scene, for example, she is shown as a teenager sitting on her father's lap, pleading with him to rescind some punishment he has meted out to Juliane. During one flashback to 1955 the sisters are also shown watching a film about the Nazi concentration camps. They find it so shocking that they are sick afterwards in the toilets. The final flashback to 1968 shows the sisters as young adults watching a film about Vietnam with Wolfgang, and all three are visibly affected by it.

Although these flashbacks highlight the shared influences that have shaped the sisters' different lives, they stop at 1968 and do not show when and how Marianne became a terrorist or how Juliane became involved in the women's movement. Since the flashbacks are constructed from Juliane's viewpoint, their inclusion suggests that her meetings with Marianne trigger a process of remembering the past. Indeed, on occasions von Trotta clearly indicates that something in the present has reminded Juliane of some aspect of her past. The first flashback, for instance, occurs during their meeting at the museum. They buy two cups of hot chocolate, sit down and talk animatedly until they notice that skin has formed on the undrunk chocolate. There is a cut from a shot of the two cups to Juliane's thoughtful face to a flashback of the two infant sisters sitting at the breakfast table watching their hot chocolate go cold while their father offers up morning prayers. This process, combined with the inhumanity of the prison system, begins to transform Juliane's sympathetic stance into a desire to understand and identify with her sister. For instance, she simulates the forced-feeding process that Marianne is subjected to after going on hunger strike, to find out what it feels like and what her sister is having to endure.

When Marianne subsequently dies in prison Juliane's identification with her intensifies dramatically. Unhappy with the official explanation of suicide, she embarks on an obsessive investigation into her sister's death. Following in Marianne's footsteps, she breaks off her ten-year relationship with Wolfgang and isolates herself from personal contact. She meticulously sorts through her sister's things, conducts detailed medical research and finally makes a dummy in order to carry out a reconstruction of Marianne's death. When she finally has the evidence she needs she telephones a newspaper only to find they are no longer interested in what is now considered yesterday's news.

In the meantime, however, Jan has been attacked and badly burned because, so it is thought, someone found out who his real mother was. Unable to help Marianne, Juliane now decides to accept responsibility for Jan and takes him home with her. When he tears up a picture of Marianne that she had pinned to her study wall, Juliane tells him he is wrong to do so and says she will tell him about his mother. The film ends with Jan demanding 'begin, begin'. It is as if, after resenting Marianne and then identifying with her, Juliane has finally absorbed her sister to find a new position of equilibrium.

Although *The German Sisters* is clearly concerned with the spate of terrorism that dominated West German political life during the seventies, von Trotta's handling of her subject matter did not satisfy the film's critics. As Ellen Seiter has observed:

> If [*The German Sisters*] is read as a historical film about Gudrun Ensslin ... why does the film concentrate on the psychological ordeal of the character based on Christiane Ensslin?.... The narrative structure conspicuously excludes information such as Ensslin's involvement in the student movement in Berlin in the 1960s ... the terrorists' isolation from the political left in Germany.... We see the consequences of the terrorist actions of Marianne portrayed as personal tragedy – her

husband's suicide, her suffering and death in prison, the attack on her son – but we never understand the decisions which led to those actions.[20]

In fact, by focusing on the way Marianne's politics are experienced as an unwelcome intrusion in Juliane's life in the first part of the film, the film can be viewed as initially representing terrorism as something which has nothing to do with Juliane, rather than as exploring the terrorist issue. Marianne's attitude, her lifestyle, her desertion of her family all mark her out as 'other', even as inhuman, to Juliane. As a result, Marianne becomes the fanatical terrorist of the popular imagination and the tabloid press. However, the flashbacks function to humanize her, to show that she actually shares the same family and German history as Juliane. Although Juliane's act of remembering does not explain how terrorism developed in Germany, it nevertheless highlights the need to acknowledge the past in order to understand the present. The way in which her subsequent identification with and absorption of Marianne leads her to accept responsibility for Jan suggests that real change can only be effected if she comes to terms with the past.

The German title of the film translates literally as *The Leaden Times*. Von Trotta chose this title as it described, for her, the experience of growing up in West Germany during the fifties:

> We felt that there was a past of which we were guilty as a nation but we weren't told about in school. If you asked questions, you didn't get answers. We all grew up with that burden. Only afterwards, in the sixties, when society was a little more open minded, did we find out about our past and what we had done.[21]

Thus, von Trotta's film is not 'about' terrorism. The Ensslin sisters are only, as the director has termed it, 'the point of departure'.[22] Rather the film is addressing the need to remember and face one's own history, and von Trotta therefore regards the film as an overdue act of mourning for the country's Nazi past. Consequently, the film is about what it means or feels like to be a member of the post-war generation in Germany:

> Christiane Ensslin and I belong to the same generation.... In this picture there are many things which have more to do with me rather than Christiane. At the same time there are things that have nothing to do either with her or with me, but with my imaginative vision of a woman of our generation, a vision that has somehow assumed the essence of reality.[23]

Although the question of a feminine aesthetic has repeatedly been raised with reference to women's filmmaking, many women directors have in fact rejected the concept. Some, such as Helke Sander and Helga Reidemeister, regarded any discussion of a feminine aesthetic in filmmaking as premature, since women had only recently begun to gain access to the means of feature film production.[24] In contrast, Jutta Brückner pointed to the diversity of filmmaking practices that had already emerged among women filmmakers – which is indeed evidenced by the four films discussed above – as proof that there could be no single feminine aesthetic.[25] Still others warned against interpreting certain filmmaking practices as 'feminine' when they in fact arose out of economic necessity.

Of course, any discussion of a feminine aesthetic with regard to women's filmmaking also tends to reinforce the categorization of films by women as 'women's films'. Although Sander, von Alemann and others had initially appropriated the term to designate films made by women about women, they quickly found it only served to ghettoize their work, and thus most filmmakers came to vehemently oppose its use. Margarethe von Trotta even declared: 'I would like to eliminate this genre description from the face of the earth.'[26]

Nevertheless, the directors of films such as those discussed above agreed that their work did more than simply foreground women's real-life experiences. Such a description of their work would suggest they simply filmed 'what was there', as if their films had more in common with *cinéma-vérité* or drama-documentaries than with feature film production. Yet as von Trotta stressed, the real Ensslin sisters and their lives were only her point of departure for *The German Sisters*. The incident concerning the teenage Juliane wearing black trousers to school is, for instance, von Trotta's memory, not Christiane Ensslin's. Despite the explicitly autobiographical nature of *Germany, Pale Mother*, even Sanders-Brahms asserts: 'The story of me and Lene did not happen exactly as it was shown in the film.... [It is] a story, constructed from personal experiences and from the experiences of many women, with whom I spoke, of whom I made tape recordings and sketches, etc.'[27] The manner in which several directors have discussed their work suggests that what they regard as a major defining characteristic is the way in which their films 'defamiliarize' reality.

The notion of art's potential capacity to 'defamiliarize' has been in circulation in one form or another since the Renaissance, but was first clearly theorized by a group of linguists and students of literature in Russia in the early twentieth century with regard to literature. In an attempt to define literature the Russian Formalists argued that what uniquely distinguished it from other written texts was its ability to 'defamiliarize' or make strange the way we habitually view the world. According to Formalist Viktor Shklovsky our perception of the world becomes automatized through habit:

> We do not see [objects] in their entirety but rather recognize them by their main characteristics. We see the object as though it were enveloped in a sack. We know what it is by its configuration, but we see only its silhouette.[28]

Rather than reflecting reality or offering a transparent 'window on the world', the Formalists maintained that literature constructs a particular representation of it which distorts and disrupts the habitual modes of perception of everyday life. The purpose of literature is therefore to impart a renewed awareness of reality:

> Art exists that one may recover the sensation of life; it exists to make one feel things, to make the stone *stoney*. The purpose of art is to impart the sensation of things as they are perceived and not as they are known.[29]

Although women filmmakers in Germany did not directly reference the concept of defamiliarization, the parallels between the approach some took to their film work and the Formalists' arguments are unmistakable. With regard to *Ticket of No Return*, for instance, Ulrike Ottinger has asserted:

> I don't think it is adequate to show things 'as they are' in a film....

There was a counter-movement ten years ago against formalist films; even fiction films then presented things 'as they were'.... In my film *Bildnis einer Trinkerin*, quasi-documentary scenes alternate with extremely stylized ones. I introduced this technique because I realized that Berlin filmmakers often made the quasi-documentary with tremendously precise film content, but formally lifeless. The public for these films has already developed a critical consciousness and watches a familiar reality on film – so familiar that the public doesn't see, or doesn't want to see, what goes on around them.[30]

When interviewed about her subsequent film, *Freak Orlando* (1981) she again reiterated these ideas. Consciously referencing Virginia Woolf's *Orlando* and Tod Browning's film *Freaks* (1932), Ottinger's film is about a figure called Orlando who changes sex and wanders through the history of western culture encountering many freaks and outsiders:

There is something deeply disturbing about actually seeing someone of one's own species who is simply different. Which means that there is also, under certain circumstances, the possibility of being like that oneself; or of course, that also shows one something of oneself. It's quite normal for that to arouse fears – and that is disturbing. Which is exactly what I find interesting. I think it's very important that there are things in our everyday life which disturb and engage us again and again, since that causes us to think. As far as I'm concerned, artistic works, and it doesn't matter whether it's painting or theatre or whatever, should also create this kind of disturbance. Certainly it should entertain, but it should really also produce this disturbance.[31]

In a similar vein, Jutta Brückner has stressed that:

We must not just constitute images out of the small banalities of daily life; to do only that is false realism. Rather, we must find new forms to narrate private life, to recognize collective gestures in the most banal ones: for example, the way a wife hands her husband a cup of tea in the morning. To what extent does this collective gesture destroy me because it has nothing to do with me and makes me into a trained dog? I am trying to disrupt the habitual ways in which people see.[32]

By undertaking 'a "vertical" investigation' of what a particular situation 'feels like', each of the four films discussed above can certainly be said to have a 'defamiliarizing' effect. *Germany, Pale Mother* 'defamiliarizes' the way we have come to view the Second World War as a time of death and destruction, and the fifties as a period of prosperity for Germany. *Ticket of No Return* reveals West Berlin as an isolated island in contrast to the way it is popularly thought of as a symbol of western 'freedom'. Von Alemann shows that 'history' is not something which is 'out there' and can be simply documented, while von Trotta 'defamiliarizes' the dominant perception of German terrorists. Each film can also be viewed as complying with Shklovsky's demand that art 'impart the sensation of things as they are perceived and not as they are known'.

At the same time, however – despite their overwhelming rejection of a feminine aesthetic – some directors did also argue that many of their films were in some way specifically 'feminine'. In an interview Marianne Rosenbaum, for instance, asserted: 'I am a feminist and think that *Peppermint Freedom* could never have been made by a man.'[33] Helga Reidemeister also maintained that 'certain films ... could only have been made by a woman',[34] This was not just a subjective impression on the part of the filmmakers, but one which was shared by viewers. When reviewing Sanders-Brahms's *Germany, Pale Mother* Linda Christmas contrasted it with Fassbinder's *Die Ehe der Maria Braun / The Marriage of Maria Braun* (1979), which explores the same period of German history: 'To see the films on consecutive days showed all too clearly that there is indeed a male and a female way with the world.'[35]

When pressed on the subject, several filmmakers felt that the difference between their films and those made by many men stemmed from the way they perceived their surroundings. Indeed, Reidemeister coined the term 'camera eye of a woman'.[36] Although she works as a video artist, Ulrike Rosenbach succinctly summarized these feelings:

[I am] convinced that men have totally different psychic and social imprints to women. That they consequently also have totally different ways of viewing things, but not the only possible or true way. Therefore, of course, women produce different art if they work consciously.[37]

According to Margarethe von Trotta, when women organize or think about their reality 'we do not separate intellect from feeling, big events from little ones ... we make no distinction between the private and the political, between public and personal life.' And she continues:

> We have retained some of the anti-hierarchical perception of matri-archy. In the matriarchal order everyone was equal, because they were all children of mothers. The mother's love was granted unconditionally, you didn't have to earn it through achievement or merit. The patri-archal order introduced the favourite son, he had to earn the father's love through service and obedience. That was the beginning of hier-archical thinking which gave rise to the separating out of individual areas, gradually gave rise to the difference between the public and the private.[38]

The consequence of this is that, women working consciously as women express themselves more associatively than men. With specific reference to the way women remember, Claudia von Alemann argued that 'women remember differently, more metaphorically, associatively, in a more disorderly way... [They] proceed differently than men when they try to remember.'[39] This results in films which, in Ottinger's words, tend to 'show us how something is' rather than what happens.[40] Thus, with regard to her earlier film *Schwestern – oder Die Balance des Glücks / Sisters, or the Balance of Happiness* (1979) von Trotta has observed:

> I think that the manner in which this film is made is perhaps tied to a woman. How the characters and their feelings are portrayed – *the stress lies not in the story but rather in the emotional flow which runs through this story* – is perhaps a specifically feminine manner of expression.[41] (my emphasis)

The 'vertical investigation' of what something feels like, of what it means, which is undertaken in each of the four films discussed above can therefore equally be regarded as a specifically feminine 'way of looking'. Indeed, it is precisely this 'way of looking' that Silvia Bovenschen appears to suggest constitutes a feminine aesthetic. In an article entitled 'Is there a feminine aesthetic?' Bovenschen examines old and new ways of appraising women's artistic capabilities.[42] She explores at some length the way patriarchy has functioned to exclude women from the sphere of artistic production and then used that exclusion to argue that women 'are incapable of art'.[43] When the women's movement eased women's entry into this realm of activity, however, various approaches were adopted in an attempt to describe the products of women's artistic endeavours. Although women were recognized as men's equals and could therefore be equally creative, 'equality' denied for Bovenschen their obvious differences, and could not account for the different kinds of art women were beginning to produce. A different tack was to discuss women's art in terms of a historical female counterculture; but the few women who had managed to work as artists in the past had, according to Bovenschen, been largely absorbed into male traditions. She therefore concluded: 'No matter which tack I take, I am left with the frustrations and difficulties inherent in positive definitions.'[44]

In order to advance her discussion, Bovenschen returned to the fact of women's traditional under-representation in the realm of artistic production. She suggested that women's historical absence as artists could also be evidence of 'a different (female) relationship to detail and generality, to motionlessness and movement, to rhythm and demeanour'. It could indicate that

> women have different assumptions with regard to their sensory approach, their relationship to matter and material, their perception, their experience, their means of processing tactile, visual and acoustic stimuli, their spatial orientation and temporal rhythm.[45]

She stresses that there is no concrete proof that women do actually have a different relationship from men to their surroundings, but maintains that such a difference would produce what can be regarded as 'specifically feminine modes of perception'.[46] Consequently, women artists who consciously work as women would necessarily produce art which differs from male artistic traditions, and this would of course compound their inability to enter the masculine realm of artistic production. Thus Bovenschen answers her own question in the affirmative – yes, there is a feminine aesthetic.

However, she avoids formulating an exact description of what constitutes a feminine aesthetic, precisely because it stems from a mode of perception rather than from a way of *doing*. This means it cannot be reduced to a list of readily identifiable features, or what she terms 'an unusual variant of artistic production'.[47] Nevertheless she does give an indication of what might constitute a feminine aesthetic, or 'a feminine approach to art'[48] by comparing a description of books written by men to one of a woman's writing. She quotes Dorothy Richardson on 'the masculine manner of writing':

> ... the self-satisfied, complacent, know-all condescendingness of their handling of their material.... Bang, bang, bang on they go, these men's books, like an LCC tram, yet unable to make you forget them, the authors for a moment.[49]

In contrast, Virginia Woolf has the following to say of Richardson's own writing:

> She has invented, or, if she has not invented, developed and applied to her own uses, a sentence which we might call the psychological sentence of the feminine gender. It is of a more elastic fibre than the old, capable of stretching to the extreme.... Other writers of the opposite sex have used sentences of this description and stretched them to the extreme. But there is a difference. Miss Richardson has fashioned her sentence *consciously, in order that it may descend to the depths and investigate the crannies of Miriam Henderson's consciousness. It is a woman's sentence, but only in the sense that it is used to describe a woman's mind* by a writer who is neither proud nor afraid of anything that she may discover in the psychology of her sex.[50] (my emphasis)

But both Bovenschen and the filmmakers stress that specifically feminine modes of perception – and by implication a feminine aesthetic – are not biologically determined. They do not emanate from some eternal female essence. Bovenschen regards women's different perceptual modes rather as the inevitable outcome of the very different way most women experience the world as compared to men:

> The exclusion of women from vast areas of production and the public sphere has directed women's imagination along other lines, not to speak of women's responsibility for the biological and social reproduction of the species, as well as the economic, if they are working.[51]

In a similar vein, when Jutta Brückner discussed her film *Laufen lernen/Learning to Run* (1980) about a forty-year-old housewife and mother of two who starts to re-evaluate her life, she asserted:

> I think a housewife has a different perception of space and time to – well, especially to men, but also to women who work and who spend a lot of time outside the home.[52]

Thus, it is possible to argue that the concept of 'defamiliarization' and the notion of a 'feminine aesthetic' are in fact two ways of discussing the same phenomenon. Despite the reservations expressed by the filmmakers, it would appear that the concept of a feminine aesthetic can in fact offer an equally, if not more, productive approach to their work. Rather than attempting categorically to define or delineate women's filmmaking, the concept can be viewed as a critical framework which permits the acknowledgement of a common element that stems from the specifics of women's experience without obfuscating the very diverse nature of the kinds of films being made.

SIX

A Change of Direction

During the 1980s the situation of women filmmakers in West Germany undoubtedly improved. Whereas in the seventies Helke Sander and others had complained bitterly about the way institutional sexism had prevented them from pursuing their careers, *Frauen und Film* editor Karola Gramann could state in 1990 that women's projects are no longer rejected because of their subject matter or because the director is a woman.[1] By the early 1980s a significant number of women had established themselves as directors, and as the decade progressed a few also started to gain access to far bigger budgets than had previously been possible. For her film *Rosa Luxemburg* (1985) Margarethe von Trotta secured a budget of DM6 million, while Ulrike Ottinger raised DM3.5 million for *Johanna d'Arc of Mongolia* (1989). Although these sums are relatively small by Hollywood standards, they are more in line with the budgets the West German industry was allocating to commercial films during the mid eighties.[2]

Younger women, such as Doris Dörrie and Pia Frankenberg, have also found it considerably easier to establish themselves as film directors. Born in 1955, Dörrie had a documentary treatment accepted by Bavarian Television while still at film school in Munich. Her graduation film, *Der erste Walzer/ The First Waltz* (1978) was selected for two major German film festivals (Hof and Berlin), and subsequently broadcast by Bavarian television. After leaving film school she made a string of documentaries and feature films for various television stations, including *Dazwischen/In Between* (1981). Such were the audience ratings for the latter that a German television company decided to back her first cinema feature, *Mitten ins Herz/Straight Through the Heart* (1983). Reflecting upon her career Dörrie – in direct contrast to most women of Sander's generation – has asserted: 'All in all I have been treated very well.'[3]

Born in 1957, Pia Frankenberg came to directing by the path of co-producing, writing and assistant directing. Although she has made only two features to date (after initially experimenting with shorts), her first, *Nicht nichts ohne dich/Not Nothing Without You* (1985), is a comedy and suggests that she experienced none of the problems Sander elucidates in *Die allseitig reduzierte Persönlichkeit/The All-round Reduced Personality – Redupers* (1977). There are in fact some quite startling similarities between the two films – both are filmed in black and white, both directors play themselves, and both films explore the life of a female character in her work and as a single parent. However, the similarity ends there. Whereas Sander's character, Edda, was beset with financial problems and found the demands of single parenthood taxing, Frankenberg's character, Marthe, is successful and lives quite comfortably. While for Edda life was a constant battle for survival, Marthe's easy life has made her neurotic, with her main worry being whether she has become superficial. With Frankenberg's humorous approach – especially her ability to laugh at herself – and in view of Marthe's neurosis, many critics have compared her to Woody Allen.[4]

Despite these success stories, some of the difficulties experienced in the 1970s persisted into the eighties. In fact, in 1985 two feminist film critics maintained that seventeen years after the birth of the new women's movement 'sexism, in the film sector as elsewhere, has basically not changed'.[5] More recently, in 1989, a group of young women filmmakers called Trick 17 found themselves reiterating many of the complaints made by their older colleagues in the late seventies:

> We don't find our situation as women in the film sector very easy. From time to time we get the impression that it is difficult to be taken seriously. We have to work harder than men to prove the seriousness and quality of our work. In addition to the external resistance there are the private difficulties with personal partners.[6]

As one of the still relatively few women who sit on film festival selection committees, even Karola Gramann concedes that in many respects attitudes to women's work have not changed so very much:

> I try to look at women's work carefully and with patience, because some of the women's films are different, so you have to look closely ... and I found myself in the position where my colleagues would say, 'Oh well, there's a film for Karola' ... and I got really mad at one point and I said, 'Maybe you should look at the films, not me.' ... What I am trying to say is that I think that a lot of work still needs to be done.[7]

Some women have also continued to experience difficulties in securing funding for their projects. Marianne Rosenbaum's script for her film *Peppermint Frieden / Peppermint Freedom* (1983) was turned down for funding by the Bavarian Film Promotion agency, the FFA and the BMI. In order to attract financing she had to form her own production company with her collaborator Gerard Saman, a tax consultant and a lawyer, and persuade Peter Fonda to star in the film. They were then able to find backers willing to invest in the project for tax purposes. Even a well-established director like Helma Sanders-Brahms found it difficult to fund her film *Flügel und Fesseln / The Future of Emily* (1984). The project was eventually realized with the help of French money, the actors agreeing to work for very little payment. In the late eighties Monika Treut had enormous difficulties raising money for her lesbian coming-out story *Die Jungfrauen Maschine / The Virgin Machine* (1988). After rewriting the script three times she managed to obtain a miniscule budget of DM322,000 from the Hamburg Film Office and the Hamburg television station.

However, during the eighties there have been changes in the film subsidy system which have exacerbated the persisting effects of institutional sexism. Throughout the seventies Germany's social-democratic party, the SPD, remained in power with support of the Free Democratic Party (FDP). In 1982, however, the FDP switched sides to support the right-wing CDU/CSU and in doing so forced an election which returned the CDU/CSU to power. The most far-reaching consequence of this change in government for the film sector has been the subsequent appointment of Friedrich Zimmermann as Minister of the Interior. He has attempted to assume absolute control over how funds for film projects are allocated and has demonstrated his overwhelming preference for big budget, commercially orientated, Hollywood-style 'entertainment' films to the detriment of all other types of filmmaking: 'The taxpayer does not wish to be provoked, he wants to be entertained.'[8] The more experimental and innovative filmmakers, both male and female, have been the obvious and most immediate casualties of such a film policy. During Zimmermann's first year in office he withdrew aid already awarded to Herbert Achternbusch's *Das Gespenst/ The Ghost* (1983) and refused a subsidy for the filmmaker's project *Der Wanderkrebs/ The Wandering Cancer* (1984). Among the first women to suffer were Elfi Mikesch and Monika Treut, who also had BMI funding withdrawn from their film *Verführung: die grausame Frau/ Seduction: The Cruel Women* (1984–85) shortly after it had been awarded. The project was eventually realized on a modest budget of DM380,000 raised via regional funding initiatives.

However, this has also meant that filmmakers have found it increasingly difficult to secure financing for any projects of socio-political or cultural significance, and that such projects frequently manage to attract only low-budget funding. Although Ottinger succeeded in raising substantial finance for *Johanna d'Arc of Mongolia* (1989), it took her over three years to do so. The net effect of this revised film policy has been to erode the subsidy system that enabled the critically acclaimed New German Cinema to emerge. Indeed, innumerable critics and filmmakers have agreed that the era of the New German Cinema is now over.[9] Such claims have of course been fuelled by a number of filmmakers leaving Germany during the eighties to work abroad and by the emergence of the pan-European co-production as a means of financing the ever-increasing costs of feature film production.

The changed situation in the eighties has equally had consequences for West Germany's feminist film culture. The combination of improved professional opportunities for women filmmakers and diminishing state support for a culturally motivated cinema, together with the general improvement in women's position in society, have functioned effectively to dissipate it. Admittedly, initiatives such as *Frauen und Film* and the *Verband der Filmarbeiterinnen* have remained intact, and a number of films continue to be made which explore the workings of patriarchal ideology. Among these is Helke Sander's latest film, *Die Deutschen und ihre Männer/ The Germans and Their Men* (1990), a semi-documentary about a woman who goes to Bonn in search of a husband. The film's fictional character interviews real politicians and people on the street to highlight the way German men accept responsibility for and are ashamed of their German history, but do not accept the same responsibility for the way men treat women. Although Sander sees and wittily draws a highly illuminating parallel here, the men interviewed clearly distinguish between the two as totally separate areas: one is political while the other is purely personal. As if to confirm Gramann's assertion that attitudes towards women's film work have also not changed a great deal, Sander includes footage of Chancellor Helmut Kohl refusing to be interviewed for the film. The viewer cannot help but wonder if he would have reacted in the same way had be been confronted with a male director and film crew.

Although vestiges of the vibrant feminist film culture that emerged at the end of the seventies are still in evidence, in the course of the eighties it has nevertheless largely given way to two broad, polarized trends. One is considered by many to be 'totally devoid of feminist polemic',[10] while the other could be loosely described as 'post-feminist'.

Firstly, as professional opportunities for women improved in the film sector, an increasing number of women started to work within mainstream cinema. This is not to suggest that women directors necessarily 'went commercial' – indeed, very few films by women have made money – but several started to make feature films that adhered more closely to the conventions of mainstream cinema. Although a substantial number of the films continued to focus on female protagonists, they did not – in view of the revised film policy – demonstrate the deep concern with socio-political questions or pursue the 'quest for alternative images and counter-representations' that characterized much of the New German Cinema. Consequently, they have on the whole aroused far less interest than the critically acclaimed women's cinema of the late seventies and early eighties.

Ingemo Enström is one of the directors whose recent work forms part of this first trend. Based on Klaus Mann's novel *Journey into Freedom*, her film *Flucht in den Norden/Flight North* (1985) is set in 1933 and begins with Johanna, a young German woman, arriving in Finland after she has fled the spectre of Nazism. She is met by a woman friend and they indulge in a brief passionless affair. Johanna is then taken to stay at the family estate of a friend, where she embarks on a far more passionate affair with landowner Ragnar. After a few days she and Ragnar set off on a journey that takes them across the endless and timeless expanses of Finland. As they travel further and further north, Johanna finds herself increasingly removed from the political reality of her opposition to Nazism. When they eventually reach the Polar Sea, Johanna decides she must return to Germany.

Although the film purports to address the question of political responsibility, the process by which Johanna comes to her decision mainly comprises innumerable sex scenes between her and Ragnar, interspersed with shots of breathtakingly beautiful landscapes and sunsets and accompanied by very little dialogue. This repetitiveness proved too much for at least one critic at the film's premiere at the 1986 Berlin Film Festival: 'After I had seen the fourth or fifth sunset – sometimes accompanied by the sound of a flute, sometimes not – I left the cinema.'[11] The sex and sunset scenes dominate the film to such an extent that rather than exploring the issue of political responsibility, the film can only be said to use it as a flimsy excuse for making an 'arty' film about heterosexual love.

Furthermore, the film tends to reinforce the dominant perception of heterosexuality as the 'norm' rather than offer lesbianism as a serious alternative. Having initially responded to her woman friend's sexual advances, Johanna then rejects and avoids her. The actual affair serves no narrative purpose and appears to have been included in the film only so that the option of lesbian sexuality could be rejected in favour of heterosexuality. Furthermore, the contrast between lesbian sex as passionless and straight sex as extremely passionate suggests that heterosexual love is a far more satisfying or worthwhile experience. Indeed, in certain scenes Johanna is thrown into an instant state of sexual pleasure as soon as Ragnar penetrates her.

Alexandra von Grote's *Novembermond/November Moon* (1984) fared slightly better with the critics and in fact proved popular among some audiences because of its highly sympathetic representation of a lesbian relationship. The film opens in Berlin in 1939. The Jewish daughter of a well-known political cartoonist, a young woman called November, decides to leave for Paris. There she finds work in a café run by a woman who had been her father's lover in the 1920s. The woman's son falls in love with November, but November falls for his sister, Ferial, who reciprocates. When war is declared Ferial and her mother send

November to stay with some relations in the country. November is, however, discovered by the occupying Germans and taken to work in a Nazi brothel. She escapes and returns to Ferial in Paris, who hides her in her flat for the rest of the war. In order to divert suspicion Ferial does secretarial work for the Nazi Information Department. Although she succeeds in protecting November, her neighbours denounce her as a collaborator and eventually publicly humiliate her by shaving her head.

Since it is set during the Nazi era – albeit in France rather than Germany – von Grote's film invites comparison with other women's films which locate their protagonists in or reference that period of German history. Films such as Helma Sanders-Brahms's *Germany, Pale Mother* (1979–80) and Margarethe von Trotta's *The German Sisters* (1981), however, use their protagonists to comment on the experience of living through certain periods of German history and to foreground how personal history informs contemporary reality (see chapter five). Consequently, each film in some way 'stands for the human condition in general'.[12] In marked contrast, von Grote's film uses the historical period merely as a colourful background against which to explore love between two women. It offers no useful insight into the experience of living in Nazi-occupied France. Indeed, English language publicity material for the film described it as 'a love story of two women caught up in the chaos and the turmoil *that war can bring.*' (my emphasis) The fact that it is the Second World War, the fact of November's racial origins and her father's political sympathies are incidental. They simply function to heighten the dramatic tension against which the love story is played out and as impediments to be overcome in the course of true love. As a result, videomaker Ulrike Zimmermann argues that all the film does is to state: 'There are lesbians and they're beautiful.'[13] For the little the film actually says about lesbian sexuality – despite its sympathetic portrayal of the relationship – November and Ferial could easily be replaced by a heterosexual couple.

In marked contrast to her earlier work, the last three films of Margarethe von Trotta have also met with little critical acclaim. *Rosa Luxemburg* (1985) explores the life of the eponymous political radical committed to the ideal of socialist democracy who co-founded the German Communist Party in 1918. After an abortive left-wing revolution in 1919, Luxemburg and her close associate Karl Liebknecht were brutally murdered by remnants of the German Imperial army. The film attempts to depict both the development of Rosa's passionate political engagement *and* her family background, together with the trials and tribulations of her later private life. It not only shows her making speeches at political gatherings, how she was imprisoned during the First World War for her ardent pacifist beliefs, and her reluctant participation in the 1919 revolution which she judged premature, but also includes flashbacks to her childhood, focuses on her long affair with Leo Jogiches and reveals a subsequent shortlived affair with the much younger son of a friend. According to von Trotta this latter affair was a well-kept secret and she only stumbled upon its existence accidentally when wading through over two thousand of Luxemburg's letters in the course of her research. Although the film won the prize for best film in the 1986 Federal film awards, it suffers from over-ambitious aims. By trying to offer an all-encompassing look at Luxemburg's life, von Trotta has produced a rather confusingly episodic bio-pic which fails to fully explore the role Luxemburg played in German history.

In her two most recent productions, *Paura e amore/ Three Sisters* (1988) and *L'Africana/ The Return* (1990), von Trotta has left the realms of German history altogether. The former is set in Italy and is about three sisters – 'a Chekhov's *Three Sisters* for nowadays' according to the director.[14] The eldest, Valia, is a literature academic who embarks on an affair with Massimo, a married science professor. Massimo, however, soon throws Valia over for her sister Maria, who is married to Frederico, a television comedian. The youngest sister, Sandra, is still a student, studying to become a doctor of medicine. Although the film sets up a tension between art and science, suggesting the former possesses eternal values of some kind which science in the form of nuclear technology and television threatens but cannot totally destroy, this sub-plot remains undeveloped. Rather, the film concentrates with depressing seriousness on the emotional agonies to which the various characters subject each other, the deceptions they practice, and their inability to find real happiness.

The Return, set in Paris, also focuses on the relationship between three people – this time, two women and a man. Anna is in hospital with an unspecified but life-threatening illness. She persuades her husband, Michel, to write to her friend Marthe who is working in

Africa and ask her to return to Paris. Marthe arrives and as the film unfolds we discover that she and Anna used to be lovers. After they split up Marthe met Michel, who in turn fell in love with and married Anna. Anna now believes that her illness is a form of punishment for hurting Marthe by taking Michel away from her. As this film also examines the way its characters hurt each other, swap partners and are unable to satisfactorily resolve their situation, it is almost as if von Trotta has simply refilmed *Three Sisters*, changing the names. Both films are Italian, French and West German co-productions and can be regarded as prime examples of projects which, by trying to transcend cultural and national boundaries, have become totally characterless. Suzi Feay's description of *Three Sisters* adequately describes them both: 'It's a Euro production: multi-lingual cast puréed in a blender and poured out like glop.'[15]

A notable exception to this rather depressing trend has been Doris Dörrie's comedy *Männer/Men* (1985). The film explores the lives of two apparently different men, both in their mid thirties: Julius, a married and highly successful designer who is having an affair with his secretary, and Stephan, a graphic designer who prefers to work in a fast-food restaurant than become a corporate executive – in short, a hippy drop-out. Stephan is having an affair with Julius's wife Paula. When Julius finds out about his wife's affair, he ends his own affair and 'drops out' himself in order to find out why Paula is attracted to Stephan. Concealing his real identity, Julius befriends Stephan and moves into his communal flat. Gradually, however, Julius takes Stephan in hand, smartens him up and gets him a 'proper' job with an advertising company. As Stephan becomes a carbon copy of Julius, the affair with Paula goes stale and eventually Julius returns home to resume his life with Paula.

Although Dörrie's film, like those of Engström, von Grote and von Trotta discussed above, deals with personal relationships, it is by contrast an amusing send-up of very familiar male behaviour. At the same time, it focuses specifically on Germany's 1968 generation. As Dörrie asserts: 'I wanted to know what happened to those people, how they established themselves, what they do now.'[16] The director conducted fieldwork, eavesdropping on men's conversations to find out; and the film suggests that the youngsters of 1968 traded rebellion in for an easy life of conformity. Stephan may have retained a 'drop-out' image but, as Dörrie observes, he quickly adapts to the new yuppie lifestyle that Julius offers him: 'It's easy for Julius to change him because Stephan's leftist ideas are all surface. He doesn't believe them anymore. He dreams about Porsches.'[17]

To the surprise of all those involved in the production, including Dörrie herself, *Men* met with both critical and box-office success. The German press acclaimed the film for its 'enrapturing charm and disarmingly funny dialogue, comparable with classics like Billy Wilder and Ernst Lubitsch'.[18] According to Dörrie, the film even appealed to the left press: 'I was surprised that the left press in Germany didn't come down on *Men*. They seemed relieved that Stephan admits he likes fancy cars. They were enchanted.'[19]

Initially released in twenty prints, the number in distribution quickly rose to 230 to meet audience demand. *Men* became the most successful German film of 1986 with just under five million admissions on the domestic market. It was the first film by a woman to enjoy this kind of box-office success since May Spils's *Zur Sache Schätzchen/ Go to it, Baby* (1967). (Despite winning the award for best film in 1986, von Trotta's *Rosa Luxemburg* (1985) attracted a total audience of only 519,000.) Dörrie's film also managed to repeat its success in the US. On its first day of opening in New York, it took over ten million dollars; 'on a day,' according to one appreciative critic, 'it rained so hard you were crazy to go out.'[20]

Men also signalled the introduction of humour into women's filmmaking. In reviewing von Trotta's earlier work, one critic made a comment that would be equally applicable to many of her female colleagues: 'There is ... an unnerving absence of humour.'[21] In contrast by the late eighties several women directors had turned, if not to outright comedy, then at least to low-key humour. Pia Frankenberg's *Not Nothing Without You* (1985), discussed earlier, was released in the same year as Dörrie's film. The following year Verena Rudolph made *Francesca* (1986), a spoof bio-pic, which purports to document the life of Francesca, a foundling child who rose to stardom and fame in cultural and religious circles. Francesca is, however, entirely fictional and this allows Rudolph to make the most outrageous claims for her character – ranging from screen goddess to miracle-working saint – and to have a total disregard for plausibility. In 1987 von Trotta, Helke Sander and Helma Sanders-Brahms also made their first foray into comedy with *Felix* (1987), a so-called episode film, co-directed with Christel Buschmann. The film follows the wanderings of Felix, a 'new man' in his thirties, after his girlfriend walks out on him. Each director directs a segment of the film, bringing her own distinctive style to bear, and producing a humorous, gently paced exploration of social interaction in the late eighties.

However, none of these films managed to make the mark that *Men* did. Indeed, the success of Dörrie's film has made it something of a critical yardstick against which to measure other films by women. Given its similar focus, *Felix* has been almost universally appraised in comparison with *Men*, usually negatively. One critic, for instance, maintained that he would 'rather see Doris Dörrie's *Men* twice than *Felix* once',[22] while another asserted:

> I can't dispel the impression that with *Felix* the four [women directors] are struggling in the shadow of another German woman director who has won unaccustomed popularity for the German film: Doris Dörrie.[23]

The other broad trend that emerged in women's filmmaking during the eighties was the explicit exploration of women's sexuality. This work grew out of a desire to construct a self-determined female identity, and has generated a debate around the notion of a women's erotic cinema. Since this was very much concerned with a 'quest for alternative images and counter-representations', it has succeeded in attracting only low-budget funding or has been financed from the film-makers' personal resources.

As the women's movement began to win recognition for the principle of equal rights for women and to achieve some political reform, women working in film and other areas of cultural production started to identify the earlier emphasis on acknowledging and fore-grounding women's authentic experiences as reactive:

> A case of reacting to what 'they' say about us, how 'they' represent us, i.e. from the image of the *femme fatale* of classical Hollywood narrative cinema to the exploitative objectifications of women's bodies to sell consumer products. . . . There is a sense in which this 'other' image of us has negated our own visions (of ourselves), stopped us from seeing ourselves in the ways in which we might possibly like to, perhaps the way in which we could fantasize.[24]

Having examined the way in which women experience patriarchy, a number of filmmakers therefore moved on to try to formulate what they, as women, wanted in its place; to construct a self-determined female identity. One or two isolated women filmmakers had in fact already highlighted the fact that this second step was a crucial element in any campaign for women's emancipation. The research that Ula Stöckl carried out for her film *Neun Leben hat die Katze / The Cat has Nine Lives* (1968) led her to preface the film with the statement: 'Women have never had so many opportunities to organize their lives themselves. But first they have to learn that they have the ability to want.'[25]

In *Madame X – Eine absolute Herrscherin / Madame X – An Absolute Ruler* (1977) Ulrike Ottinger also suggested that equal rights were of little use if women had not formulated their own wants. A lesbian tyrant who sails a Chinese junk, Madame X sends a message to all women promising them gold, love and adventure on the high seas. In a highly stylized, anti-realist narrative seven women throw up their conventional lives and jobs to join her. By constructing Madame X as a tyrant who paradoxically promises freedom, however, Ottinger demonstrates that simply being given the opportunity to do something does not necessarily result in emancipation. Indeed the director has asserted: 'The leitmotif throughout the film is about the prohibition imposed on women to make their own experiences.'[26] Rather than embarking upon new lives on Madame X's junk, the women eventually end up reproducing the traditional hierarchical patterns of behaviour from which they were trying to escape. As power relations, jealousies and discontentment intensify, the adventure ends in death for all the women who were seduced by Madame X's promises.

It was only during the early eighties, however, that a significant number of women filmmakers actually started to explore the question of female identity. To do this, as Birgit Hein explains, they returned to women's sexuality, an area which women video/performance artists such as Valie Export and Ulrike Rosenbach had begun to explore a decade earlier:

> The worst form of oppression which women have to suffer is their sexuality. The repression goes so deep that many women even willingly relinquish their sexuality. To win back desire, to show it in its total diversity and to break existing taboos is for me the most important task for contemporary women artists.[27]

Since the patriarchal order constructs women's sexuality as essentially 'passive', filmmakers such as Hein and Monika Treut have argued that what patriarchy fundamentally represses in women is their aggression. Treut, for instance, has observed: 'I was thinking about images of women, about what images are most suppressed or repressed, and it was the image of the cruel woman.'[28] For Hein, the fact that some feminists have argued that aggression is an emotion totally alien to women is an indication of how successful patriarchy has been in this repression.[29] In order to 'win back desire' several filmmakers therefore rejected the image of the 'gentle' woman, as they termed her, that had characterized much feminist filmmaking and is typified in the work of Margarethe von Trotta. Treut, for instance, asserted:

> Today ... we're in the fortunate position of having a whole range of images of women.... But that doesn't mean that we like all of them. One, for instance, that we absolutely can't bear is that of the loving and kind women's relationship which has above all plagued the German film. Even if women were always so understanding and nice to one another! Women can be just as mean and nasty, especially the gentle ones.[30]

As the image of the 'cruel woman' is an important figure in the work of de Sade and Sacher-Masoch a number of filmmakers turned initially to portraying the practice of sado-masochism, an avenue of exploration which has proved highly controversial in feminist circles. For those factions denying the possibility of female aggression, the aggressor-victim nature of the relationship between those involved makes it a patriarchal discourse and hence one that necessarily precludes the possibility of female emancipation. According to some theorists, even if a woman becomes the aggressor, 'she is not cruel for her own sake, or for her own gratification.'[31] It has also been deemed highly censorable because sado-masochism is generally regarded as a form of sexual violence, like rape. However, Treut maintains that to reduce sado-masochism to the practice of sexual violence against an unwilling victim is to misunderstand the sado-masochistic universe. For her this neglects the possibility of sexual pleasure and personal expression that can arise from 'playing' with feelings of power and helplessness. Having studied the writings of both de Sade and Sacher-Masoch for her dissertation, Treut argues:

For me it's not about real brutality.... I'm interested in the liberating possibility of a game which appropriates images and projections of cruel women in order to draw pleasure and sovereignty from them.[32]

In this context, Treut and others view sado-masochism more as an art form which, like other art forms, offers the possibility of personal expression. In 1983 Treut filmed an interview with Carol, a member of New York's lesbian subculture, who explains these ideas further:

I'm doing S/M for a lot of years, but not calling it S/M, playing dominant and submissive games, dressing up, spanking, bondage.... When I put someone in bondage, it's sort of an art form for me. S/M is an art form. It's very creative. I identify as a top, but I'm switchable, so that sometimes I'm submissive. When I'm depressed, hurting about something, I have a friend put me into bondage and it makes me feel a lot better, makes me feel very safe. And if I put someone in bondage I take great care for their comfort and their well-being, not only their physical, but their emotional well-being. S/M is communication and really getting into people's emotions.[33]

One of the first films to draw on sado-masochism and one that clearly uses the practice for its 'liberating' possibilities was Elfi Mikesch's *Das Frühstück der Hyäne/ The Hyena's Breakfast* (1983). Beautifully filmed in black and white, this short, poetic film focuses on Maria, a woman who has left her male lover. She finds, however, that she cannot escape his attempts to control her life just by leaving him. As she enters her flat at the beginning of the film she finds a message from him on her answerphone: 'Maria, can you hear me? It's me, why don't you ring me? You know that I'm waiting for you to call.' After getting herself a drink she returns his call. Instead of talking to him, however, she leaves the handset dangling so that his voice forms the soundtrack of the film. By turns he pleads with her to come back, accuses her of cruelty and capriciousness, and suggests she needs him, that she has 'strayed' and that her rightful place is with him:

Why won't you come back, what's the matter? ... When you went away from me – I never imagined that you'd be crazy enough not to come back. I guess it's one of your caprices or fantasies or whatever.... It's cruel what you're doing. Your cruelty is beyond limits. You're ruining your life – through your own cruelty.... You have to confess, at least to me, that what you have done is thoughtless.... I'm ready to take responsibility for you. I completely forgive you. I told my mother that I've devoted my life to the sole purpose of bringing you back to the right path.

As her ex-lover's voice pervades the room, Maria roams around the flat, first pacing up and down, then sitting down, then getting up again only to flop down again on the sofa or bed. Mikesch's use of atmospheric lighting, her relentlessly mobile camerawork and abrupt editing combine with Maria's restlessness to create a sense of tension. Although she has left her lover, it is as if part of her is still powerless to resist his domination of her. Eventually Maria picks up a scarf and starts playing with it. She ties it round her head, gagging her mouth, but spits it out. Then she ties her ankles together with a belt, laughing as she does so. With her ankles still bound Maria starts to play with some ropes and begins to playfully whip herself over her shoulder as she fantasizes about another woman clad from head to toe in leather. Eventually the voice of Maria's ex-lover falls silent. Afterwards there is a knock at the door and as Maria opens it her fantasy woman enters.

By replacing Maria's ex-male lover with a new female lover – whether real or fantasy – the film tends towards the simplistic suggestion that lesbian sexuality will solve the problems Maria encountered in her heterosexual relationship. However, when Maria indulges in her sado-masochistic fantasy or 'game' she is completely alone. Mikesch appears to be suggesting therefore that Maria is symbolically acting out the oppression she knows she will experience if she gives into the demands she hears her ex-lover making on the phone. By acting out that oppression on herself Maria effectively places herself rather than her ex-lover in control of her life, since she is controlling what happens to her body. She therefore wins her autonomy and achieves the possibility of formulating her own sexual identity. The leather-clad woman that Maria welcomes into her flat at the end of the film can thus be regarded as symbolizing freedom of choice, rather than the actual choice itself.

Mikesch explored these ideas again and developed them further in her next film, *Verführung: Die grausame Frau / Seduction: The Cruel Woman* (1984–85), which she co-directed with Monika Treut. A feature-length film, *Seduction* is about a pleasure palace run by Wanda, a professional tyrant, somewhere in the Hamburg docklands. Using a highly episodic narrative, the film follows Wanda through various encounters with her paying admirers and faithful servants. The film also charts the initiation of Wanda's 'innocent' American lover, Justine, into the sado-masochistic universe. On the night of her arrival at the beginning of the film she is given a guided tour of the pleasure place and its 'toys'. Initially horrified, Justine gradually becomes fascinated and then begins to participate.

Although there are a few brief moments when Mikesch and Treut show either mental torture or physical pain being inflicted by one person on another, there is very little actual sex or nudity in *Seduction* and no final act of total domination-submission. Instead the film constantly foregrounds the pleasure palace as a place where a paying public can go and act out or see acted out their sexual fantasies. In one scene, for instance, a man and two women act out a scene of whipping in a room for a man who pays them to do so and then sits and watches. At times Wanda and members of her entourage stage tableaux while an audience watches. On yet another occasion, we see Wanda playing back a videotape of herself taunting a man while she talks direct to camera, commenting on what is happening in the tape. The acting in much of the film is also very theatrical, with the characters often consciously posing as if deliberately to create a particular image for someone else's gratification. Some sequences are more like filmed performance pieces than scenes from a feature film. Consequently, rather than offering what one critic terms 'hard-core action',[34] *Seduction* explores sado-masochism as a form of role playing or theatre. Indeed, in one scene Justine complains to Wanda that she can no longer play the role of nurse because she hates role playing and hates wearing white. As if to underline the representational nature of sado-masochism still further, Mikesch and Treut frequently use mirrors to film the reflection of a character, rather than the actual character.

By showing the theatrical nature of the practices indulged in at Wanda's pleasure palace, the film constructs the participants as consenting individuals. As such, they are motivated by their own desire, and Justine's initiation can be regarded as representing an 'awakening' of her sexual desires. By highlighting the need for consent and sexual desire to be present if sado-masochistic practices are to be pleasurable, *Seduction*, like Mikesch's earlier film, represents sado-masochism as a means of realizing a self-determined sexuality, of exercising control over one's own body.

As if to silence possible critics of this argument, Treut has pointed to the actual experience of viewing the film. She asserts that the film itself functions like classic masochist desire. By refusing to show the 'hard-core action' one might expect to see in a film about sado-masochism, *Seduction* arouses a desire in its audience and then indefinitely post-pones its fulfilment.[35] As a result, we, the film's audience not only watch but are drawn into and experience the sado-masochistic universe. Furthermore, having paid to see and remaining to watch the film, we can be said to participate in that universe of our own volition and thus remain in control of our situation.

The implication of the audience in this way obviously suggests that we all have sado-masochistic desires and fantasies of some kind even though we may not necessarily realize them by indulging in sado-masochistic practices. However, on occasions the film also deliberately blurs the boundary between fantasy and reality. In response to Justine's complaint about playing a nurse, for instance, Wanda asserts she is *not* in fact role playing but *is* a nurse. Towards the end of the film Wanda also enters a room full of mirrors. As she wanders between the mirrors her reflection is itself reflected and re-reflected, so that it becomes unclear which image is the real Wanda. This suggests that even if we do not realize our fantasies they nevertheless inform our 'real' or daily lives. This implies that for women the appropriation of the image of the cruel women in their fantasy lives can also have liberating possibilities. Indeed, according to one of the film's few appreciative critics, *Seduction* suggests that:

> [women] can fantasize without going further; and that by doing so, they might be granting themselves a freedom unhindered by the limits of their bodies or the boundaries of their consciences.[36]

The film can therefore be regarded as a fantasy rather than a represen-tation of sado-masochistic practices, a fantasy which makes its audience aware of certain aspects of their own desire.

Another film which explores the liberating possibilities of sado-masochism is Cleo Übelmann's *Mano Destra* (1985). Filmed in black and white, this short primarily comprises a series of tableaux of a woman, dressed in a skin-tight bodice and high heels, bound in various positions in a large, white, empty room. Occasionally another woman, a 'dominatrix' figure dressed in a leather jacket and cap, appears in order to put the 'victim' into bondage. The camera is always static and the eye is drawn to the bound woman since she occupies centre frame and is positioned against a featureless background. Each shot of her also lasts far longer than is necessary for the eye to register the image. This allows the viewer to dwell on the image of the bound woman and absorb details such as how neatly and carefully her bonds are tied, the pristine whiteness of the ropes, the doubled-up position of her body and the way she gently flexes her muscles within her bonds. As the camera persists in an unrelenting gaze, the sense of restriction becomes almost palpable.

The woman is not, however, simply tied up, but bound in a manner which makes her body appear very angular; her face is usually turned away from the camera. This has the effect of transforming her into a sort of human sculpture, an art object. The black-and-white film stock compounds this by emphasizing the contrast between her black bodice and the white ropes to make the images visually stunning. The process of viewing the film therefore becomes like looking at a painting or photograph. As if to confirm Übelmann views sado-masochism as an art form, there is a sequence where the 'dominatrix', dressed in ordinary clothes, is hanging framed photos of her bound 'victim' on a wall. However, the bound woman is not a passive object, displayed solely for the viewer's consumption. In one scene she is shown inspecting the bondage equipment before her partner ties her up, which suggests she is in control of her situation. Indeed, the scene is reminiscent of an escape artist or circus performer checking his or her equipment before performing some death-defying act. Furthermore, she glances at the camera while performing her inspection, as if to make sure the audience understands that she, not the viewer, is in control.

Like *Seduction, Mano Destra* does not fulfil audience expectations of what a film about sado-masochism will be like. At no point during the film does the 'dominatrix' act aggressively towards or exercise real power over her partner. She appears to be there only to assist the other woman, not to dominate her. Indeed, they very rarely appear in frame together – we may see part of the 'dominatrix's' arm or leg as she ties her 'victim' up, but that is all. However, the prolonged shots, combined with the noise of insistent, banging footsteps on the sound-track, do produce a sense of extreme tension and discomfort. At some screenings of the film this has proved unbearable for a number of viewers and resulted in screams from the audience.[37] It is as if, by voluntarily subjecting herself to bondage, the 'victim' is winning back control of her body by denying her audience any pleasure from her body as visual spectacle.

Although these films succeeded in generating some debate around female desire, pornography and eroticism, the interest in sado-masochism has waned during the course of the decade. *Seduction* and *Mano Destra* rapidly became cult films for a lesbian sub-culture both in Germany and abroad, but sado-masochism appears to have had a limited potential for exploring and formulating a general self-deter-mined female identity. Nevertheless, the concern with female identity is still very much in evidence and attention has remained focused on women's sexuality. Continuing the exploration of women's capacity for aggression, some films, such as Birgit and Wilhelm Hein's collage film *Kali-Filme/The Kali Films* (1987–88), have dealt with women's actual violence.[38] Although Birgit Hein finds the cruel woman image in *Seduction* interesting, she nevertheless argues that:

> the aggression is institutionalized … there are men who come to their place, they want to have their dominatrix. The aggressiveness in *Die grausame Frau* is not strong enough, not subversive enough in my opinion. It still belongs to the codes, to the way … it doesn't go further than the broad acceptance. … It's a very nice film, I like it as a film, but some parts of it are also too picturesque. I would say that *Die grausame Frau* is not enough![39]

The Heins' *Kali Films* comprise nine segments, all of which deal with fantasies about sexuality and violence that are largely taboo in dominant western culture. One segment in particular, however, focuses on women's aggression by editing together clips from horror movies and women's prison films. It begins with women prisoners, often semi-naked, attacking and fighting with fellow female prisoners, moves on to clips showing women rioting and attacking their female guards, and climaxes with women using guns, knives and other sharp instruments to attack, penetrate, castrate and kill men. The segment becomes an orgy of blood, sexual aggression and unrelenting violence. Although some critics have argued that 'the images arouse a powerful sense of women taking power, "fighting back",'[40] many women viewers have also been appalled and unwilling to believe that women could possibly be so violent. Hein herself admits that at first she was not interested in the women's prison films, but asserts that what eventually drew her to them was the fact that they did not correspond to 'official' representations of women. In addition to the unusual sight of women being extremely aggressive, they offer a rare representation of women as sexually confident, self-assured and challenging. Although many women may have as much trouble identifying with or 'recognizing' the Heins' images of violent women as Treut does with von Trotta's gentle women, for Birgit Hein they nevertheless offer a means of expanding the way women are represented in dominant culture.

Adopting another tack altogether, Monika Treut's first solo feature, *The Virgin Machine* (1988), is a humorous lesbian coming-out story. Beautifully filmed in black and white, it is about Dorothee, a Hamburg journalist who is investigating romantic love. She watches couples sitting on the river bank, even using binoculars to get a closer look, and takes photographs of them. Although she interviews people and writes about it as well, romantic love is nevertheless absent from her own relationship with her boyfriend Hans. Dissatisfied, Dorothee starts to look elsewhere and the film hints at a sexual relationship with her brother. Failing to find what she is looking for in Germany, Dorothee departs for San Francisco where she meets Susie Sexpert, an authority on and active participant in the city's gay sub-culture. Susie introduces Dorothee to San Francisco's lesbian sex industry: a world of dykes on bikes, all-women strip shows, dildoes of all shapes and sizes, lesbian call-girl services and the like. Dorothee also spies on a couple who occupy the hotel room next to hers and indulge in sado-masochistic practices.

Although fascinated by this new strange world, Dorothee initially persists in her search for romantic love and seems to have been rewarded when she meets Ramona, a lesbian sex therapist, who takes her off for a highly romantic date and a night of sex. But it turns out that, for Ramona, Dorothee is just another client, and she charges Dorothee for both her time and her expenses. This brings about a sexual 'awakening' for Dorothee which dispels her dreams of romance.

It is as if she realizes that romantic love is a myth which, by encapsulating the promise of happiness, prevents women from pursuing their own sexual pleasure. Although Dorothee fails to find love with Ramona, she does experience sexual desire and this permits her to start pursuing her own sexual pleasure by participating in the lesbian sex industry. The final scene shows Dorothee symbolically casting off her old life by throwing the photos she took in Hamburg – images of romance – into the sea.

The women Dorothee meets in San Francisco have, by creating their own lesbian sex industry, clearly placed themselves in control of their own lives. Not only do they bar men from their clubs, but they actively enjoy their self-determined sexual activities. In one scene, for instance, Ramona, dressed in a man's suit, skilfully mimics the act of male masturbation with the aid of a beer bottle while doing a semi-strip for a highly appreciative female audience. In another, Susie proudly shows Dorothee her collection of dildoes and tells her with great pleasure about how she uses them. In marked contrast to the anti-pornography campaign launched in Germany in the same year by feminist activist Alice Schwarzer, *The Virgin Machine* suggests that it is not so much that women object to the sex industry itself, but rather to the fact that they have had little or no say in it.

Consequently, although the film focuses on lesbian sexuality, it also stresses the need for women to have freedom of choice with regard to their sexuality. Treut emphasizes this by making Dorothee a journalist. Rather than representing her as making a simple transition from one sexuality to another, Treut shows her investigating and assessing various possible options. The resolution to the film is therefore represented as a conscious choice, rather than as the only alternative or the spontaneous emerging of a repressed sexuality. Although the film has an episodic narrative and frequently uses camera angles and a style of editing more associated with avant-garde filmmaking, Treut's use of humour and the narrative device of a journalistic investigation also make *The Virgin Machine* – unlike *Seduction* and *Mano Destra* – far more accessible to a wider audience.

In contrast to both the Heins' and Treut's films, Claudia Schillinger's short film, *Between* (1989) is far more personal since it attempts to explore the nature of her own sexuality:

Women are usually represented from a male perspective. What really interests me is to see myself or to look for myself, but also to find representations which I really find sexual or which correspond to that.[41]

The film opens with a woman in a red dress wandering through a green field. She lies down, falls asleep and starts to dream. A series of black-and-white images follow − occasionally intercut with a colour shot of the dreaming woman − offering a range of sexual fantasies: a female torso with material bound across her breasts, the shadow of a chain, a woman combing her hair and looking at the camera, a naked gyrating female torso with a dildo attached, a woman touching and feeling her own body, a naked person lying face down on a bed, a close-up shot of a vagina as a woman aggressively masturbates, two bodies lying across a bed together.

Although several of the images clearly show a woman using her body for her own pleasure, others are ambiguous. It is not clear if the body lying face down on the bed is male or female, whether the two bodies lying together are a woman and a man or two women, whether the material covering the breasts on one of the torsos is an attempt to hide them − to make the female male − or a form of bondage. It is as if Schillinger is playing with a whole range of fantasies to suggest that her own sexuality is in fact structured by a number of different sexual desires.

One of the casualties of the changed circumstances of the eighties has been the highly acclaimed *Frauenfilm*. Although its demise is to be regretted, the work of West Germany's first generation of women filmmakers has nevertheless left an indelible mark on German cinema.

After working several years as a film editor, Dagmar Hirtz moved into directing and realized her first feature film, *Unerreichbare Nähe/Final Call* (1984). She attributes her success in this transition directly to the influence of and role models offered by such women:

For me, meeting women like Margarethe von Trotta (who co-wrote the screenplay) − who preceded me along this path, who had the confidence, who fought for and successfully realized their own films − has been crucial.[42]

Furthermore, the film projects of these older women have provided invaluable opportunities for women like Hirtz who wished to follow in their footsteps to gain practical experience of filmmaking. After collaborating with Margarethe von Trotta on *Das zweite Erwachen der Christa Klages/ The Second Awakening of Christa Klages* (1977) and working with directors such as Elfi Mikesch, Claudia von Alemann and Helke Sander, Margit Czenki went on to direct her first feature film *Komplizinnen/Accomplices* (1987) about a woman who is sentenced to seven years' imprisonment. Pia Frankenberg also gained invaluable experience working with Ulrike Ottinger on her film *Freak Orlando* (1981) before becoming a director herself.

As filmmaking has proved a highly unreliable source of income for most women in West Germany, directors such as Claudia von Alemann, Jutta Brückner, Christel Buschmann, Jeanine Meerapfel, Elfi Mikesch, Cristina Perincioli, Marianne Rosenbaum, Helke Sander and Gisela Tuchtenhagen have also taken teaching jobs in the country's film and television schools and art colleges. Not only do younger women now have the role models that Sander, von Trotta and others lacked, but female students can benefit directly from their knowledge and experience.

The women filmmakers of what was once West Germany may not have succeeded in achieving their 50 per cent demands, but due to the improved general position of women in society and the campaigning work undertaken by the country's first generation of women directors they at least – according to Brückner – 'feel stronger as individuals'.[43]

These factors have, of course, considerably eased women's entry into the profession. Although the vibrant feminist film culture that emerged at the end of the seventies has been dissipated, it has nevertheless ensured that women directors have become a permanent fixture in German cinema.

Notes

Introduction: The Absent Directors

1. Eric Rentschler, *West German Film in the Course of Time*, Bedford Hills 1984, p. 4.

2. Thomas Elsaesser, *New German Cinema: A History*, Basingstoke 1989, p. 52.

3. *Geschichten vom Kübelkind/Stories of a Bucket Baby* (1969) and *Das goldene Ding/The Thing of Gold* (1971).

4. Elsaesser, p. 185.

5. Quoted in Robert Russett and Cecile Starr, *Experimental Animation*, revised edn, New York 1988, p. 77.

6. Ibid.

7. See, for instance 'Gestern und Heute; Gespräch mit Herthe Thiele', *Frauen und Film* no. 28, June 1981, p. 32.

8. See, for instance, B. Ruby Rich, 'From Repressive Tolerance to Erotic Liberation: *Mädchen in Uniform*', in Mary Ann Doane, Patricia Mellencamp and Linda Williams, eds, *Re-Vision, Essays in Feminist Film Criticism*, Los Angeles 1984, pp. 100–30. German feminist film critics, however, disagree with this evaluation; see, for instance, Helen Fehervary, Claudia Lenssen and Judith Mayne, 'From Hitler to Hepburn: A Discussion of Women's Film Production and Reception', in *New German Critique* nos 24–25, Fall-Winter 1981–2, pp. 172–85. In this discussion Lenssen argues that lesbianism is only an underlying theme of the film and asserts that German critics view the film as part of a cinematic tradition that emerged in the pre-Nazi era, analysing it in terms of the Prussian morality and the forms of censorship that prevailed at the time.

9. Helge Herberle, 'Notizen zur Riefenstahl-Rezeption', in *Frauen und Film* no. 14, Dec 1977, p. 33. This and all subsequent quotations from German language sources are my own translations.

10. Quoted in Erwin Leiser, *Nazi Cinema*, London 1974, p. 138.

11. Peter Nowotny, 'Leni Riefenstahl', in Hans-Michael Bock, ed., *Cinegraph: Lexikon zum deutschsprachigen Film*, Munich 1984, p. E2.

12. Leontine Sagan did direct one other film. After making *Maidens in Uniform* Sagen went to England, where Alexander Korda engaged her to direct *Men of Tomorrow* (1932), a film about Oxford student life.

13. Programme notes, Goethe Institute, London 1990.

14. Quoted in Christian-Albrecht Gollub, 'May Spils and Werner Enke – Beyond Pure Entertainment?', in Klaus Phillips, ed., *New German Filmmakers*, New York 1984, p. 306.

15. Ibid., p. 308.

16. With the setting up of the Berlin and Munich schools the Ulm Institute eventually discontinued its own practical training programme and concentrated on research and theoretical work.

17. Figures are taken from Renate Möhrmann, *Die Frau mit der Kamera*, Munich 1980, p. 34.

18. Ibid., p. 106.

19. Eva Hiller, 'Interview mit Claudia Alemann', *Frauen und Film* no. 5, 1975, p. 11.

20. Möhrmann, p. 17.

21. Helke Sander, 'Vorwort der Redaktion: von "Film und Frau" zu "Frauen und Film",' *Frauen und Film* no. 1 (reprint), July 1975, p. 6.

22. Monika Funke Stern and Helge Heberle, 'Das Feuer im Innern des Berges. Ein Gespräch mit Danièle Huillet von Helge Heberle und Monika Funke Stern', *Frauen und Film* no. 32, June 1982, p. 5.

23. Christian-Albrecht Gollub, p. 305.

24. Marc Silberman, 'Women Filmakers in West Germany: A Catalog', *Camera Obscura* no. 6, Fall 1980, pp. 123–52.

25. Marc Silberman, 'Women Filmmakers in West Germany: A Catalog (Part 2)', *Camera Obscura* no. 11, 1983, pp. 133–45.

26. Rentschler, p. 143.

27. John Sandford, *The New German Cinema*, London 1980.

28. Anton Kaes, 'Distanced Observers: Perspectives on the New German Cinema', *Quarterly Review of Film Studies* vol. 10, no. 3, Summer 1985, p. 240.

29. Timothy Corrigan, *New German Film. The Displaced Image*, Austin 1983.

30. Ibid., p. xiii.

31. James Franklin, *New German Cinema*, London 1986, p. 40.

32. Hans Günther Pflaum and Hans Helmut Prinzler, *Cinema in the Federal Republic of Germany*, Bonn 1983, pp. 76–9.

33. Ibid., p. 77.

34. Prinzler's und Pflaum's book was first published in German in 1979. When it was translated in the early eighties the book was revised and updated for the English-speaking market. The marginalization of women filmmakers has emerged largely as a result of this process and is less apparent in the German original.

35. *Literature/Film Quarterly* vol. 7, no. 3, 1979.

36. *Wide Angle* vol. 3, no. 4, 1980.

37. *Quarterly Review of Film Studies* vol. 5, no. 2, Spring 1980.

38. *New German Critique* nos 24–25, Fall/Winter 1981–2.

39. *Discourse* no. 6, Fall 1983.

40. Marc Silberman, 'Introduction: From the Outside Moving In', *Jump Cut* no. 27, July 1982, p. 41.

41. Ibid.

42. Franklin, pp 39–40.

43. Rentschler, p. 4.

44. Ibid.

45. *Jump Cut* no. 27, July 1982; no. 29, Feb 1984; no. 30, Mar 1985.

46. Klaus Phillips, *New German Filmmakers*, New York 1984.

47. *Film Criticism* vol. 9, no. 2, Winter 1984–5.

48. *Literature/Film Quarterly* vol. 13, no. 4, 1985.

49. Thomas Elsaesser, *New German Cinema: A History*, Basingstoke 1989.

50. Eric Rentschler, ed., *German Film and Literature: Adaptations and Transformations*, New York and London 1986; and Anton Kaes, *From 'Hitler' to 'Heimat': The Return of History as Film*, Cambridge and London 1989.

51. Rentschler's book, which encompassses the entire history of German cinema, also includes a film by New German Cinema directors Straub and Danièle Huillet. Huillet, however, has never been associated with feminist film culture in West Germany.

52. Rentschler, *West German Film in the Course of Time*, p. 59.

53. Sandford, p. 6.

54. The National Film Theatre in London, for instance, presented a season of films by West German women directors in August 1986. In 1987 the Tyneside Film Festival screened a selection of German lesbian films. London's Institute of Contemporary Arts and Goethe Institute also presented various programmes of women's films from West Germany during the eighties.

55. See L. Heck-Rabi, *Women Filmmakers: A Critical Reception*, Metuchen and London 1984, pp. 1–25.

56. Richard Roud, ed., *Cinema, A Critical Dictionary: The Major Filmmakers*, London 1980.

57. Jill Forbes, 'Agnes Varda. The Gaze of the Medusa?', *Sight & Sound*, Spring 1989, p. 122.

Chapter 1: A Divided History

1. From a speech given by Spyros Skouras, Head of Twentieth-Century Fox, quoted in Thomas H. Guback, *The International Film Industry*, Bloomington 1969, p. 125.

2. Klaus Phillips, ed., *New German Filmmakers*, New York 1984, p. xiii.

3. Quoted in John Sandford, *The New German Cinema*, London 1980, p. 156.

4. Quoted in Thomas Elsaesser, 'The Postwar German Cinema', in Tony Rayns, ed., *Fassbinder*, London 1976, p. 2.

5. Paul Virilio, *War and Cinema. The Logistics of Perception*, London 1989, p. 9.

6. Helmut Herbst, 'New German Cinema, 1962–83: A View From Hamburg', *Persistence of Vision* no. 2, Fall 1985, p. 70.

7. Thomas Elsaesser, *New German Cinema: A History*, Basingstoke 1989, p. 20.

8. Hans Günther Pflaum and Hans Helmut Prinzler, *Film in der Bundesrepublik Deutschland*, Munich 1982, p. 134.

9. R.C. and M.E. Helt, *West German Cinema Since 1945: A Reference Book*, London 1987, p. 8.

10. All figures taken from Helt, pp. 8–9.

11. Joe Hembus, *Der deutscher Film kann gar nicht besser sein*, Bremen 1961, p. 88, quoted in Sheila Johnston, 'The Author as Public Institution: The "New" Cinema in the Federal Republic of Germany', *Screen Education* nos 32–3, 1979–80, p. 72.

12. Elsaesser has, however, suggested that another reason exists for this. He maintains that 'the political bias of the awards was unmistakable; the Minister regularly honoured films with a distinct anti-communist and pro-NATO slant.' *New German Cinema*, p. 20. So, the withholding of the awards in 1961 could equally be attributable to the lack of politically 'suitable' entries. Nevertheless, the fact remains that the prizes were also intended to celebrate 'quality' films and went unawarded that year.

13. Quoted in Jan Dawson, 'A Labyrinth of Subsidies', *Sight & Sound* vol. 50, no. 1, 1981, p. 16.

14. Ingrid Scheib-Rothbart and Ruth McCormick, 'Edgar Reitz: Liberating Humanity and Film', in Phillips, p. 255.

15. Quoted in Dawson, 'Labyrinth', p. 17.

16. Kluge's *Yesterday Girl* (1965–66), Schaaf's *Tattooing* (1967) and Werner Herzog's *Lebenszeichen/Signs of Life* (1967).

17. Schamoni's *It* (1965), Schlöndorff's *Young Törless* (1966) and Kluge's *Die Artisten in der Zirkuskuppel: ratlos/Artists Under the Big Top: Perplexed* (1967).

18. Quoted in Phillips, *New German Filmmakers*, p. xvii.

19. Ibid., p. xviii.

20. Resolution of the 139th session of the Bundestag, 1968, quoted in Hermann Gerber, ed., *Kuratorium junger deutscher Film: Zielsetzung, Entwicklung, Förderungsweise*, Munich 1977, p. 10.

21. Elsaesser, 'The Postwar German Cinema', p. 14.

22. Quoted in Hans Günther Pflaum and Hans Helmut Prinzler, *Cinema in the Federal Republic of Germany*, Bonn 1983, p. 99.

23. Quoted in Dorin Popa, ed., *Kurbel-Brevier: Handbuch für die Film- und Videoarbeit*, Frankfurt-am-Main 1985, p. 117.

24. Elsaesser, *New German Cinema*, p. 15.

25. Quoted in Dawson, 'A Labyrinth', p. 17.

26. Rentschler, *West German Film*, p. 46.

27. See, for instance, the comments of Eckart Schmidt in *Deutsche Zeitung* in September 1977: 'Filmmakers like Kluge, Herzog, Geissendörfer and Fassbinder, all of whom have collected subsidies more than once, and who despite such public funding are incapable of directing a success, should in future be barred from receiving subsidies. Film subsidy is no pension fund for failed filmmakers.' Quoted in Elsaesser, *New German Cinema*, p. 37.

28. Sandford, *The New German Cinema*, p. 6.

29. Ibid., p. 149.

30. Claudia Lenssen, 'Frage an Wilhelm Roth', *Frauen und Film* no. 15, Feb 1978, p. 32.

31. Elsaesser, *New German Cinema*, p. 25.

32. Eric Rentschler, 'American Friends and the New German Cinema: A Study in Reception', *New German Critique* nos 24–5, Fall/Winter 1981–2, p. 23.

33. Marc Silberman, 'Jutta Brückner, Cristina Perincioli, and Helga Reidemeister Conversing Together Finally', *Jump Cut* no. 27, July 1982, p. 48.

34. The SPD is West Germany's social-democratic party. However, they aband-

oned their position as a socialist workers' party in the late fifties and remain left-wing only in comparison to the CDU/CSU.

35. Margit Mayer, 'The German October of 1977', *New German Critique* no. 13, Winter 1978, p. 160.

36. Quoted in Elsaesser, *New German Cinema*, p. 313.

37. Jan Dawson, 'The Sacred Terror: Shadows of Terrorism in the New German Cinema', *Sight & Sound* vol. 48, no. 4, 1979, p. 243.

38. See the September 1977 interview with Hans Geissendörfer as referenced by Rentschler, *West German Film*, p. 135.

39. Eric Rentschler, 'Deutschland im Vorherbst: Literature Adaptation in West German Film', *Kino (German Film)* no. 3, Summer 1980, p. 16.

40. Dawson, 'The Sacred Terror', p. 243.

41. Charlotte Delorme, 'Zum Film "Die bleierne Zeit" von Margarethe von Trotta', *Frauen und Film* no. 31, Feb 1982, p. 55.

42. See, for instance, Dawson, 'The Sacred Terror', p. 243 and E. Ann Kaplan, 'Discourses of Terrorism, Feminism, and the Family in von Trotta's "Marianne and Juliane"', *Persistence of Vision* no. 2, Fall 1985, pp. 61–8. The project was turned down by two television companies, WDR and ZDF, before it received partial funding from a third, SFB.

43. Rentschler, 'Deutschland im Vorherbst', p. 18.

44. Rentschler, *West German Film*, p. 58.

45. Ula Stöckl's *Haben Sie Abitur?* (1967) and *Neun Leben hat die Katze* (1968), Oimel Mai and Marion Zemann's *Duniel* (1967), Claudia von Alemann's *Fundevogel* (1967), Dore O's *Kaldalon* (1970), Oimel Mai's *Die Liebe ist eine Himmelsmacht* (1967) and *Shivas Children* (1967), and Mischa Gallé's *Die Ohrfeige* (1970). Stöckl's film *Neun Leben hat die Katze* was the single feature film. Two further features co-directed by women, were funded by the *Kuratorium*, during this period, namely Danièle Huillet and Jean-Marie Straub's *Chronik der Anna Magdalena Bach / Chronicle of Anna Magdalena Bach* (1968) and *Das goldene Ding / The Thing of Gold* (1971) directed by Ula Stöckl, Edgar Reitz, Alf Brustellin and Nicos Perakis. However, it is arguable that the involvement of male colleagues in these films played a significant role in the projects being awarded funding. With regard to *The Thing of Gold*, Stöckl has asserted that Reitz received the funding for the project, not her. See Renate Möhrmann, *Die Frau mit der Kamera*, Munich 1980, p. 58.

46. Claudia Lenssen, 'Women's Cinema in Germany', *Jump Cut* no. 29, Feb 1984, p. 49. An example of this kind of sexism can be found in the way in which *Deutschland im Herbst/Germany in Autumn* (1978) was promoted as a model for political film work at a press conference held during the 1978 Berlin Film Festival. According to a group of women filmmakers, producers and journalists it was suggested that the film was the first in which filmmakers had collectively reacted directly to political events. In an open letter to the mostly male directors they drew attention to the fact that as feminists they had been engaged in political film work that addressed current events in the Federal Republic for the past ten years. See 'Offener Brief an den Filmverlag der Autoren und die Regisseure des Films "Deutschland im Herbst"', *Frauen und Film* no. 16, June 1978, pp. 22–3.

47. Eva Hiller, 'Interview mit Claudia Alemann', *Frauen und Film* no. 5, 1975, p. 13.

48. Barbara Bronnen and Corinna Brocher, *Die Filmemacher. Zur neuen deutschen Produktion nach Oberhausen*, Munich 1973.

49. Eva Hiller, Claudia Lenssen, Gesine Strempel, 'Gespräch mit Ula Stöckl', *Frauen und Film* no. 12, June 1977, p. 8.

50. Helke Sander, 'Feminismus und Film: "I like chaos, but I don't know, whether chaos likes me"', *Frauen und Film* no. 15, Feb 1978, p. 7.

51. Rita Pohland, 'Doris Dörrie: Männer sind ihr Glück', *Cinema (West Germany)* no. 3, March 1986, p. 35.

52. Helke Sander, 'Nimmt man dir das Schwert, dann greife zum Knüppel', *Frauen und Film* no. 1, 1974, p. 39.

53. Renate Fischetti, 'Interview with Heidi Genée', *Jump Cut* no. 30, March 1985, p. 65.

54. This was the motivation behind such initiatives as the first international Seminar on Women's Films held in Berlin in November 1973 (organized by Claudia von Alemann and Helke Sander) and the founding of the feminist film journal *Frauen und Film*. These will be discussed in chapter four.

55. Hiller, 'Interview mit Claudia Alemann', p. 13.

56. Christel Buschmann, 'Interview mit Erika Runge', *Frauen und Film*, no. 12, June 1977, p. 24. Renate Möhrmann also reported that during the early sixties Ula Stöckl found that 'the prejudices against women in television companies were enormous.' Möhrmann, p. 48.

57. Fischetti, p. 65.

58. See Hiller, 'Interview mit Claudia Alemann', p. 13.

59. Jutta Brückner, 'Adler und Maulwurf', *Frauen und Film* no. 27, Feb 1981, p. 6.

60. Marc Silberman, 'Interview with Helke Sander: Open Forms', *Jump Cut* no. 29, Feb. 1984, p. 60.

61. Helga Reidemeister, 'On Documentary Filmmaking', *Jump Cut* no. 27, July 1982, pp. 45–6.

62. Lenssen, 'Women's Cinema in Germany', p. 50.

63. Quoted in Margret Köhler, 'Blitzableiter für manches Gewitter', *Film-Korrespondenz* no. 4, 16 February 1988, p. 6.

64. Claudia Lenssen, 'Der Spass an der Arbeit in der Frauengruppe mit sachkundigen ahnungslosen Männern. Ein Gespräch mit Gesine Strempel über 3 Jahr in der Projektkommission der Filmförderungsanstalt', *Frauen und Film* no. 34, Jan 1983, p. 23.

65. Quoted in Elsaesser, *New German Cinema*, p. 25.

66. Marc Silberman, 'Interview with Christina Perincioli. Women's Movement Art', *Jump Cut* no. 29, Feb 84, p. 52.

67. Dagmar Beiersdorf, 'Von einer guten Sache ... kann man nie genug kriegen', *Zitty* no. 5/86, 27 February–12 March 1986, p. 91.

68. Silberman, 'Interview with Helke Sander', p. 59.

69. Silberman, 'Jutta Brückner, Christina Perincioli, and Helga Reidemeister', p. 48.

70. Elsaesser, *New German Cinema*, p. 67. In contrast, Helke Sander, for instance, was unsuccessful in realizing any of her projects between 1973 and 1977. See Helke Sander, 'Der Herren machen das selber, dass ihnen die arme Frau feind wird', in Hans Prinzler and Eric Rentschler, eds, *Augenzeugen: 100 Texte neuer deutscher Filmemacher*, Frankfurt-am-Main 1988, pp. 80–8.

71. Sander, 'Nimmt man das Schwert', pp. 34–5.

72. Möhrmann, p. 55. The description Möhrmann offered Stöckl of herself was a quote taken from an article written by Karsten Witte for the *Frankfurter Rundschau*, 9 October 1978.

73. Hiller, 'Interview mit Claudia Alemann', p. 16.

74. Silberman, 'Jutta Brückner, Christina Perincioli, and Helga Reidemeister', p. 48.

75. Hiller, 'Interview mit Claudia Alemann', p. 15.

76. See, for instance, James Franklin, *New German Cinema*, London 1986; and Ulrich Gregor, *Geschichte des Films ab 1960*, Munich 1978.

Chapter 2: Critical Reception

1. Gerald Clarke, 'Seeking Planets that do not Exist: The New German Cinema is the Liveliest in Europe', *Time* 20 March 1978.

2. See, for instance, Jan Dawson, 'A Labyrinth of Subsidies', *Sight & Sound* vol. 50, no. 1, 1981, pp. 14–20; Eric Rentschler, *West German Film in the Course of Time*, Bedford Hills 1984; and Thomas Elsaesser, *New German Cinema: A History*, Basingstoke 1989.

3. Clarke, p. 51.

4. Charles Eidsvik, 'Behind the Crest of the Wave: An Overview of the New German Cinema', *Literature/Film Quarterly* vol. 7, no. 3, 1979, p. 174.

5. See Elsaesser, p. 75.

6. Eidsvik, pp. 169–70.

7. François Truffaut, 'A Certain Tendency of the French Cinema' originally appeared in *Cahiers du Cinéma* no. 31, Jan 1954; reprinted in Bill Nichols, ed., *Movies and Methods*, London 1976, pp. 224–37.

8. Edward Buscombe, 'Ideas of Authorship', in John Caughie, *Theories of Authorship*, London 1981, p. 23.

9. See Rudolph Arnheim, *Film*, London 1933; and Vachel Lindsay, *The Art of the Moving Picture*, New York 1970.

10. Manuel Alvarado, *Authorship, Origination and Production*, London 1982, p. 15.

11. Most notably by Andrew Sarris and Peter Wollen. See, for instance, Sarris's 'Notes on the Auteur Theory in 1962', *Film Culture* no. 27, Winter 1962–3; and Wollen's *Signs and Meanings in the Cinema*, London 1969.

12. John Sandford, *The New German Cinema*, London 1980, p. 16.

13. Ibid.

14. Quoted in Sheila Johnston, 'The Author as Public Institution', *Screen Education* nos 32–3, 1979–80, p. 72.

15. The Bauhaus was an art college set up in Germany in 1919. In contrast to earlier forms of art education which had been confined to learning a particular skill, the Bauhaus trained its students in a variety of media. Although this was not due to any conscious privileging of individual authorship, it was designed to make them 'all-rounders'. The Bauhaus was closed down on the instructions of the Nazi government in April 1933.

16. Quoted in Johnston, p. 74.

17. Hans Günther Pflaum and Hans Helmut Prinzler, *Film in der Bundesrepublik Deutschland*, Munich 1979, p. 85.

18. Hermann Gerber, ed., *Kuratorium junger deutscher Film. Zielsetzung, Entwicklung, Förderungsweise*, Munich 1977, p. 7.

19. See Elsaesser, p. 24.

20. Ibid., p. 28.

21. Quoted ibid., p. 29.

22. Quoted ibid., p. 28.

23. Clarke, p. 51.

24. See, for instance, Rentschler, *West German Film*, p. i; or Anton Kaes, 'Distanced Observers: Perspectives on the New German Cinema', *Quarterly Review of Film Studies* vol. 10, no. 3, Summer 1985, p. 241.

25. Clara Burckner, 'Critical Observations on the Changed Situation of the German Film d'Auteur and the Possibilities it has of Reaching the Viewer', in Goethe Institute, ed., *Basis Film: A Berlin Model of Film Production and Distribution*, London 1987, p. II/2–3.

26. Ibid., p. II/2.

27. Ronald Holloway, 'The Backbone of German Cinema', *Kino (German Film)* no. 3, Summer 1980, p. 25.

28. Eric Rentschler, 'Deutschland im Vorherbst: Literature Adaptation in West German Film', *Kino (German Film)* no. 3, Summer 1980, p. 16.

29. Eidsvik, p. 177.

30. Lester Friedman, 'Cinematic Techniques in *The Lost Honour of Katherina Blum*', *Literature/Film Quarterly* vol. 7, no. 3, 1979, p. 251.

31. Ibid., p. 248.

32. Ibid.

33. Ibid., p. 245.

34. Rentschler, 'Deutschland im Vorherbst', pp. 14–15.

35. Ibid., p. 14.

36. James Franklin, *New German Cinema*, London 1983. p. 82. It should also be remembered that Brecht objected to G.W. Pabst's film version of *The Threepenny Opera* (1931) on similar grounds.

37. Alvarado, p. 10; there are obviously exceptions to the assertion that cultural artefacts were authorless prior to the Renaissance, such as poetry attributed to the author-figures of Homer and Chaucer, but on the whole creativity was deemed to be the 'sole prerogative of God'.

38. Eric Rentschler, *West German Film in the Course of Time*, Bedford Hills 1984.

39. Thomas Elsaesser, *New German Cinema: A History*, Basingstoke 1989.

40. See, for instance, Richard Collins and Vincent Porter, *WDR and the Arbeiterfilm: Fassbinder, Ziewer and Others*, London 1981. Although Ziewer has more recently achieved auteur status, Collins and Porter give an extensive account of the political and institutional contexts.

41. Lynne Layton, 'Peter Lilienthal: Decisions Before Twelve', in Klaus Phillips, ed., *New German Filmmakers*, New York 1984, p. 230.

42. Ibid., p. 232.

43. See, for instance, Ulrike Ottinger's comments in Renate Möhrmann, *Die Frau mit der Kamera*, Munich 1980, p. 189; Ingemo Engström's in Uta Berg-Ganschow and Gesine Strempel, 'Gespräch mit Ingemo Engström', *Frauen und Film* no. 22, Dec 1979, p. 13; and Ula Stöckl's in Eva Hiller, Claudia Lenssen, Gesine Strempel, 'Gespräch mit Ula Stöckl', *Frauen und Film* no. 12, June 1977, p. 4.

44. See Cristina Perincioli's comments in Marc Silberman, 'Interview with Christina Perincioli. Women's Movement Art', *Jump Cut* no. 29, Feb 1984, p. 52. Helma Sanders-Brahms, for instance, has expressed 'a burning desire for a career, and all that

implies'. Quoted in 'Derek Malcolm on the Radical Filmmaking of Helma Sanders-Brahms: Future Tense', *The Guardian*, 25 April 1985, p. 19.

45. There are exceptions, of course, such as the British Documentary Movement of the thirties.

46. Karl Scheffler, *Die Frau und die Kunst*, Berlin 1908, p. 29, quoted in Gisela Ecker, ed., *Feminist Aesthetics*, London 1985, p. 26.

47. John Berger, *Ways of Seeing*, London 1972, p. 47.

48. Sandford, p. 140.

49. Robert Acker, 'The Major Directions of German Feminist Cinema', *Literature/Film Quarterly* vol. 13, no. 4, 1985, p. 245.

50. Ibid., p. 248. A similar example can be found in Elsaesser, *New German Cinema*. On the one hand he asserts that 'some of the most remarkable examples of West German filmmaking in general during the 1970s came from women' (p. 185), yet he also maintains that documentary filmmaker Klaus Wildenhahn 'influenced at least initially the films that came out of the women's movement' (p. 176). Elsaesser's assertion may be better founded since Wildenhahn taught at the DFFB and a far larger number of women attended the Berlin school than studied at Ulm. However, it is still indicative of a tendency to find a male originator for female film production.

51. Hans Günther Pflaum and Hans Helmut Prinzler, *Cinema in the Federal Republic of Germany*, Bonn 1983, p. 77.

52. Franklin, p. 34.

53. Hans Günther Pflaum, ed., *Jahrbuch Film 78/79*, Munich 1979, p. 46. See also Karl Saurer, *Kölner Stadt-Anzeiger*, 9 March 1978, who asserted that Sander's film was one of 'the most discussed and most approved of films at the "8th International Forum of Young Film"'; or Wolfram Schütte, *Frankfurter Rundschau*, 21 April 1978, who singled it out as 'one of the most important films of the Federal film year'.

54. Christel Buschmann, 'Gespräch zwischen Margarethe von Trotta und Christel Buschmann', *Frauen und Film* no. 8, June 1976, p. 30.

55. Of the few that have it should be noted that two, Helma Sanders-Brahms's *Heinrich* (1976–77) and Heidi Genée's *Grete Minde* (1977), won Federal Film Prizes.

56. See, for instance, Franklin, p. 39. He stresses the documentary backgrounds of women filmmakers and the politically and socially committed nature of their feature films. In the course of developing a more sophisticated analysis of New German Cinema, Elsaesser describes the work of such directors as 'semi-documentary' (p. 233). He also identifies them as belonging to what he terms a 'cinema of experience' which he describes as including films which deal with 'the aspirations of ... disadvantaged groups as recorded through the voices and images of those immediately concerned and affected. Ideally, the form a film of this kind takes is determined by the nature of the experience itself, its most authentic expression and manifestation. To this extent, the medium is treated as (ideally) transparent.' (p. 207)

57. Birgit Hein, 'Die Radikalität der Avantgarde', in Hans Prinzler and Eric Rentschler, eds, *Augenzeugen: 100 Texte neuer deutscher Filmemacher*, Frankfurt-am-Main 1988, p. 222.

58. Buschmann, 'Gespräch zwischen Margarethe von Trotta', p. 31.

59. Ibid., p. 30.

60. Monika Funke Stern and Helge Heberle, 'Das Feuer im Innern des Berges. Ein Gespräch mit Danièle Huillet von Helge Heberle und Monika Funke Stern', *Frauen und Film* no. 32, June 1982, pp. 5–6.

61. The collective film projects undertaken by male directors, such as *Germany in Autumn* (1978) have not suffered similar critical neglect largely due precisely to the fact that those involved were already established *auteurs*.

62. Marc Silberman, 'Interview with Helga Reidemeister: The Working Class Family', *Jump Cut* no. 27, July 1982, p. 44.

63. Marc Silberman, 'Interview with Ulrike Ottinger: Surreal Images', *Jump Cut* no. 29, Feb 1984, p. 56.

64. Feminism has provided the context for a discussion of women's films to such an extent that it has also reinforced the classification of women's film work on the basis of gender rather than medium. With regard to *Frauen und Film*, for instance, the editors observed that 'in bookshops it is seldom to be found under film where it belongs, but under women'. See 'Vorwort der Redaktion zum Nachdruck der Nr. 1', *Frauen und Film* no. 1, 1974, p. 2. Indeed Elsaesser asserts that the work of many women directors has effectively 'sidestepped' being labelled as New German Cinema. (p. 297)

65. See, for example, Thomas Elsaesser, 'The Heimatfilm', in Goethe Institute, ed., *Deutscher Heimatfilm*, London 1988, p. II/1–14.

66. Sandford, p. 56.

67. Franklin, p. 34.

Chapter 3: The Women's Movement

1. Quoted in Hilke Schlaeger, 'The West German Women's Movement', *New German Critique* no. 13, Winter 1978, p. 63.

2. Alice Schwarzer, ed., *Alice Schwarzer: So fing es an! Die neue Frauenbewegung*, Munich 1983, p. 13.

3. Ibid.

4. Quoted in Marc Silberman, 'Women Filmmakers in West Germany: A Catalog', *Camera Obscura* no. 6, 1980, p. 140.

5. Schwarzer, p. 15.

6. Ibid., p. 16.

7. Ibid., p. 20.

8. Ibid., p. 127.

9. Ibid., p. 66.

10. Ibid., p. 53.

11. Helke Sander, 'Feminismus und Film: "I like chaos, but I don't know, whether chaos likes me"', *Frauen und Film* no. 15, Feb 1978, p. 8.

12. Schwarzer, p. 73.

13. Quoted in Gudrun Lukasz-Aden and Christel Strobel, eds, *Der Frauenfilm*, Munich 1985, p. 110.

14. Marc Silberman, 'Interview with Christina Perincioli, Women's Movement Art', *Jump Cut* no. 29, Feb 1984, p. 52.

15. Marc Silberman, 'Interview with Erika Runge, "One Brick in a Large House"', *Jump Cut* no. 29, Feb 1984, p. 54.

16. Silberman, 'Interview with Christina Perincioli', p. 52.

17. See, for example, the round-table discussion between Uta Berg-Ganschow, Helge Heberle, Claudia Lenssen, Helke Sander, Gesine Strempel, Sigrid Vagt and

Hildegard Westbeld, 'Die "gute Mutter". Gespräch über "Von wegen 'Schicksal'" von Helga Reidemeister', *Frauen und Film* no. 20, May 1979, pp. 21–39; see also Hans Günther Pflaum and Hans Helmut Prinzler, *Cinema in the Federal Republic of Germany*, Bonn 1983, pp. 67–8.

18. Silberman, 'Interview with Christina Perincioli', p. 52.

19. Renate Fischetti, 'Interview with Heidi Genée', *Jump Cut* no. 30, Mar 1985, p. 65.

20. Quoted in Schwarzer, p. 15.

21. Quoted in ICA programme notes.

22. Given these splits in the movement and its lack of a national coordinating body, some observers have commented on the problematic nature of trying to construct a coherent or 'objective' overview of the movement. See, for instance, Schlaeger, p. 61 and Schwarzer, p. 95.

23. Schlaeger, p. 67.

24. Helke Sander, Überlegungen zum Verhältnis von Kunst und Politik', in Silvia Eiblmayr, Valie Export, Monika Prischl-Maier, eds, *Kunst mit Eigen-Sinn. Aktuelle Kunst von Frauen. Texte und Dokumentation*, Munich 1985, p. 90.

25. Sander, 'Feminismus und Film', pp. 6–8.

26. The editors, 'Vorwort der Redaktion zum Nachdruck der Nr. 1', *Frauen und Film* no. 1 (reprint), July 1975, p. 2.

27. Marc Silberman, 'Interview with Ula Stöckl, Do Away with Taboos', *Jump Cut* no. 29, Feb 1984, p. 55.

28. Lisa Katzman, 'The All-round Reduced Personality: Redupers, Women's Art in Public', *Jump Cut* no. 29, Feb 1984, p. 60.

29. Quoted in Silberman, 'Women Filmmakers in West Germany: A Catalog', p. 131.

30. Quoted in Lukasz-Aden and Strobel, p. 47.

31. See, for instance, Renate Möhrmann, *Die Frau mit der Kamera*, Munich 1980, pp. 83–98.

32. Marc Silberman, 'Interview with Jutta Brückner, Recognizing Collective Gestures', *Jump Cut* no. 27, July 1982, p. 47.

33. Helke Sander, 'Nimmt man dir das Schwert, dann greife zum Knüppel', *Frauen und Film* no. 1 (reprint), July 1975, p. 37. Heidi Genée also expresses this opinion in Renate Fischetti, 'Interview with Heidi Genée', *Jump Cut* no. 30, Mar 1985, p. 65.

34. Patricia Harbord, 'Interview with Jutta Brückner', *Screen Education* no. 40, Autumn/Winter 1981–2, p. 51.

35. Ibid., p. 52.

36. Gottfried Knapp, *Süddeutsche Zeitung*, 10 June 1978.

37. With regard to *Years of Hunger* Jutta Brückner has asserted that: 'A lot of men have told me they identify with Ursula, too. Well, her problem is that she doesn't want to be forced into a classic gender role – she admires her father, his politics, she's trying to become a whole person, to develop her masculine qualities as well as her feminine ones – both sorts of qualities are present in every human being. So of course, Ursula's oppression is about the oppression of men, too' (Harbord, p. 52). With regard to Sander's film *Redupers*, film academic Philip Hayward has stressed that: 'For me the film also transcended its (very important) gender specific and made *me* (as a male) identify with the human predicament of the character and her social situation. I found

the film really affecting.' (From unpublished notes.)

38. Gottfried Knapp, 'Eingemauert in Berlin', *Süddeutsche Zeitung*, 10 July 1978. See also Lukasz-Aden and Strobel, p. 61.

39. Helen Fehervary, Claudia Lenssen, Judith Mayne, 'From Hitler to Hepburn: A Discussion of Women's Film Production and Reception', *New German Critique* nos 24–25, Fall/Winter 1981–2, p. 181.

40. Marc Silberman, 'Jutta Brückner, Christina Perincioli, and Helga Reidemeister, Conversing Together Finally', *Jump Cut* no. 27, July 1982, p. 47.

41. Gretchen Elsner-Sommer, untitled interview with Cristina Perincioli, *Jump Cut* no. 29, Feb 1984, p. 52.

42. Quoted in Silberman, 'Women Filmmakers in West Germany', p. 135.

43. Uta Berg-Ganschow and Gesine Strempel, 'Gespräch mit Ingemo Engström', *Frauen und Film* no. 22, Dec 1979, p. 7.

44. Silberman, 'Jutta Brückner, Christina Perincioli, and Helga Reidemeister', p. 47. See also Eva Hiller, 'Interview mit Claudia Alemann', *Frauen und Film* no. 5, 1975, p. 15.

45. See, for instance, Klaus Phillips, ed., *New German Filmmakers*, New York 1984. Reinhard Hauff 'emphatically rejects the notion that the director should ultimately be given all the credit for a film's success, views himself as totally dependent on his cameraman, editor, writer, and actors, and considers it his working philosophy to obtain optimum results in close cooperation with cast and crew' (p. 232). In James Franklin, *New German Cinema*, London 1986, Fassbinder is described as searching 'for a means of creating collective art' in his early film work (p. 132). Alexander Kluge also tried to realize a 'cooperative cinema' (see Eric Rentschler, *West German Film In the Course of Time*, Bedford Hills 1984, pp. 195–6).

46. *Germany in Autumn* (1978), directed by Alf Brustellin, Rainer Werner Fassbinder, Alexander Kluge, Maximiliane Mainka, Edgar Reitz, Katia Rupé, Hans Peter Cloos, Bernhard Sinkel and Volker Schlöndorf; *The Candidate* (1980), directed by Alexander Kluge, Stefan Aust, Volker Schlöndorff and Alexander von Eschwege; *War and Peace* (1982), directed by Alexander Kluge, Stefan Aust, Volker Schlöndorff and Axel Engstfeld.

47. Charles Eidsvik, 'Behind the Crest of the Wave: An Overview of the New German Cinema', *Literature/Film Quarterly* vol. 7, no. 3, 1979, p. 174.

48. Before moving into directing, Heidi Genée also worked as an editor for over ten years, establishing herself as one of the top editors in the New German Cinema. Among the directors she worked with are Kluge, Ula Stöckl, Ulrich Schamoni, Peter Lilienthal, Erika Runge, Bernhard Sinkel, Alf Brustellin, Uwe Brandner, May Spils and Ulf Miehe. A number of other women, such as Ila von Hasperg, Annette Dorn, Ursula West, Jane Seitz-Sperr, Maximiliane Mainka, Heidi Handorf, have worked as editors for Ulrike Ottinger, Fassbinder, Werner Schroeter, von Trotta, Edgar Reitz, Helma Sanders-Brahms, Kluge, Schlöndorff, Christel Buschmann, Reinhard Hauff, Herzog and Herbert Achternbusch. Seitz-Sperr has moreover edited two of West German cinema's recent international productions, namely Wolfgang Petersen's *Unendliche Geschichte/The Neverending Story* (1984) and Jean-Jacques Annaud's *Der Name der Rose/The Name of the Rose* (1986). Women have also played a key role as women producers for the New German Cinema. As director of *Basis Film* Clara Burckner, for instance, has been involved in helping realize Christian Ziewer's film *Der Aufrechte Gang/Walking Tall* (1976) and Helke Sander's *Redupers* (1977). Renée Gundelach helped set up Wim

Wenders's production company Road Movies and produced his film *Der amerikanische Freund/The American Friend* (1976) and Peter Handke's *Die linkshändige Frau/The Left-Handed Woman* (1978).

49. Sheila Johnston, 'Hanna Schygulla', in Hans-Michael Bock, ed., *Cinegraph. Lexikon zum deutschsprachigen Film*, Munich 1984, p. E3.

50. These actresses have also acted in the films of Peter Handke, Ingemo Engström, Hans Geissendörfer, Herzog, Helma Sanders-Brahms, Peter Lilienthal, Reinhard Hauff, Straub, Wenders, Marianne Lüdcke, Doris Dörrie, Jeanine Meerapfel and Heidi Genée. See Thomas Elsaesser, *New German Cinema: A History*, Basingstoke 1989, pp. 284–9 for a discussion of the role of actors and actresses in the New German Cinema.

51. Egon Netenjacob, 'Filmen für eine bessere Gesellschaft', *Fernsehen und Film* no. 3 Mar 1970, p. 24.

52. In an interview conducted by the author on 6 November 1988, Monika Treut gives this as her reason for leaving the Hamburg women's media centre, *Bildwechsel.*

53. See, for instance, Berg-Ganschow and Strempel, 'Gespräch mit Ingemo Engström', pp. 13–14.

54. Fehervary, Lenssen, Mayne, p. 181.

55. Quoted in Saskia Baron, 'The Go-Between', *City Limits* 10–16 May 1985, p. 13.

56. Quoted in Jane Root, 'She, who is what she is . . .', *Monthly Film Bulletin* vol. 53, no. 634, Nov 1986, p. 331.

57. Dagmar Beiersdorf, 'Von einer guten Sache . . . kann man nie genug kriegen', *Zitty* no. 5/86, 27 Feb–12 Mar 1986. See also Uta Berg-Ganschow, Helge Heberle, Claudia Lenssen, 'Mysteriöse Trivialität und eine gewisse Unschärfe, Elfi Mikesch im Gespräch,' *Frauen und Film* no. 24, June 1980, pp. 19–20, and Hiller, pp. 14–15.

58. Silberman, 'Jutta Brückner, Christina Perincioli, and Helga Reidemeister', p. 47.

59. Rita Pohlandt, 'Doris Dörrie, Männer sind ihr Glück', *Cinema (West Germany)* no. 3, Mar 1986, p. 35.

60. See Sander, 'Feminismus und Film', pp. 8–9.

61. Ibid., p. 9.

62. Helke Sander, 'Der Herren machen das selber, dass ihnen die arme Frau feind wird', in Hans Prinzler and Eric Rentschler, eds, *Augenzeugen: 100 Texte neuer deutscher Filmemacher*, Frankfurt-am-Main 1988, p. 83.

63. Marc Silberman, 'Interview with Helke Sander, Open Forms', *Jump Cut* no. 29, Feb 1984, p. 59.

64. Silberman, 'Jutta Brückner, Christina Perincioli, and Helga Reidemeister', p. 48.

65. Sander, 'Nimmt man dir das Schwert', pp. 20–1.

66. See, for example, John Sandford, *The New German Cinema*, London 1980, p. 140.

67. Sander, 'Nimmt man dir das Schwert', p. 14.

68. Ibid., p. 29.

69. Ibid., p. 27.

70. Monica Jacobs, 'Civil Rights and Women's Rights in the Federal Republic of Germany Today', *New German Critique* no. 13, Winter 1978, p. 173.

71. Of the terrorists being sought by police during the seventies, approximately 60 per cent were women.

72. Quoted in Jacobs, p. 166.

73. Ibid., p. 167.

74. Schwarzer, p. 25.

75. Quoted in Sander, 'Nimmt man dir das Schwert', pp. 31–2.

76. See Lukasz-Aden and Strobel, p. 163.

77. 'Titelbild', *Frauen und Film* no. 5, p. 3.

78. See Möhrmann, p. 88.

79. Schwarzer, p. 25.

80. Sheila Johnston, John Ellis, 'The Radical Film Funding of ZDF', *Screen* vol. 23, no. 1, May–June 1982, p. 62.

81. Harbord, p. 48.

82. Johnston, Ellis, p. 66.

83. Silberman, 'Jutta Brückner, Cristina Perincioli, and Helga Reidemeister', p. 48.

84. Robert Acker, 'The Major Directions of German Feminist Cinema', *Literature/Film Quarterly* vol. 13, no. 4, 1985, p. 247.

85. Lukasz-Aden and Strobel, p. 74.

86. Munich 1985. Their book does not deal solely with German films, nor only with films by women. However, a sufficient number are included by German women to reveal the thematic and formal diversity of their work.

Chapter 4: Institutional Initiatives

1. Dörte Haak, *Verfassungsklage, 35 Filmarbeiterinnen gegen Regierung der BRD*, Cologne 1988, p. 2.

2. Renate Möhrmann, *Die Frau mit der Kamera*, Munich 1980, p. 25.

3. Helke Sander, 'Nimmt man dir das Schwert, dann greife zum Knüppel', *Frauen und Film* no. 1, July 1975, p. 18.

4. See, for instance, Edgar Reitz's comments, quoted in Jan Dawson, 'A Labyrinth of Subsidies', *Sight & Sound* vol. 50, no. 1, 1981, p. 17.

5. Möhrmann, p. 28.

6. Editorial, 'Vorwort der Redaktion zum Nachdruck der Nr. 1', *Frauen und Film* no. 1 (reprint), July 1975, p. 3.

7. Ibid., p. 4.

8. Editorial, 'In eigener Sache', *Frauen und Film* no. 11, Mar 1977, p. 2. *Courage* was a feminist magazine.

9. Editorial, 'Vorwort der Redaktion', p. 3.

10. Quoted by the editors, 'Die Filmemacherin Helma Sanders-Brahms', *Frauen und Film* no. 13, Oct 1977, p. 21.

11. See Miriam Hansen, 'Messages in a Bottle?', *Screen* vol. 28, no. 4, Autumn 1987, p. 34.

12. From an unpublished interview conducted by the author with Monika Treut on 6 November 1988 in London.

13. The Editors, 'Wird eine Frau Leiterin der Berliner Filmfestspiele?', *Frauen und Film* no. 6, 1975, p. 17.

14. Christel Buschmann, 'Fragen an Alexander Kluge', *Frauen und Film* no. 15, Feb 1978, p. 27.

15. See also Möhrmann, p. 95, where Helke Sander asserts that the presence of women in Basis-Film and at ZDF played a crucial role in her securing funding for her film *Die allseitig reduzierte Persönlichkeit/The All-round Reduced Personality* (1977).

16. Sander, 'Nimmt man dir das Schwert', pp. 13–14.

17. Claudia Lenssen, 'Fragen an Wilhelm Roth,' *Frauen und Film* no. 15, Feb 1978, p. 33.

18. See, for instance, Barbara Creed, 'Pornography and Pleasure: The Female Spectator', *Australian Journal of Screen Theory* nos 15–16, 1983, pp. 67–88.

19. Christel Buschmann and Claudia Lenssen, 'Wenn der Hahn kräht auf dem Mist, ändert sich das Wetter, oder es bleibt, wie es ist. Fragen von Christel Buschmann und Claudia Lenssen an: Klaus Eder, Alexander Kluge, Dr Günter Struve, Robert Backheuer, Wilhelm Roth, Dr Günter Rohrbach, Manfred Hohnstock, Volker Baer, Dr Gerd Albrecht', *Frauen und Film* no. 15, Feb 1978, pp. 22–62.

20. Ibid., p. 22.

21. Ibid., p. 39.

22. Ibid., p. 23.

23. Ibid., p. 39.

24. Ibid., p. 34.

25. Ibid., p. 42.

26. Quoted in Möhrmann, p. 42.

27. *Frauen und Film* no. 22, Dec 1979, p. 27.

28. Petra Hallter, 'Versuch eines Resumés: Zwei Jahre Verband der Filmarbeiterinnen e.V.', *Filmfaust* no. 27, April/May 1982, p. 52.

29. Ibid.

30. Ibid.

31. The Association's newsletter is very similar to that produced by the Women's Film, Television and Video Network in Britain before the organization lost its funding.

32. 'Verfassungsklage', in Hans Helmut Prinzler and Eric Rentschler, eds, *Augenzeugen: 100 Texte neuer deutscher Filmemacher*, Frankfurt-am-Main 1988, pp. 37–8.

33. Quoted in Patricia Clough, 'SPD Elects a Woman Vice-Chairman', *The Independent*, 2 September 1988, p. 8.

34. From author's unpublished interview.

35. 'Filmgruppe im Frauenzentrum Köln', *Frauen und Film* no. 18, Dec 1978, p. 50.

36. Hildegard Westbeld, 'Autonom und Subversiv: Kino von Frauen für Frauen', *Frauen und Film* no. 15, Feb 1978, p. 63.

37. Quoted in Gesine Strempel, '... es kommt drauf an, sie zu verändern', *Frauen und Film* no. 5, 1975, pp. 28–9.

38. Westbeld, p. 64. The women's film group in Cologne also reported a similar level of interest in their early days; see 'Filmgruppe im Frauenzentrum Köln', p. 50.

39. Eva Hiller, Claudia Lenssen, Gesine Strempel, 'Gespräch mit Ula Stöckl', *Frauen und Film* no. 12, June 1977, p. 6.

40. 'Filmgruppe im Frauenzentrum Köln', p. 51.

41. See Möhrmann, p. 42.

Chapter 5: 'Is There a Feminine Aesthetic?'

1. Filmstelle VSETH/VSU, *Frauen hinter der Kamera. Postmoderne im Kino*, Zurich 1988, p. 13.

2. Amos Vogel, 'Poetry and the Film: A Symposium', *Film Culture* no. 29, Summer 1963, p. 171.

3. Luce Irigaray, *Le Langage des dements*, Paris 1973, p. 351, quoted in Toril Moi, *Sexual/Textual Politics*, London 1985, p. 127. Although Irigaray is referring to people suffering from senile dementia, as Moi points out, the description has 'a familiar ring' and seems a particularly apt description of women's role within patriarchy.

4. Helma Sanders-Brahms, *Deutschland, bleiche Mutter. Film-Erzählung*, Hamburg 1980, p. 113.

5. Ibid.

6. Ibid., p. 112.

7. Ibid., p. 113.

8. Ibid., p. 114.

9. Ibid., p. 112.

10. Ibid., p. 9.

11. Angelika Bammer, 'Through a Daughter's Eyes: Helma Sanders-Brahms's *Germany, Pale Mother*', *New German Critique* no. 36, Fall 1985, p. 105.

12. Renate Möhrmann, *Die Frau mit der Kamera*, Munich 1980, p. 155.

13. Sanders-Brahms, p. 9.

14. Ibid., p. 11.

15. Roswitha Mueller, 'Interview with Ulrike Ottinger', *Discourse* no. 4, Winter 1981–82, p. 120.

16. Ibid., p. 115.

17. See Erica Carter, 'Interview with Ulrike Ottinger', *Screen Education* no. 41, Winter/Spring 1982, p. 36.

18. Möhrmann, p. 114.

19. Ibid.

20. Ellen Seiter, 'The Political is Personal: Margarethe von Trotta's "Marianne and Juliane"', in Charlotte Brunsdon, ed., *Films for Women*, London 1986, pp. 114–15.

21. Carol Bergman, 'Sheer Madness: An Interview with Margarethe von Trotta', *Cineaste* vol. 13, no. 4, 1984, p. 47.

22. 'Margarethe von Trotta on her Film "Leaden Times"', *Kino*, April 1981, p. 12.

23. Ibid.

24. See, for instance, Helke Sander, 'Feminism and Film', *Jump Cut* no. 27, July 1982, p. 49, and Marc Silberman, 'Interview with Helga Reidemeister: The Working Class Family', *Jump Cut* no. 27, July 1982, p. 45.

25. See Marc Silberman, 'Jutta Brückner, Christina Perincioli, and Helga Reidemeister. Conversing together finally', *Jump Cut* no. 27, July 1982, p. 48.

26. Quoted in Christian-Albrecht Gollub, 'Volker Schlöndorff and Margarethe von Trotta: Transcending the Genres', in Klaus Phillips, ed., *New German Filmmakers*, New York 1984, p. 298.

27. Sanders-Brahms, pp. 115 and 125.

28. Viktor Shklovsky, 'Art as Technique', in Lee Lemon and Marion Reis, trans., *Russian Formalist Criticism – Four Essays*, Nebraska 1965, p. 11.

29. Ibid., p. 12.

30. Marc Silberman, 'Interview with Ulrike Ottinger. Surreal Images', *Jump Cut* no. 29, Feb 1984, p. 56.

31. Carter, pp. 38–9.

32. Marc Silberman, 'Interview with Jutta Brückner. Recognizing Collective Gestures', *Jump Cut* no. 27, July 1982, p. 46.

33. Jane Root, 'Memories of Childhood, Dreams of Freedom. Interview with Marianne Rosenbaum', *Monthly Film Bulletin* vol. 52, no. 613, Feb 1985, p. 42.

34. Silberman, 'Interview with Helga Reidemeister', p. 45.

35. Linda Christmas, 'The Screen Test', *Guardian*, 24 September 1980.

36. Silberman, 'Interview with Helga Reidemeister', p. 45.

37. Ulrike Rosenbach, *Ulrike Rosenbach*, Cologne 1982, p. 115.

38. Margarethe von Trotta, 'Eine weibliche Filmästhetik', in Hans Prinzler and Eric Rentschler, eds, *Augenzeugen: 100 Texte neuer deutscher Filmemacher*, Frankfurt 1988, p. 200.

39. Quoted in Marc Silberman, 'Women Working. Women Filmmakers in West Germany: A Catalog (Part 2)', *Camera Obscura* no. 11, 1983, pp. 143–4.

40. Carter, p. 37.

41. Quoted in Christian-Albrecht Gollub, p. 298.

42. Silvia Bovenschen, 'Is There a Feminine Aesthetic?', in Gisela Ecker, ed., *Feminist Aesthetics*, London 1985, pp. 23–50.

43. Ibid., p. 27.

44. Ibid., p. 32.

45. Ibid., p. 48.

46. Ibid., p. 37.

47. Ibid., p. 49.

48. Ibid., p. 43.

49. Ibid., p. 49.

50. Quoted ibid., p. 49.

51. Ibid., p. 49.

52. Patricia Harbord, 'Interview with Jutta Brückner', *Screen Education* no. 40, Autumn/Winter 1981–2, p. 53.

Chapter 6: A Change of Direction

1. From an interview with Karola Gramann, conducted by Rebecca Coyle on 23 March 1990 in Sydney for Radio Two's *Media Magazine*.

2. See Jorn Rossing Jensen, 'West German Focus', *Screen International* no. 535, 15–22 Feb 1986, p. 30.

3. Ibid.

4. Hans-Jürgen Jagau, 'Eine gewisse Anarchie', *Zitty* no. 6/86, 13–26 March 1986, pp. 90–1.

5. Karola Gramann and Heide Schlüpmann, 'Frauenbewegung und Film – die letzten zwanzig Jahre', in Gudrun Lukasz-Aden and Christel Strobel, eds, *Der Frauenfilm*, Munich 1985, p. 255.

6. From an interview with Ruth Becht, Margit Weber, Ira Zamjatnins, Leonore Poth, conducted by the author on 22 March 1989.

7. Coyle-Gramann interview.

8. Quoted in H.B. Moeller, 'West German Women's Cinema: The Case of Margarethe von Trotta', *Film Criticism* vol. 9, no. 2, Winter 1984–5, p. 66.

9. See, for instance, Thomas Elsaesser, *New German Cinema*, Basingstoke 1989, p. 319, and Anton Kaes, 'Distanced Observers: Perspectives on the New German Cinema, *Quarterly Review of Film Studies* vol. 10, no. 3, Summer 1985, p. 238. Monika Treut also expressed a similar view in an interview conducted by the author on 6 November 1988 in London.

10. Margret Köhler, 'Blitzableiter für manches Gewitter', *Film-Korrespondenz* no. 4, 16 Feb 1988, p. 6.

11. CHP, 'Gepflegte Langeweile', *TAZ Berlinale* 18 Feb 1986.

12. Jill Forbes, 'Novembermond (Novembermoon)', *Monthly Film Bulletin* vol. 54, no. 647, Dec 1987, p. 358.

13. From an interview with Ulrike Zimmermann, conducted by the author on 23 February 1989 in Hamburg.

14. Quoted in Cynthia Kee, 'Sisters in Sorrow', *The Observer*, 20 Nov 1988.

15. Suzi Feay, 'Three Sisters', *Time Out* no. 1060, 12–19 Dec 1990, p. 32.

16. Jane Root, 'In the belly of the whale and sharing flats with men: Doris Dörrie discusses her researches with Jane Root', *Monthly Film Bulletin* vol. 53, no. 634, Nov 1986, p. 331.

17. Quoted in Marcia Pally, 'Open Dörrie', *Film Comment* vol. 22, no. 5, Sept–Oct 1986, p. 44.

18. Rita Pohlandt, 'Männer sind ihr Glück', *Cinema (W. Germany)* no. 3, March 1986, p. 35.

19. Pally, p. 44.

20. Ibid., p. 42.

21. Phillip French, 'Heller Wahn', *The Observer*, 10 July 1983, p. 31.

22. Leo Schönecker, 'Felix', *Film-Dienst* no. 2, 26 January 1988, p. 31.

23. Katrin Müller, 'Quartett am Bett', *Tip* 21 Jan–3 Feb 1988.

24. Kathleen Maitland-Carter, 'Too Much Talk About Sexuality and Not Enough Sex', *Independent Media* no. 91, September 1989, p. 16.

25. 'Ula Stöckl', in Hans-Michael Bock, ed., *Cinegraph. Lexikon zum deutschsprachigen Film*, Munich 1984, p. D1.

26. Roswitha Mueller, 'Interview with Ulrike Ottinger', *Discourse* no. 4, Winter 1981–2, p. 121.

27. Quoted in the London Filmmakers' Coop programme notes for July 1989.

28. From an interview with Monika Treut, conducted by the author on 6 November 1988 in London.

29. From an interview with Birgit Hein, conducted by the author on 8 February 1989 in Cologne.

30. 'Die Wahl der Qual – Der Filmemacher Frank Ripploh sprach mit den beiden Frauen', *Tip* 3/86, p. 48. Birgit Hein also echoes this view in my interview with her: 'For instance, Margarethe von Trotta – I find these women, as she represents them awful, they make me sick.'

31. Angela Carter, *The Sadeian Woman*, London 1979, p. 21.

32. Monika Treut, 'Die Zeremonie der blutenden Rose. Vorüberlegungen zu einem Filmprojekt', *Frauen und Film* no. 36, Feb 1984, p. 35.

33. From Monika Treut's film *Bondage* (1983), quoted in ibid., p. 42.

34. C. Carr, *Village Voice*, 14 Jan 1986.

35. 'Die Wahl der Qual', p. 49.

36. Christine Cremen, 'Female Fantasies that Celebrate Sexual Freedom', *The Australian*, 17 May 1988, p. 12.

37. See Moira Sweeney, 'Towards a New Erotica', *Independent Media* no. 92, Oct 1989, p. 21.

38. Although not many women have chosen to explore this avenue, another film which features a form of women's violence is Karin Albers's film *Das Schwarze Dreieck/ The Black Triangle* (1987) which shows a woman performing an act of self-mutilation.

39. This and the following observations are from the Knight–Hein interview.

40. Kathleen Maitland-Carter, p. 16.

41. From an interview with Claudia Schillinger, conducted by the author on 16 February 1989 in Berlin.

42. Quoted in Gudrun Lukasz-Aden and Christel Strobel, p. 61.

43. Jutta Brückner, '20 Jahre "Frauenfilm"', unpublished article, given to the author on 14 June 1989.

Bibliography

English and German books and articles focusing specifically on women directors and their work:

Robert Acker, 'The Major Directions of German Feminist Cinema', *Literature/Film Quarterly* vol. 13, no. 4, 1985, pp. 245–9.

Willi Baer and Hans Jürgen Weber, *Schwestern oder die Balance des Glücks. Ein Film von Margarethe von Trotta*, Frankfurt am Main 1979.

Angelika Bammer, 'Through a Daughter's Eyes: Helma Sanders-Brahms's "Germany, Pale Mother", *New German Critique* no. 36, Fall 1985, pp. 91–109.

Uta Berg-Ganschow, Helge Heberle, Claudia Lenssen, Helke Sander, Gesine Stempel, Sigrid Vagt and Hildegard Westbeld, 'Die "gute Mutter". Gespräch über "Von wegen 'Schicksal'" von Helga Reidemeister', *Frauen und Film* no. 20, May 1979, pp. 21–39.

Uta Berg-Ganschow and Gesine Strempel, 'Gespräch mit Ingemo Engström', *Frauen und Film* no. 22, Dec 1979, pp. 6–14.

Uta Berg-Ganschow, Helge Heberle and Claudia Lenssen, 'Mysteriöse Trivialität und eine gewisse Unschärfe, Elfi Mikesch im Gespräch,' *Frauen und Film* no. 24, June 1980, pp. 15–28.

Uta Berg-Ganschow and Wolfgang Jacobsen, 'Gespräch mit Ingemo Engström', *Film (W. Germany)* no. 5, May 1986, pp. 23–5.

Mo Beyerle, Noll Brinckmann, Karola Gramann, Katherine Sykora, 'Ein Interview mit Birgit Hein', *Frauen und Film* no. 37, 1984, pp. 95–102.

Hans-Michael Bock, ed., *Cinegraph: Lexikon zum deutschsprachigen Film*, Munich 1984.

Noll Brinckmann, 'Schwere Zeiten für Schauspieler. Beobachtungen zu "Heller Wahn" und "Der Schlaf der Vernunft"', *Frauen und Film* no. 40, Aug 1986, pp. 4–12.

Jutta Brückner, 'Women Behind the Camera', in Gisela Ecker, ed., *Feminist Aesthetics*, London 1985, pp. 120–24.

BIBLIOGRAPHY

Christel Buschmann, 'Gespräch zwischen Margarethe von Trotta und Christel Busch-mann', *Frauen und Film* no. 8, 1976, pp. 29–33.

Christel Buschmann, 'Interview mit Erika Runge', *Frauen und Film* no. 12, June 1977, pp. 24–7.

Erica Carter, 'Interview with Ulrike Ottinger', *Screen Education* no. 41, Winter/Spring 1982, pp. 34–42.

Charlotte Delorme, 'On the Film "Marianne and Juliane" by Margarethe von Trotta', *The Journal of Film & Video* vol. 37, no. 2, Spring 1985, pp. 47–51.

Thomas Elsaesser, 'Mother Courage and Divided Daughter', *Monthly Film Bulletin* vol. 50, no. 594, July 1983, pp. 176–8.

Thomas Elsaesser, '"It started with these Images" – Some Notes on Political Film-making after Brecht in Germany: Helke Sander and Harun Farocki', *Discourse* no. 7, Spring 1985, pp 95–120.

Thomas Elsaesser, 'Public Bodies & Divided Selves: German Women Film-makers in the 80s', *Monthly Film Bulletin* vol. 54, no. 647, Dec 1987, pp. 358–61.

Helen Fehervary, Claudia Lenssen and Judith Mayne, 'From Hitler to Hepburn: A Discussion of Women's Film Production and Reception', *New German Critique* nos 24–5, Fall–Winter 1981–2, pp. 172–85.

Reiner Frey and Christian Göldenboog, 'Rebellinen wider eine bleierne Zeit. Ein Inter-view mit Margarethe v. Trotta über ihren Film "bleierne Zeit"', *Filmfaust* no. 24, Oct–Nov 1981, pp. 29–36.

Regina Halter, Eva Hiller, Renate Holy, 'Die Filmemacherin Helma Sanders-Brahms' and reviews of her films, *Frauen und Film* no. 13, Oct 1977, pp. 21–43.

Miriam Hansen, 'Visual Pleasure, Fetishism and the Problem of Feminine/Feminist Discourse: Ulrike Ottinger's "Ticket of No Return"', *New German Critique* no. 31, Winter 1984, pp. 95–108.

Miriam Hansen, 'Messages in a Bottle?', *Screen* vol. 28, no. 4, Autumn 1987, pp. 30–39.

Patricia Harbord, 'Interview with Jutta Brückner', *Screen Education* no. 40, Autumn/Winter 1981–2, pp. 48–57.

Helge Heberle, Claudia Lenssen, Hille Sagel, Helke Sander and Gesine Strempel, 'Publikumserfahrungen. Gespräch zu dem Film "Die allseitig reduzierte Persön-lichkeit"', *Frauen und Film* no. 17, Sept 1978, pp. 49–55.

Helge Heberle and Monika Funke Stern, 'Das Feuer im Innern des Berges. Ein Gespräch mit Danièle Huillet', *Frauen und Film* no. 32, June 1982, pp. 4–12.

Eva Hiller, 'Interview mit Claudia Alemann' and reviews of her films, *Frauen und Film* no. 5, 1975, pp. 10–42.

Eva Hiller, Claudia Lenssen and Gesine Strempel, 'Gespräch mit Ula Stöckl' and reviews of her films, *Frauen und Film* no. 12, June 1977, pp. 3–23.

Barbara Hyams, 'Is the Apolitical Woman at Peace?: A Reading of the Fairy Tale in "Germany, Pale Mother"', *Wide Angle* vol. 10, no. 3, 1988, pp. 40–51.

Gary Indiana, 'Valie Export', *On Film* no. 9, Winter 1978–9.

Annette Insdorf, 'Rosa Luxemburg: More Than a Revolutionary', *The New York Times*, 31 May 1987.

E. Ann Kaplan, 'Female Politics in the Symbolic Realm: Von Trotta's Marianne and Juliane ("The German Sisters") (1981)', in Kaplan, *Women & Film. Both Sides of the Camera*, London 1983.

E. Ann Kaplan, 'Discourses of Terrorism, Feminism and the Family in von Trotta's Marianne and Juliane', *Persistence of Vision* no. 2, Fall 1985, pp. 61–8.

BIBLIOGRAPHY

Joanna Kiernan, 'Films by Valie Export', *Millenium Film Journal* nos 16–18, Fall–Winter 1986–7, pp. 181–7.

Julia Knight, 'Vestal Vision', *Independent Media* no. 95, Jan 1990, pp. 20–21.

Gertrud Koch, 'Die Internationale tanzt', *Konkret* no. 4, April 1986, pp. 72–6.

Gertrud Koch and Heide Schlüpmann, 'Spiegelungen. Ein Gespräch mit Birgit und Wilhelm Hein', *Frauen und Film* no. 43, Dec 1987, pp. 27–36.

Barbara Koenig Quart, 'Sheer Madness', and Carol Bergman, 'Sheer Madness. An Interview with Margarethe von Trotta', *Cineaste* vol. 13, no. 4, 1984, pp. 46–9.

Dietrich Kuhlbrodt, 'Porträt Experimentalfilm 2, Wilhelm und Birgit Hein', *epd Film* 1/87, pp. 12–14.

Annette Kuhn, 'Encounter between Two Cultures. A Discussion with Ulrike Ottinger', *Screen* vol. 28, no. 4, Autumn 1987, pp. 74–9.

Annette Kuhn with Susannah Radstone, eds, *The Women's Companion to International Film*, London 1990.

Gudrun Lukasz-Aden and Christel Strobel, eds, *Der Frauenfilm*, Munich 1985.

Kathleen Maitland-Carter, 'Too Much Talk About Sexuality and Not Enough Sex', *Independent Media* no. 91, Sept 1989, pp. 16–18.

Judith Mayne, 'Female Narration, Women's Cinema: Helke Sander's "The All-Round Reduced Personality/Redupers"', *New German Critique*, nos 24–5, Fall/Winter 1981–2, pp. 155–71.

Renate Möhrmann, *Die Frau mit der Kamera*, Munich 1980.

Renate Möhrmann, 'Occupation: Woman Artist', in Gisela Ecker, ed., *Feminist Aesthetics*, London 1985, pp. 150–61.

Hans-Bernhard Moeller, 'West German Women's Cinema: The Case of Margarethe von Trotta', *Film Criticism* vol. 9, no. 2, Winter 1984–5, pp. 51–66.

Roswitha Mueller, 'Interview with Ulrike Ottinger', *Discourse* no. 4, Winter 1981–2, pp. 108–26.

Roswitha Mueller, 'The Mirror and the Vamp', *New German Critique* no. 34, Winter 1985, pp. 176–93.

Egon Netenjacob, 'Filmen für eine bessere Gesellschaft. Gespräch mit den Filmerinnen Erika Runge und Ilona Perl', *Fernsehen und Film* no. 3, March 1970, pp. 21–4.

Ulrike Ottinger, *Madame X – eine absolute Herrscherin*, Frankfurt 1979.

Marcia Pally, 'Open Dörrie', *Film Comment* vol. 22, no. 5, September–October 1986, pp. 42–5.

Anita Prammer, *Valie Export. Eine multimediale Künstlerin*, Vienna 1988.

Helga Reidemeister, 'Gegen die schöne Illusion, daß "reiner" Dokumentarfilm heute noch realisierbar ist, gezeigt am Beispiel der Produktionshintergründe zum Film "der gekaufte Traum"' and other contributions, *Frauen und Film* no. 13, October 1977, pp. 12–20.

Frank Ripploh, 'Die Wahl der Qual. Auf der letztjährigen Berlinale heftig umstritten, kommt Elfi Mikeschs und Monika Treuts Film "Verführung – Die grausame Frau" jetzt ins Kino', *Tip* 3/86, pp. 46–8.

Ruth Perlmutter, 'Two New Films by Helke Sander and Ulrike Ottinger', *Film Criticism* vol. 9, no. 2, Winter 1984–5, pp. 67–73.

B. Ruby Rich, 'She Says, He Says: The Power of the Narrator in Modernist Film Politics', *Discourse* no. 6, Fall 1983, pp. 31–46.

Jane Root, 'Memories of Childhood, Dreams of Freedom. Jane Root interviews Marianne Rosenbaum', *Monthly Film Bulletin* vol. 52, no. 613, February 1985, pp. 41–2.

BIBLIOGRAPHY

Ulrike Rosenbach, *Ulrike Rosenbach*, Cologne 1982.

Helke Sander, 'Nimmt man dir das Schwert, dann greife zum Knüppel', *Frauen und Film* no. 1, 1974, pp. 12–48.

Helke Sander, 'Überlegungen zum Verhältnis von Kunst und Politik', in Silvia Eiblmayr, Valie Export, Monika Prischl-Maier, eds, *Kunst mit Eigen-Sinn. Aktuelle Kunst von Frauen. Texte und Dokumentation*, Munich 1985, pp. 89–92.

Helma Sanders-Brahms, *Deutschland, bleiche Mutter. Film-Erzählung*, Hamburg 1980.

Albert Schwarzer, *Begleitheft zum Film "Peppermint Frieden" von Marianne S.W. Rosenbaum*, Duisburg 1987.

Ellen Seiter, 'The Political is Personal: Margarethe von Trotta's "Marianne and Juliane"', in Charlotte Brunsdon, ed., *Films for Women*, London 1986, pp. 109–16.

Marc Silberman, 'Cine-Feminists in West Berlin', *Quarterly Review of Film Studies* vol. 5, no. 2, Spring 1980, pp. 217–32.

Marc Silberman, 'Women Filmmakers in West Germany: A Catalaog', *Camera Obscura* no. 6, Fall 1980, pp. 123–52.

Marc Silberman, 'Women Filmmakers in West Germany: A Catalog (Part 2)', *Camera Obscura* no. 11, 1983, pp. 132–45.

Marc Silberman, ed., 'Film and Feminism in Germany Today', *Jump Cut* no. 27, July 1982, pp. 41–53.

Marc Silberman, ed., 'German Film Women', *Jump Cut* no. 29, Feb 1984, pp. 49–64.

Marc Silberman, ed., 'German Women's Film Culture', *Jump Cut* no. 30, March 1985, pp. 63–9.

Kaja Silverman, 'Helke Sander and the Will to Change', *Discourse* no. 6, Fall 1983, pp. 10–30.

Yvonne Spielmann, 'Porträt Experimentalfilm 4. Elfi Mikesch', *epd Film* 11/87, pp. 10–13.

Bion Steinborn and Carola Hilmes, '"Frieden" hat für uns Deutsche einen amerikanischen Geschmack. Ein Gespräch mit Marianne S.W. Rosenbaum', *Filmfaust* no. 39, May–June 1984, pp. 27–31.

Moira Sweeney, 'Towards a New Erotica', *Independent Media* no. 92, Oct 1989, pp. 19–21.

Margarethe von Trotta and Luisa Franca, *Das zweite Erwachen der Christa Klages*, Frankfurt am Main 1980.

Margarethe von Trotta, *Heller Wahn*, Frankfurt am Main 1983.

Margarethe von Trotta, *Rosa Luxemburg*, Nördlingen 1986.

Verband der Filmarbeiterinnen, *Frauen Film Handbuch*, Berlin 1984.

Verband der Filmarbeiterinnen, *Verfassungsklage. 35 Filmarbeiterinnen gegen Regierung der Bundesrepublik Deutschland*, Cologne 1988.

Ginette Vincendeau, 'Misunderstood Mother and Forgotten Father. An Interview with Helma Sanders-Brahms', *Monthly Film Bulletin* vol. 52, no. 616, May 1985, pp. 141–2.

Hans Jürgen Weber in Zusammenarbeit mit Ingeborg Weber, eds, *Die bleierne Zeit. Ein Film von Margarethe von Trotta*, Frankfurt am Main 1981.

Kraft Wetzel, 'Neuland jenseits des Kinomarktes. Deutsche Filme auf der Berlinale '87', *epd Film* 6/87, pp. 22–6.

Patricia White, 'Madame X of the China Seas', *Screen* vol. 28, no. 4, Autumn 1987, pp. 80–95.

English books, journals and articles on New German Cinema and German film. These are useful background reading and some provide further information on women's filmmaking:

Richard Collins and Vincent Porter, *WDR and the Arbeiterfilm: Fassbinder, Ziewer and Others*, London 1981.

Timothy Corrigan, *New German Film. The Displaced Image*, Austin 1983.

Jan Dawson, 'The Sacred Terror', *Sight & Sound* vol. 48, no. 4, Autumn 1979, pp. 242–5.

Jan Dawson, 'A Labyrinth of Subsidies', *Sight & Sound* vol. 50, no. 1, 1981, pp. 14–20.

Charles Eidsvik, 'The State as Movie Mogul', *Film Comment* vol. 15, Mar–April 1979, pp. 60–6.

Thomas Elsaesser, *New German Cinema: A History*, Basingstoke 1989.

James Franklin, *New German Cinema*, London 1986.

Gillian Hartnoll and Vincent Porter, eds, *Alternative Filmmaking in Television: ZDF – A Helping Hand*, London 1982.

R.C. and M.E. Helt, *West German Cinema Since 1945: A Reference Book*, London 1987.

Sheila Johnston, 'The Author as Public Institution. The "New" Cinema in the Federal Republic of Germany', *Screen Education* nos 32–3, 1979–80, pp. 67–78.

Sheila Johnston and John Ellis, 'The Radical Film Funding of ZDF, *Screen* vol. 23, no. 1, May–June 1982, pp. 60–73.

Anton Kaes, *From 'Hitler' to 'Heimat'. The Return of History as Film*, Cambridge and London 1989.

Hans Günther Pflaum and Hans Helmut Prinzler, *Cinema in the Federal Republic of Germany*, Bonn 1983.

Klaus Phillips, ed, *New German Filmmakers*, New York 1984.

Hans Prinzler and Eric Rentschler, eds, *West German Filmmakers on Film*, New York 1988 (also published in German under the title *Augenzeugen: 100 Texte neuer deutscher Filmemacher*, Frankfurt am Main 1988).

Eric Rentschler, *West German Film in the Course of Time*, Bedford Hills 1984.

Eric Rentschler, *German Film and Literature. Adaptations and Transformations*, New York and London 1986.

John Sandford, *The New German Cinema*, London 1980.

Discourse no. 6, Fall 1983.

Literature/Film Quarterly vol. 7, no. 3, 1979.

Literature/Film Quarterly vol. 13, no. 4, 1985.

New German Critique nos 24–5, Fall/Winter 1981–2.

Persistence of Vision no. 2, Fall 1985.

Quarterly Review of Film Studies vol. 5, no. 2, Spring 1980.

Wide Angle vol. 3, no. 4, 1980.

The Filmmakers

ALEMANN, Claudia von (born 1943)

Studied sociology and art history, then film at the Ulm Institute (1964–68). *Einfach/Simple* (1966), *Lustgewinn/Pleasure* (1967), *Fundevogel/Found Bird* (1967), *Das ist nur der Anfang – der Kampf geht weiter/It's Only the Beginning, the Struggle Goes On* (1969), *Brigitte* (1970), *Algier/Algiers* (1970), *Kathleen und Eldridge Cleaver/Kathleen and Eldridge Cleaver* (1970), *Tu luc van doan – Aus eigner Kraft/Through One's Own Strength* (1971), *Es kommt drauf an, sie zu verändern/The Point is to Change It* (1972–73), *Namibia* (1973), *Filme der Sonne und der Nacht: Ariane Mnouchkine/Films of Sun and Night: Ariane Mnouchkine* (1977), *Reise nach Lyon/Blind Spot* (1980), *Das Frauenzimmer/The Women's Room* (1981), *Nebelland/Fogland* (1981–82), *Die Tür in der Mauer/The Door in the Wall* (1984).

BEHRENS, Gloria (born 1948)

Studied ballet, then film at the Munich School for Film and Television (1967–70). *Die Kinder vom Hasenbergl/The Children of the Hasenbergl* (1971), *Der Herr unserer Hoffnung/The Master of our Hope* (co-dir 1971), *Geschichten von Franz und seinen Freunden/Stories of Franz and his Friends* (1975–76), *Christinas Reise/Christina's Journey* (1980), *Rosi und die grosse Stadt/Rosi and the Big City* (1980), *La Vagabonde on the Blue Eye* (1981).

BEIERSDORF, Dagmar (born 1946)

Studied drama and journalism, then worked as an assistant director and actress. *Puppe kaputt/Broken Doll* (1977), *Dirty Daughters* (1981), *Die Wolfsbraut/The Wolf Girl* (1985), *Der sexte Sinn/The Sixth Sense* (1985).

BREITEL, Heide (born 1941)

Studied photography and then film editing, has specialized in documentary filmmaking. *Der letzte Kuss/ The Last Kiss* (co-dir 1977), *Vergesst es nie, wie es begann! – Ernst Busch/Never Forget How it Began* (co-dir 1978), *Küche – Theater – Krankenhaus/ Kitchen – Theatre – Hospital* (co-dir 1979), *Die kleinen Kleberinnen/ The Little Splicers* (co-dir 1980), *Zwischen den Bildern/ Between the Pictures* (co-dir 1981), *Im Jahr der Schlange/ In the Year of the Snake* (1982), *Wenn der Wald stirbt, stirbt die Seele/ When the Forest Dies, the Soul Dies* (co-dir 1983).

BRÜCKNER, Jutta (born 1941)

Studied political science and philosophy; from 1973 worked as a scriptwriter for Bavarian television. *Tue recht und scheue niemand/ Do Right and Fear No-one* (1975), *Ein ganz und gar verwahrlostes Mädchen/ A Thoroughly Demoralized Girl* (1977), *Hungerjahre/ Years of Hunger* (1979), *Laufen lernen/ Learning to Run* (1980), *Die Erbtöchter/ The Daughters' Inheritance* (co-dir 1982), *Kolossale Liebe/ Colossal Love* (1984), *Ein Blick – und die Liebe bricht aus/ One Glance and Love Breaks Out* (1986).

BUSCHMANN, Christel (born 1942)

Studied German and Romantic Literature, then worked as a journalist and translator. *Gibbi Westgermany* (1980), *Comeback* (1982), *Auf Immer und Ewig/ For Ever and Ever* (1985), *Felix* (co-dir 1987), *Ballhaus Barmbek – Let's Kiss and Say Goodbye* (1988).

CZENKI, Margit (born 1942)

Worked in remedial education; from 1971 spent five years in prison for bank robbery, then worked with children and in women's projects, then as scriptwriter and assistant director for Margarethe von Trotta, Elfi Mikesch, Claudia von Alemann, and others. *Komplizinnen/ Accomplices* (1988).

DEPPE, Gardi (born 1939)

Studied acting, then film at the Berlin Academy for Film and Television (1970–73), from 1973 worked for television. *Women's Camera* (1970), *Xenia will erzählen/ Xenia Wants to Talk* (1970), *The Pigs* (1971), *Kinder für dieses System – Paragraph 218/ Children for This System– Paragraph 218* (1973), *Helfen können wir uns nur selbst/ Only We Can Help Ourselves* (1973–74), *Später kannst du ja auch studieren/ You Can Study Later on as Well (1976)*, *Frauen im Widerstand 1933–45/ Women in the Resistance 1933–45* (1977), *Ich will weg von Heroin/ I Want to Give up Heroin* (1980).

DÖRRIE, Doris (born 1955)

Studied drama, acting and film in the US, then film at the Munich School for Film and Television (1975–78). *Der erste Walzer/ The First Waltz* (1978), *Hättest was Gscheits gelernt/ If ya'd Only Learned Something Practical* (1978), *Paula aus Portugal/ Paula from Portugal* (1979), *Von Romantik keine Spur: Martina (19) wird Schäferin/ No Trace of Romance: Martina (19) Becomes a Shepherdess* (1980–81). *Dazwischen/ In Between* (1981), *Unter Schafen/ Among Noisy Sheep* (1981), *Mitten ins Herz/ Straight Through the Heart* (1983), *Im Innern des Wals/ In the Belly of the Whale* (1984), *Männer/ Men* (1985), *Paradies/ Paradise* (1986), *Ich und Er/ Me and Him* (1988), *Geld/ Money* (1989), *Happy Birthday, Türke!/ Happy Birthday* (1990).

DURBAHN, Birgit (born 1952)

Co-founded the women's media centre Bildwechsel; has specialized in video. *Walpurgisnacht/ Walpurgis Night* (co-dir 1979), *Unter-Rock* (co-dir 1980), *Fotos und Collagen von Monika Neuser/ Photos and Collages by Monika Neuser* (co-dir 1981), *Mit den besten Wünschen/ With Best Wishes* (co-dir 1982), *Fotomorgana* (1983), *Auch den Körpern der Frauen ist nicht mehr zu trauen/ Even Women's Bodies can no Longer be Trusted* (co-dir 1983–84), *Klischee: Lesben im Film/ Cliché: Lesbians in Film* (co-dir 1985), *Rocking Neetze* (co-dir 1985), *Werbewelten: Frauenabteilung/ Advertising Worlds: Women's Department* (1985).

ENGSTRÖM, Ingemo (born 1941, Finland)

Studied psychology, medicine and literature, then film at the Munich School for Film and Television (1967–70). *Candy Man* (1968), *Dark Spring* (1970), *Zwei Liebende und die Mächtigsten dieser Erde/ Two Lovers and the Powerful on Earth* (1973), *Kampf um ein Kind/ Fight for a Child* (1974–75), *Erzählen/ Telling Stories* (co-dir 1975), *Fluchtweg nach Marseille/ Escape Route to Marseille* (co-dir 1977), *Letzte Liebe/ Last Love* (1979), *Flucht in den Norden/ Flight North* (1985).

EXPORT, Valie (born 1940, Austria)

Studied textiles, then worked as a film extra, model, script girl and assistant film editor, and from 1967 moved into performance art, filmmaking, expanded cinema, video, photography and installation work; 1967–69 collaborated extensively with Peter Weibel. *Menstruationsfilm* (1967), *Cutting* (1967–68), *Abstract Film No. 1* (1968), *VALIE EXPORT* (co-dir 1968), *Instant Film* (co-dir 1968), *Auf + zu + ab + an* (1968), *Ping Pong* (1968), *333* (1968), *Tapp- und Tastkino* (1968), *Splitscreen – Solipsismus* (1968), *Vorspann* (co-dir 1968), *Ohne Titel xn/ Ohne Titel No. 1* (co-dir 1968), *Ohne Titel Nr. 2* (co-dir 1968), *Das Eine* (1968), *Der Kuss* (co-dir 1968), *Ein Familienfilm von Waltraut Lehner* (co-dir 1968), *Ars lucis* (1968), *Gesichtsgrimassen* (1968), *A World Cinema* (co-dir 1968–75), *Eine Reise ist eine Reise wert* (co-dir 1969), *Das magische Auge* (co-dir 1969), *Bewegte Bilder über sich bewegende Körper* (1969–73), *Split Reality* (1970), *Facing a*

Family (1971), *Die unterbrochene Linie* (1971–72), *Schnitte* (1972–75), *Remote ...
Remote* (1973), *mann & frau & animal* (1973), *Adjungierte Dislokationen* (1973),
Zeit und Gegenzeit (1973), *Interrupted Movement* (1973), *Autohypnose* (1973), *Sehtest*
(1973), *Die süsse Nummer: Ein Konsumerlebnis* (1973), *Asemie* (1973), *Hyperbulie*
(1973), *Raumsehen und Raumhören* (1974), *Body Politics* (1974), *Bewegungs-
imaginationen* (1975), *Implentation* (1975), *Inversion* (1975), *Unsichtbare Gegner/In-
visible Adversaries* (1976), *Positiv Negative Transfinit* (co-dir 1976), *Adjungierte Dislokationen II* (1978), *I Beat It* (1978), *Menschenfrauen* (1979), *Syntagma* (1983), *Das
bewaffnete Auge* (1984), *Die Praxis der Liebe/The Practice of Love* (1984), *Tischbemerk-
ungen – November 1985* (1985), *Die Zweiheit der Natur* (1986), *Sieben Frauen – Sieben
Sünden/Seven Women – Seven Sins* (co-dir 1985), *Yukon Quest* (co-dir 1986), *Mental
Images oder der Zugang zur Welt* (co-dir 1987), *Maschinenkörper – Körpermaschinen –
Körperraum* (1988), *Dokumente zum Internationalen Aktionismus* (1988), *Unica* (1988).

FRANKENBERG, Pia (born 1957)

Studied acting and theatre, then started working in film sector as assistant
director, producer and scriptwriter. *Sehnsucht nach dem ganz anderen/Yearning
for Something Totally Different* (1981), *Nachtbilder/Night Pictures* (co-dir 1982), *Der
Anschlag/The Attack* (1983–84), *Nicht nichts ohne dich/Not Nothing Without You*
(1985), *Brennende Betten/Burning Beds* (1987).

GENÉE, Heidi (born 1938)

Studied film (1956–59), from 1960 worked extensively as an assistant director
and film editor. *Hinter Ihnen dreht einer/One of Them is Turning Behind You*
(1967), *Frühnachrichten/Early News* (1968), *Grete Minde* (1977), *Guten Morgen,
Gulliver/Good Morning, Gulliver* (1978), *Auch der Herbst hat schöne Tage/Even
Autumn has Beautiful Days* (1979), *1 + 1 = 3* (1979), *Stachel im Fleisch/Thorn in
the Flesh* (1981), *Kraftprobe/Test of Strength* (1981).

GROTE, Alexandra von (born 1944)

Studied drama, philosophy, psychology, romantic literature and acting; from
1970 worked in television and as a journalist. *Weggehen um anzukommen/
Leaving in Order to Arrive* (1981–82), *Novembermond/November Moon* (1985), *Time
is Money* (1987).

HAFFTER, Petra (born 1953)

Studied journalism, drama and political science, from 1974 worked in radio
and television, then moved into writing, producing and directing films; co-
founder of the Association of Women Film Workers. *Zensur/Censorship* (co-dir
1977), *Alles hat hier seinen Preis/Everything has its Price Here* (1977), *Morgen geht
die grosse Reise los/The Big Journey Starts Tomorrow* (co-dir 1978), *Wahnsinn, das
ganze Leben ist Wahnsinn/Madness, Life is Total Madness* (1979), *Vom anderen*

Stern/From Another Planet (1982), *Der Kuss des Tigers/The Tiger's Kiss* (1988).

HEIN, Birgit (born 1942)

Studied art history, from 1966 carried out joint film work with husband Wilhelm Hein, has specialized in and become an authority on experimental film and expanded cinema (all films co-directed with Wilhelm Hein). *S & W* (1967), *Ole* (1967), *Und Sie?* (1967), *Grün* (1968), *Werbefilm Nr. 1: Bamberg* (1968), *Rohfilm* (1968), *Reproductions* (1969), *625* (1969), *Square Dance* (1969), *Work in Progress Teil A* (1969), *Sichtbarmachung der Wirkungsweise optischer Gesetze am einfachen Beispiel* (1969), *Work in Progress Teil B* (1970), *Porträts* (1970), *Auszüge aus einer Biographie* (1970), *Madison/Wis* (1970), *Replay* (1970), *Foto-Film* (1970), *Reproduktionsimmanente Ästhetik* (1970), *Porträts. 4. Nina I–III* (1971), *Autobahn. 2 Teile* (1971), *Work in Progress Teil C* (1971), *Work in Progress Teil D* (1971), *Doppelprojektion I* (1971), *I Want You To Be Rich* (1971), *Altes Material* (1971), *Zoom – lange Fassung* (1971), *Zoom – kurze Fassung* (1971), *Videotape I* (1971), *Liebesgrüsse* (1971), *Yes to Europe* (1971), *Porträts. Kurt Schwitters I, II, III* (1972), *Porträts* (1972), *Doppelprojektionen II–V* (1972), *Aufblenden/Abblenden* (1972), *Dokumentation* (1972), *Fussball* (1972), *Ausdatiertes Material* (1973), *God Bless America* (1973), *Stills* (1973), *London* (1973), *Zu Lucifer Rising von Kenneth Anger* (1973), *Strukturelle Studien* (1974), *Jack Smith* (1974), *Künstlerfilme I* (1974), *Künstlerfilme II* (1974), *Porträts II* (1975), *Materialfilme I* (1976), *Materialfilme II* (1976), *Porträts III* (1977), *Kurt Kren. Porträt eines experimentellen Filmmachers* (1978), *Verdammt in alle Ewigkeit* (1978–79), *Superman und Superwoman* (1980), *Die Medien und das Bild. Andy Warhols Kunst* (1981), *Love Stinks – Bilder des täglichen Wahnsinns* (1982), *American Grafitti* (1982), *Verbotene Bilder* (1984–85), *Die Kali-Filme/The Kali Films* (1987–88).

HIRTZ, Dagmar (born 1941)

From 1964 worked as film editor, then as assistant director. *Streifzüge/Raids* (1972), *Unerreichbare Nähe/Final Call* (1983).

HOLLDACK, Claudia (born 1943)

Worked in theatre, then studied photography, from 1967 worked in television and from 1969 as assistant director. *1000 Lieder ohne Ton/A Thousand Songs Without Sound* (1976), *Kaiserin aus der Laube/The Empress in the Summerhouse* (1977), *Eva Mattes – Fragen an eine Mutter/Eva Mattes – Questions for a Mother* (1979), *Portrait eines Schauspielers/Portrait of an Actor* (1979), *Don Quichottes Kinder/Don Quixote's Children* (1981), *Vor den Vätern sterben die Söhne/The Sons Die Before Their Fathers* (1981).

HORN, Rebecca (born 1944)

Studied fine arts, then from 1970 began working in performance and with film and video. *Einhorn* (1970), *Schwarze Hörner* (1971), *Körperfarbe* (1971), *Performances 1* (1972), *Conversation 1* (1972), *Conversation 2* (1972), *Conversation 3* (1972), *Transformation* (1972–73), *Performances 2* (1973), *Exercises* (1973), *Bleistiftmaske* (1973), *Performances* (1973), *Flamingos* (1974), *Unter dem Wasser schlafen und Dinge sehen, die sich in weiter Ferne abspielen* (1974–75), *Mit beiden Händen gleichzeitig die Wände berühren – Blinzeln* (1974–75), *Zwischen den feuchten Zungenblättern* (1974–75), *Mit zwei Scheren gleichzeitig Haare schneiden* (1974–75), *Berlin – Übungen in neun Stücken* (1974–75), *Paradieswitwe* (1975), *Paradieswitwe 1 und Paradieswitwe 2* (1975), *Die Chinesische Verlobte* (1976), *Übung zu: Der Eintänzer* (1976), *Der Eintänzer/ The Dancing Cavalier* (1978), *La Ferdinanda* (1981).

HUILLET, Danièle (born 1936, France)

Spent a year studying in order to enter film school in Paris, met Jean-Marie Straub in 1954, moved to Germany in 1959 and commenced joint film work with Straub in 1962 (all films co-directed with Straub). *Machorka Muff* (1962), *Nicht versöhnt oder Es hilft nur Gewalt, wo Gewalt herrscht/ Not Reconciled or Only Violence Helps Where Violence Reigns* (1964–65), *Chronik der Anna Magdalena Bach/ Chronicle of Anna Magdalena Bach* (1967), *Der Bräutigam, Die Komödianten und der Zuhälter/ The Bridegroom, the Comedienne and the Pimp* (1968), *Les yeux ne veulent pas en tout temps se fermer ou Peutetre qu'un jour Rome se permettra de choisir a son tour. Othon/ The Eyes do not Always Want to Close or Perhaps One Day Rome will Permit itself to Choose in its Turn. Othon* (1969), *Einleitung zu Arnold Schönbergs Begleitmusik zu einer Lichtspielscene/ Introduction to Arnold Schönberg's 'Accompaniment to a Cinematographic Scene'* (1972), *Geschichtsunterricht/ History Lessons* (1972), *Moses und Aron/ Moses and Aron* (1974–75), *Fortini Cani/ The Dogs of Sinai* (1976), *Toute Revolution est un Coup de Des/ Every Revolution is a Throw of the Dice* (1977), *Dalla nube alla resistenza/ From the Cloud to the Resistance* (1978–79), *Zu früh, zu spät/ Too Early, Too Late* (1980–81), *En Rachachant* (1982), *Klassenverhältnisse/ Class Relations* (1984), *Der Tod des Empedokles/ The Death of Empedocles* (1986), *Schwarze Sünde/ Black Sins* (1989).

JUNGMANN, Recha (born 1940)

Trained and worked as an actress (1956–64), then studied film at the Ulm Institute (1964–66), spent six years in Canada, and from 1976 worked for German television. *Renate* (1968), *Etwas tut weh/ Something Hurts* (1980), *Zwischen Mond und Sonne/ Between Moon and Sun* (1981).

KASPER, Barbara (born 1945)

Studied art, then film at the Berlin Academy for Film and Television (1970–74), specialized in documentary filmmaking. *Women's Camera* (co-dir 1970), *Kaufen oder gekauft werden/ To Buy or be Bought* (co-dir 1971), *Gleicher Lohn für Mann und Frau/ Equal Wages for Men and Women* (co-dir 1971), *Betriebsschliessung –*

Betriebsverlagerung/Factory Closure – Factory Transfer (co-dir 1972–73), *Gegen Macht International/Against Power International* (co-dir 1975), *Arbeit und Leben in Singapur/Work and Life in Singapore* (co-dir 1976), *Erinnerungen an einen deutschen Betrieb, Hanomag 1933–1945/Memories of a German Factory, Hanomag 1933–45* (co-dir 1977–78), *Borsig, Berlin-Tegel* (co-dir 1980), *Aus heiterem Himmel/Out of the Clear Blue Sky* (co-dir 1982), *Arbeit im Krieg/Work During the War* (co-dir 1982), *Fremde Arbeit/Strange Work* (co-dir 1983).

KNILLI, Maria (born 1959)

Worked as a journalist, then studied film at the Munich School for film and Television (1979–83). *Fehlanzeige/Dead Loss* (1981), *Der Selbstmörder/Suicide* (1981), *Augen gerade aus/Eyes Straight Ahead* (1980–81), *Vom Kopf zur Leinwand. Regisseur Laslo Benedek erzählt/From the Head to the Screen. Director Laslo Benedek in Conversation* (1983), *Spätvorstellung/Later Performance* (1982), *Lieber Karl/Dear Karl* (1984), *Follow Me* (1988).

KUBACH, Gabi (born 1944)

Studied film at the Munich School for Film and Television (1967–71), worked for Bavarian Television. *Die Entführung/The Kidnapping* (1971), *Technologie/Technology* (co-dir 1971), *Verkaufte Träume/Sold Dreams* (1976), *Das Ende der Beherrschung/The End of Domination* (1976), *Geteilte Freunde/Shared Friends* (1978), *Rendevous in Paris* (1980), *Trauma* (1982–83).

LÜDCKE, Marianne (born 1945)

Studied acting, then film at the Berlin Academy for Film and Television (1971–74), and collaborated on several films with Ingo Kratisch. *Akkord/Piecework* (co-dir 1971), *Die Wollands/The Wolland Family* (co-dir 1972), *Lohn und Liebe/Love and Wages* (co-dir 1973), *Familienglück/Wedded Bliss* (co-dir 1975), *Die Tannerhütte/The Pine Cabin* (co-dir 1976), *Die grosse Flatter/Breakaway* (1979), *Flüchtige Bekanntschaften/Fleeting Acquaintances* (1982), *Liebe ist kein Argument/Love is no Argument* (1983).

MEERAPFEL, Jeanine (born 1943, Argentina)

Studied film at the Ulm Institute (1964–68); from 1970 worked as a freelance film critic. *Abstand/Distance* (1966), *Regionalzeitung/Regional Newspaper* (1967), *Auf der Suche nach dem Glück/Looking for Happiness* (co-dir 1969–70), *Malou* (1980), *Im Land meiner Eltern/In The Land of My Parents* (1981), *Solange es Europa noch Gibt – Fragen an den Frieden/As Long as There's Still a Europe – Questions on Peace* (co-dir 1985), *Die Kümmeltürkin geht/The Turkish Spice Lady is Leaving* (1985), *Die Verliebten/Days to Remember* (1986), *La Amiga/The Girlfriend* (1988), *Desembarcos/When Memory Speaks* (co-dir 1989).

MIKESCH, Elfi (born 1940, Austria)

Trained and worked as a photographer under the pseudonym 'Oh Muvie', from 1970 started working with super-8; from 1978 design work for *Frauen und Film*, worked extensively as camerawoman. *Family Sketch* (1976), *Ich denke oft an Hawaii/ I often Think of Hawaii* (1978), *Execution – A Study of Mary* (1979), *Was soll'n wir denn machen ohne den Tod/ What Would we do Without Death* (1980), *Macumba* (1982), *Die blaue Distanz/ The Blue Distance* (1983), *Das Frühstück der Hyäne/ The Hyena's Breakfast* (1983), *Verführung: die grausame Frau/ Seduction: The Cruel Woman* (co-dir 1984–85), *Marocain* (1989).

NEUNKIRCHEN, Dorothea (born 1942)

Studied philosophy, German and history, then drama, worked in theatre as actress for five years, then in television scriptwriting and making documentaries; also worked as camerawoman. *Das Weib liegt unten/ Woman is at the Bottom* (1976), *Die natürlichste Sache der Welt/ The Most Natural Thing in the World* (1979), *Dabbel Trabbel* (1982).

O, Dore (born 1946)

Met Werner Nekes in 1965, from 1967 joint film work with Nekes and from 1968 started making her own films; co-founder of the Hamburg Filmmakers Cooperative, specializes in experimental film. *jüm-jüm* (co-dir 1967), *Alaska* (1968), *Lawale* (1969), *Kaldalon* (1971), *Blonde Barbarei* (1972), *Kaskara* (1974), *Frozen Flashes* (1976), *Beuys* (1981), *Nekes* (1982), *Stern des Melies* (1982), *Enzyklop* (1984), *Blindman's Ball* (1988), *Candida* (1991).

OPPERMANN, Ingrid (born 1942)

Worked as stage actress, then studied film at the Berlin Academy of Film and Television (1970–73), from 1973 worked for television. *Women's Camera* (co-dir 1970), *Kinder für dieses System – Paragraph 218/ Children for this System – Paragraph 218* (co-dir 1973), *Frauen – Schlusslichter der Gewerkschaft?/ Women – At the Tail End of Trade Unions?* (1975), *Langes Fädchen – Faules Mädchen/ Long Thread – Lazy Girl* (co-dir 1979–82), *Aus heiterem Himmel/ Out of the Clear Blue Sky* (co-dir 1982).

OTTINGER, Ulrike (born 1942)

Studied art (1959–61), worked as artist and photographer, then moved into filmmaking. *Laokoon und Söhne/ Laocoon and Sons* (1972–74), *Vostell – Berlinfieber/ Vostell – Berlin Fever* (1973), *Die Betörung der blauen Matrosen/ The Bewitchment of the Drunken Sailors* (co-dir 1975), *Madame X – eine absolute Herrscherin/ Madame X – An Absolute Ruler* (1977), *Bildnis einer Trinkerin – Aller jamais retour/ Ticket of No Return* (1979), *Freak Orlando* (1981), *Dorian Gray im spiegel der Boulevardpresse/Dorian Gray in the Mirror of the Popular Press* (1983), *China – die Künste – der Alltag/China – The Arts – The People* (1985), *Sieben Frauen – Sieben Sünden/Seven Women – Seven Sins* (co-dir 1986), *Usinimage* (1987), *Johanna d'Arc of Mongolia* (1988), *Countdown* (1990).

PERINCIOLI, Cristina (born 1946), Switzerland)

Studied film at the Berlin Academy of Film and Television (1968–71). *Striking My Eyes* (1966), *Nixonbesuch und Hochschulkampf/Nixon's Visit and the University Struggle* (co-dir 1968), *Besetzung und Selbstverwaltung eines Studentenwohnheims/ Occupation and Self-Administration of a Student Hall of Residence* (co-dir 1969), *Gegeninformation in Italien/Alternative Information in Italy* (co-dir 1970), *Für Frauen – 1 Kapitel/For Women – Chapter 1* (1971), *Kreuzberg gehört uns/Kreuzberg Belongs to Us* (co-dir 1972), *Frauen hinter der Kamera/Women Behind the Camera* (1972), *Die Macht der Männer ist die Geduld der Frauen/The Power of Men is the Patience of Women* (1978), *Die Frauen von Harrisburg/The Women of Harrisburg* (1981), *Mit den Waffen einer Frau/With the Weapons of a Woman* (1986).

PEZOLD, Friederike (born 1945, Austria)

Studied art and psychology, began working with video in 1971; also works as writer and filmmaker. *New York City* (1971), *Selbstgespräch* (1972), *Die neue leibhaftige Zeichensprache eines Geschlechts nach den Gesetzen von Anatomie, Geometrie und Kinetik, Nr. 1–12* (1973–76), *Tempel der schwarz-weissen Göttin* (1977), *Toilette* (1977–79), *Der Monolog oder Gute Nacht Bayern* (1978), *Die schwarz-weisse Göttin* (1978), *Canale Grande* (1980–83), *Eines Tages* (1984–85), *Das geheime Labyrinth des Horrors oder allein gegen die Würstel* (1987–88).

PINKUS, Gertrud (born 1944, Switzerland)

Trained as a poster artist, studied set design, then worked in the theatre, from 1970 started making documentaries for television and trained as a camerawoman. *Das höchste Gut einer Frau ist ihr Schweigen/The Most Valuable Possession of a Woman is Her Silence* (1980), *Duo Valentianos* (1983–84), *Anna Göldin – Letzte Hexe/Anna Göldin – Last Witch* (1991).

REICH, Uschi (born 1949)

Studied film at the Munich School for Film and Television (1968–72), then studied romantic literature and German; from 1974 worked for television as writer and director. *Der Herr unserer Hoffnung/The Master of Our Hope* (co-dir 1971), *Technologie/Technology* (co-dir 1971), *Die Utopie des Damenschneiders, Wilhelm Weithing/The Dressmaker's Utopia – Wilhelm Weithing* (1972), *Anna* (1975), *Heimarbeiterinnen/Home Workers* (1976), *Ich heiss' Marianne/I'm Marianne* (1976), *Keiner kann was dafür/No-One Can Do Anything About It* (1978).

REIDEMEISTER Helga (born 1940)

Studied art, worked as art teacher, then studied film at the Berlin Academy of Film and Television (1973–79). *Der gekaufte Traum/ The Purchased Dream* (co-dir 1974–77), *Von wegen 'Schicksal'/ Who Says 'Destiny'* (1978–79), *Karola Bloch* (1980), *Mit starrem Blick aufs Geld/ With Money in her Eyes* (1982), *Karola und Ernst Bloch – die Tübinger Zeit/ Karola and Ernst Bloch – The Tübing Period* (1983), *DrehOrt Berlin/ Film Location Berlin* (1986–87), *Im Glanze dieses Glückes/ In the Splendour of Happiness* (co-dir 1990).

ROSENBACH, Ulrike (born 1943)

Studied sculpture, began working with video in 1971, has specialized in video art, installations, one-woman shows and documenting performance art. *Bindenmaske* (1972), *Einwicklung mit Julia* (1972), *Eine Scheibe berühren* (1972), *Brennesseltape* (1972), *Eine Frau ist eine Frau* (1972), *Der Muff und das Mädchen* (1972), *Naturkreisaktion* (1972–73), *Zeichenhaube* (1973), *Mon Petit Chou* (1973), *Der Mann sei das Haupt der Frau* (1973), *Videokonzert Improvisation mit K. Schnitzler* (1973), *Isolation is Transparent* (1973–74), *Five Point Star* (1974), *Die Perlen dort, sie waren seine Augen* (1974), *Sorry, Mister* (1974), *Der innere Widerstand sind meine Füsse* (1974), *Port of Paradise* (1975), *Madonna of the Flowers* (1975), *Tanz für eine Frau* (1975), *Glauben Sie nicht, dass ich eine Amazone bin* (1975), *Weiblicher Energie Austausch* (1976), *Reflektionen über die Geburt der Venus* (1976–78), *Zehntausend Jahre habe ich geschlafen* (1976–77), *Good Luck for a Better Art, mit K.v. Bruch* (1976), *Frauenkultur – Kontaktversuch* (1977), *Frauenkultur – Kontaktversuch* (1977–81), *Maifrau* (1977), *Mutterliebe* (1977), *Frau – Frau* (1977), *Herakles – Herkules – King Kong* (1977), *Frauenlachen – Frauenzärtlichkeit mit Andrea* (1977), *Venusdepression, Aktion mit fünf Frauen* (1977), *Signale für Hausfrauen* (1977), *Meine Verwandlung ist meine Befreiung* (1978), *Salto Mortale* (1978), *Salto Mortale II* (1978), *Meine Macht ist meine Ohnmacht* (1978), *Kleine Stücke von Julia* (1979), *Tanz um einen Baum* (1979), *Jactatio* (1979), *Die Einsame Spaziergängerin* (1979), *Lotusknospentöne* (1980), *Keine Madame Pompadour* (1980), *Requiem für Mutter* (1980), *Psyche aber, sie irrte gänzlich umher* (1980), *Psyche und Eros* (1981), *Wechselfrau im Rosenkranz* (1981), *Wechselfrau im Wechselspiel* (1981), *Grossmutter – Dokumentation einer Begegnung* (1981), *Judofrauen haben als Hilfe Boten* (1981), *Aufwärts zum Mount Everest* (1983), *Center of Cyclon* (1985), *Der Wind meiner Träume* (1988).

ROSENBAUM, Marianne (born 1940)

Studied art, then film and television at the Film Academy in Prague (1967–72); worked for German television both during and after her film studies. *Wie der kleine Herr Soldat Josef Neudenk die Logik vom Sonntag mit der Logik vom Montag verwechselte/ How the Little Soldier Josef Neudenk Confused the Logic of Sunday with the Logic of Monday* (1969), *Gedanken eines unkonzentrierten Violinstudenten/*

Thoughts of a Violin Student Who is not Concentrating (1971), *Aufhören oder Das Fest geht weiter/Stop or the Festival Continues* (1971), *Supermannspiel/Superman Game* (1973), *Peppermint Frieden/Peppermint Freedom* (1983).

RUDOLPH, Verena (born 1951)

Studied acting (1967–70), during the seventies worked in theatre, television and film as actress; then studied film at the Berlin Academy of Film and Television (1980–84). *Sommer –Samstag – Nachmittag/Summer – Saturday – Afternoon* (1981), *Grell/Dazzling* (1982), *Daheim/At Home* (1983), *Lucy* (1984), Francesca (1986).

RUNGE, Erika (born 1939)

Studied literature and theatre, from 1968 worked as a writer and filmmaker. *Warum ist Frau B. glücklich?/Why is Mrs B. Happy?* (1968), *Ich heisse Erwin und bin 17 Jahre/My Name is Erwin and I'm 17 Years Old* (1970), *Frauen an der Spitze/Women at the Top* (1970), *Ich bin Bürger der DDR/I am a Citizen of the GDR* (1973), *Michael oder die Schwierigkeiten mit dem Glück/Michael or the Problems with Happiness (1975), Opa Schulz/Grandpa Schulz* (1976), *Lisa und Tshepo – Eine Liebesgeschichte/Lisa and Tshepo – A Love Story* (1981).

SANDER, Helke (born 1937)

Studied acting, then studied German and psychology, from 1962 worked in theatre in Finland; from 1964 worked for Finnish television, then studied film at the Berlin Academy of Film and Television (1966–69); founder of the feminist film journal *Frauen und Film* (Women and Film). *Subjektitüde/Subjectivity* (1966), *Silvo* (1967), *Brecht die Macht der Manipulateure/Crush the Power of the Manipulators* (1967–68), *Kindergärtnerin, was nun?/What Now, Nursery School Teacher?* (1969), *Kinder sind keine Rinder/Children aren't Cattle* (1969), *Eine Prämie für Irene/A Bonus for Irene* (1971), *Macht die Pille frei?/Does the Pill Liberate?* (co-dir 1972), *Männerbünde/Male Leagues* (co-dir 1973), *Die allseitig reduzierte Persönlichkeit/The All-round Reduced Personality* (1977), *Der subjektive Faktor/The Subjective Factor* (1981), *Der Beginn aller Schrecken ist Liebe/The Trouble with Love* (1983), *Nr. 1 – Aus Berichten der Wach – und Patrouillendienste/No. 1 – From the Reports of Security Guards and Patrol Services* (1984), *Nr. 8 – Aus Berichten der Wach – und Patrouillendienste/No. 8 – From the Reports of Security Guards and Patrol Services* (1986), *Nr. 5 – Aus Berichten der Wach – und Patrouillendienste/No. 5 – From the Reports of Security Guards and Patrol Services* (1986), *Sieben Frauen – Sieben Sünden/Seven Women – Seven Sins* (co-dir 1986), *Felix* (co-dir 1987), *Die Deutschen und ihre Männer/The Germans and Their Men* (1990).

SANDERS-BRAHMS, Helma (born 1940)

Studied acting, then German and English (1962–65), then worked in television and subsequently trained as a film director with Sergio Corbucci and Pier Paolo Pasolini. *Angelika Urban, Verkäuferin, Verlobt/Angelika Urban, Sales Assistant, Engaged* (1970), *Gewalt/Violence* (1970), *Die industrielle Reservearmee/The Industrial Reserve Army* (1970–71), *Der Angestellte/The Employee* (1971–72), *Die Maschine/The Machine* (1972–73), *Die letzten Tage von Gomorrha/The Last Days of Gomorrah* (1973–74), *Die Erdbeben in Chile/Earthquake in Chile* (1974), *Unter dem Pflaster ist der Strand/The Beach under the Sidewalk* (1974), *Shirins Hochzeit/Shirin's Wedding* (1975), *Heinrich* (1976–77), *Deutschland, bleiche Mutter/Germany, Pale Mother* (1979–80), *Vringsveedeler Tryptichon/The Vringsveedol Triptych* (1979), *Die Berührte/No Mercy No Future* (1981), *Die Erbtöchter/The Daughters' Inheritance* (co-dir 1982), *Flügel und Fesseln/The Future of Emily* (1984), *Alte Liebe/Old Love* (1985), *Laputa* (1985–86), *Felix* (co-dir 1987), *Manöver/Manoeuvres* (1988).

SCHILLINGER, Claudia (born 1959)

Studied art, from 1984 worked with film and video, specializes in experimental film. *Fatale Femme* (1984), *Dreams of a Virgin* (1985), *Das wahre Wesen einer Frau* (1987), *Between* (1989).

SCHMIDT, Edith (born 1937)

Studied painting, then film; from 1967 worked for television, specializing in documentary filmmaking. *Schön ist die Jugendzeit/Youth is Beautiful* (co-dir 1972), *Pierburg – Ihr Kampf ist unser Kampf/Pierburg – Your Fight is Our Fight* (co-dir 1974–75), *Der Kampf der Lip-Arbeiter/The Fight of the Lip Workers* (co-dir 1975), *Das hat mich sehr verändert/It has Changed Me Greatly* (1976), *Das Land, das wir uns nehmen/The Land That We Are Taking Away* (co-dir 1981), *Ein Mensch, der zu Fuss geht, ist verdächtig/Someone Who Walks is Suspicious* (co-dir 1982–83).

SCHÖTTLE, Valeska (born 1945)

Studied theatre, romantic literature, psychology, acting, and then film at the Berlin Academy of Film and Television (1968–71). *Ob ich wen kenne/Whether I Know Someone* (1969), *Dr Hoffmann* (1970), *Wer braucht wen?/Who Needs Whom?* (1972), *Atomkraftwerk/Nuclear Power Station* (1974), *Bei den Bären, da möchte ich gerne sein/With the Bears, That's Where I'd Like to Be* (1977–78).

SEYBOLD, Katrin (born 1943, Poland)

Studied art history, from 1970 worked in film sector, from 1973 worked as assistant director, specializes in documentary film. *Die wilden Tiere/The Wild Animals* (co-dir 1969), *Akkordarbeiterin beim Osram-Konzern/Piecework Worker at the Osram Group* (co-dir 1970), *Schäfereigenossenschaft Finkhof e.G./Shepherding Cooperative e.G* (1978), *Gorleben* (1978), *Floraeninitiative Scharnhorst/Scharnhorst Women's Initiative* (1978), *Schimpft uns nicht Zigeuner/Don't Call us Gipsies* (1980), *Wir sind Sintikinder und keine Zigeuner/We are Sinti Children and not Gipses* (1980–

81), *Was uns Druck macht/ What Puts Pressure on Us* (1981), *Wir sind stark und zärtlich/ We are Strong and Gentle* (1981), *Es ging Tag und Nacht liebes Kind/ It Went on Day and Night Dear Child* (co-dir 1982).

SPILS, May (born 1941)

Studied acting, worked in theatre, then modelling. *Das Portrait/ The Portrait* (1966), *Manöver/ Maneuver* (1966), *Zur Sache Schätzchen/ Go to it, Baby* (1967), *Nicht fummeln, Liebling/ Don't Fumble, Darling* (1969), *Hau drauf, Kleiner/ Give It To Them, Lad* (1973), *Wehe, wenn Schwarzenbeck kommt/ Watch Out for Schwarzenbeck* (1978), *Aktion Schmetterling/ Campaign Butterfly* (1983), *Mit mir nicht, du Knallkopf/ Not With Me, You Idiot* (1983).

STÖCKL, Ula (born 1938)

Studied languages and worked as a secretary, then studied film at the Ulm Institute. *Antigone* (1964), *Haben Sie Abitur?/ Did you Finish School?* (1965), *Sonnabend 17 Uhr/ Saturday 5pm* (1965), *Neun Leben hat die Katze/ The Cat Has Nine Lives* (1968), *Geschichten vom Kübelkind/ Stories of a Bucket Baby* (co-dir 1969), *Das goldene Ding/ The Thing of Gold* (co-dir 1971), *Sontagsmalerei/ Sunday Painting* (1971), *Hirnhexen/ Goblins of the Mind* (1972), *Der kleine Löwe und die Grossen/ The Lion Cub and the Grown-ups* (1973), *Ein ganz perfektes Ehepaar/ A Very Perfect Couple* (1973), *Hase und Igel/ Hare and Hedgehog* (1974), *Popp und Mingel/ Popp and Mingel* (1975), *Erikas Leidenschaften/ Erika's Passions* (1976), *Eine Frau mit Verantwortung/ A Woman with Responsibility* (1978), *Die Erbtöchter/ The Daughters' Inheritance* (co-dir 1982), *Der Schlaf der Vernunft/ The Sleep of Reason* (1984), *Peter und die Tauben/ Peter and the Doves* (1984).

TREUT, Monika (born 1954)

Studied German and politics, co-founder of the women's media centre Bildwechsel, began working with video and then moved on to film. *Berlinale 80* (co-dir 1980), *Space Chaser* (co-dir 1980), *Ich brauche unbedingt Kommunikation/ I Really Need Communication* (1981), *Kotz-Bitchband* (1981), *Die Frau von Übermorgen/ The Woman from the Day After Tomorrow* (co-dir 1981), *Bondage* (1983), *Verführung: die grausame Frau/ Seduction: the Cruel Woman* (co-dir 1984–85), *Die Jungfrauen Maschine/ The Virgin Machine* (1988), *My Father is Coming* (1991).

TROTTA, Margarethe von (born 1942)

Studied German and romantic literature; then studied acting and worked extensively as stage and film actress, from 1970 writing and directing in collaboration with husband Volker Schlöndorff. *Die verlorene Ehre der Katharina Blum/ The Lost Honour of Katharina Blum* (co-dir 1975), *Das zweite Erwachen der Christa Klages/ The Second Awakening of Christa Klages* (1977), *Schwestern, oder die Balance des Glücks/ Sisters, or the Balance of Happiness* (1979), *Die bleierne Zeit/ The*

German Sisters (1981), *Heller Wahn/ Friends and Husbands* (1983), *Rosa Luxemburg* (1985), *Felix* (co-dir 1987), *Paura e amore/ Three Sisters* (1988), *L'Africana/ The Return* (1990).

TUCHTENHAGEN, Gisela (born 1943)

Studied photography, then film at the Berlin Academy of Film and Television (1968–71), and then trained as a nurse; specialized in documentary film. *Wochenschau III/ Newsreel III* (co-dir 1969), *Im Auftrag der Arbeiterbewegung/ Commissioned by the Workers' Movement* (1970), *Der Hamburger Aufstand Oktober 1923/ The Hamburg Uprising October 1923* (co-dir 1971), *Was ich von Maria weiss/ What I Know About Maria* (1972), *Die Liebe zum Land/ Love of the Land* (co-dir 1973), *Fünf Bemerkungen zum Dokumentarfilm/ Five Observations on Documentary Film* (1974), *Der Mann mit der roten Nelke/ The Man With the Red Carnation* (co-dir 1975), *Emden geht nach USA/ Emden Goes to the USA* (co-dir 1975–76), *Im Norden das Meer, im Westen der Fluss, im Süden das Moor, im Osten Vorurteile/ To the North the Sea, to the West the River, to the South the Moors, to the East Prejudices* (co-dir 1977), *Sing, Iris Sing* (co-dir 1977–78), *Lütte Lüüd üm Groot* (1978), *Der Nachwelt eine Botschaft/ A Message for Posterity* (co-dir 1979–80).

ÜBELMANN, Cleo (born 1962, Switzerland)
Self-taught artist, working with photography, slide projections and graphics. *Mano Destra* (1985).

ZIMMERMANN, Ulrike (born 1960)

Initially introduced to video at school, then joined the Hamburg women's media centre Bildwechsel, where she worked with graphics and printing, then video. *La Triviata – die eine und die andere/ La Triviata – the One and the Other* (co-dir 1983), *Free Fucking* (1985), *Touristinnen über und unter Wasser/ Women Tourists Above and Below the Water* (1986), *Venus 220 Volt* (1991).

Index

INDEX